the LIGHTWORKERS Healing Method

"Filled with insight, wisdom and 21st Century techniques. *The Lightworkers Healing Method: Be Who Your Soul Wants You To Be* is a big leap into a new dimension of healing. Thanks to Lynn for providing a brilliantly simple method for healing self and others."

Gay Hendricks, **Ph.D**.
Author of *The Big Leap and Conscious Loving*
www.hendricks.com

"We live in a slice of time in which a new spiritual complex is coming into being—one in which our perceptions of ourselves and our relationships with "our inner guides" who reside in "the world of things hidden" are being radically expanded. In this regard, Lynn McGonagill's shared insights in her book *The Lightworkers Healing Method* are right on the mark, encouraging us to reconnect with our inner sources of wisdom and power, to bring them forward into our lives, so that each of us can contribute to the rebalancing of our personal world and to bring harmony as well as power to those connected to us in our social world, and especially to those who choose to step up and into who and what they are destined to become. Lynn is an accomplished teacher and this book is highly recommended!"

Hank Wesselman, PhD. paleoanthropologist and award-winning
author of eight books including the Spiritwalker Trilogy
(*Spiritwalker, Medicinemaker* and *Visionseeker*),
Awakening to the Spirit World (with Sandra Ingerman), and
The Bowl Of Light: Ancestral Wisdom from a Hawaiian Shaman.
www.sharedwisdom.com

"I served as a Catholic Priest for 10 years and for the past 18 years as a Minister. I have been a Reiki Master and a Certified Healing Touch Practitioner for the past 20 years and worked as a Clinical Social Worker in the inpatient mental health unit at a hospital. Healing and spiritual growth have always been my passion. I always wondered why people kept coming back with the same symptoms and stories, or why change was so slow for them. *The Lightworkers Healing Method* not only answers those questions, but it also provides a system of healing and a spiritual growth vehicle.

A book with Spiritual Energy oozing out of it is very hard to come by and this one has it! As I read the book I had the feeling that Lynn was talking to me personally and not to just another face in the crowd. It is Lynn's Presence in the book that flows out into the reader that allows the Spiritual Energy to offer transformation. Lynn writes, 'You will learn to move above the heavier/lower dimensions and vibrations, and stretch for the top reaches of your range.' Sharing her own experiences and addressing questions before I asked them, I had the feeling of Lynn's support as I journeyed along a new and exciting healing and spiritual path. The book is alive and Life giving."

Rev. Robert Sanda, DMT, MSW, MA, CHTP, RM

"As a neuroscientist, I do not fully understand the mechanisms underlying the Lightworkers Healing Method (LHM), but I can see that it works. This method can dramatically improve physical health and emotional life, and can also be a tremendous aid to personal development. My 25-year-old daughter struggled with chronic pain and clinical depression for several years. Since treatment with the Lightworkers Healing Method, she has been free of both pain and depression for eight months. Even more striking, her attitude toward life has changed radically, and she tackles the most difficult challenges fearlessly. She is a different person. I recommend LHM for anyone who finds herself blocked by emotional issues, or who lives with chronic pain."

Dianne M. Broussard, Ph. D.

"I am slowly absorbing these inspired writings and putting them into practice as I read. It has been amazing to experience the encounters from utilizing these healing methods in these last several weeks. Every chapter resonates with my understandings after thirty years of practicing spiritual prayer treatments. Spirit, Life Energy, Prana, by whatever name we use is available for us, and with it the Guidance on how to cooperate with the Whole Life that flows."

Rev. Elizabeth Thompson
Senior Minister, Unity Church

"*The Lightworkers Healing Method: Be Who Your Soul Wants You To Be* is an enlightening, easy read and the LHM techniques have helped many of my most challenging patients find relief. LHM is one of my most favorite tools in my practitioner's toolbox. Thank you Lynn and the real teachers of the Lightworkers Healing Method for showing us another way."

Christina Captain, DOM, AP, SLP is a nationally board certified acupuncture physician and founder of the Family Healing Center in Sarasota, Florida, has a Masters degree in Communication Disorders, and is an expert feng shui practitioner. Christina's knowledge and enthusiasm for health and wellness have earned her a reputation as a qualified lecturer, keynote speaker, and experienced teacher throughout the United States.

"I have been touched by the Lightworkers Healing Method (LHM) for over ten years. I met Lynn when she practiced LHM on both people and animals. As a Veterinarian and a holistic practitioner I was aware of the benefits to health that were brought about by Lynn's method. The animals do not lie. How fortunate that through this book there will be a dissemination of knowledge and an expansion of healing for many.

Through Quantum Physics we learn that energy is all around us, and connects us to our surroundings. Lynn not only says that "we are truly all one," she actually shows us the way to experience this for ourselves. The door has been opened and we have been given a clear path to follow. I for one am excited about the journey!"

E.L. Brown, DVM

"Lynn McGonagill's book, *The Lightworkers Healing Method: BE Who Your Soul Wants You To Be* brings together the knowledge and methodologies of her Guides in a unique way, successfully tested over many years with many clients. In my training with shamans, energy workers of various traditions and meditation masters from the East, I can truly say that the Lightworkers Healing Method is a brilliant bringing together of some of the finest technologies of these traditions, combined with new information I have not seen elsewhere, in a vibrantly alive and personally healing way. Lynn is a warm and caring healer, and the Lightworkers Healing Method book is a practical manual full of transmitted knowledge, just the reading of which is a transmission in itself. With proper instruction, every one of us is a healer, and this is a book of proper instructions."

Bob Pasternak, JD, L Ac. is former Director of the Nyingma Institute of Colorado. A practicing Buddhist since 1969, he has been a teacher of Tibetan Buddhist philosophy and meditation since 1980. Bob has studied with shamans of Peru since 1993 and has been a practitioner of shamanic arts since1998. A psychologist and acupuncturist, Bob has clients and teaches nationwide.

"As a YogaCharya in the Kriya Yoga tradition, I was already aware that all blessings happened not from me but through me, coming through the lineage back to Babaji and from Source. I gained a tremendous amount by studying and traveling with my guru, Hariharananda Giri, for twenty years. Studying the Lightworkers Healing Method (LHM) with Lynn McGonagill for the past six years has dramatically deepened my

Kriya Yoga. I have even experienced personal visitations from Babaji during LHM healing sessions.

Three key concepts explained in this book have made the all the difference. First, the importance of our energy body's pillar of light. Next, the importance of this pillar being fully grounded in the center of the planet and reaching to the center of the Universe. And lastly, surrendering to my specific leading energies from Source—to my Guides. This has given me the quiet conviction, joy, and strength that I am in line with my soul plan and now truly serving the Universal Plan."

Hendrik Tackenberg, YogaCharya, Kriya Yoga

"As a yoga teacher and meditation practitioner for over 35 years, I have really enjoyed the expansion that studying the Lightworkers Healing Method has brought to me. I especially love this book! It's incredibly expanding to read and understandings click into place. Studying LHM has deepened my understanding of why and how the sports psychology techniques I studied in graduate school worked. Practicing LHM has changed the way I feel when teaching yoga—I feel so much more connected to Spirit and what wants to be expressed through me. I am more relaxed, authentic, and having more fun teaching than ever before!"

Betsey Downing, Ph.D., E-RYT500 is a Certified Yoga Instructor and has been teaching yoga as her full time profession since the mid-70's. She has a Ph.D. in Sports Psychology from the University of Virginia and has founded and directed several yoga centers over the span of her career.

BetseyDowning.com

the LIGHTWORKERS Healing Method

BE Who Your Soul
Wants You To Be

LYNN McGONAGILL

NEW YORK

the LIGHTWORKERS Healing Method

BE Who Your Soul Wants You To Be

Disclaimer: The Publisher and the Author make no representations or warranties with respect to the accuracy or completeness of the contents of this work and specifically disclaim all warranties, including without limitation warranties of fitness for a particular purpose. No warranty may be created or extended by sales or promotional materials. The advice and strategies contained herein may not be suitable for every situation. This work is sold with the understanding that the Publisher is not engaged in rendering legal, accounting, or other professional services. If professional assistance is required, the services of a competent professional person should be sought. Neither the Publisher nor the Author shall be liable for damages arising herefrom. The fact that an organization or website is referred to in this work as a citation and/or a potential source of further information does not mean that the Author or the Publisher endorses the information the organization or website may provide or recommendations it may make. Further, readers should be aware that internet websites listed in this work may have changed or disappeared between when this work was written and when it is read.

Lynn McGonagill asserts the moral right to be identified as the author of this work.

ISBN 978-1-61448-331-1 paperback
ISBN 978-1-61448-332-8 eBook
Library of Congress Control Number: 2012945360

Morgan James Publishing
The Entrepreneurial Publisher
5 Penn Plaza, 23rd Floor,
New York City, New York 10001
(212) 655-5470 office • (516) 908-4496 fax
www.MorganJamesPublishing.com

Cover Design by:
Rachel Lopez
www.r2cdesign.com

Interior Design by:
Bonnie Bushman
bonnie@caboodlegraphics.com

To Allen and Jamie. I Love you so much.
And Allen. Same.

CONTENTS

JESUS JUST CAME BY

Once, a very well known televangelist made an announcement that he had a vision that Christ was coming on January 19th. At first there was a deafening silence then a storm of public ridicule broke up in the media.

But then a preacher of a large church in one of the large cities in the United States made the same claim. He said he had exactly the same vision on the same day as the televangelist. He said he did not have the courage to be ridiculed so he did not come out first.

While it was easy to make fun of the televangelist, the second preacher was a very respectable person held in high esteem even by the president of the country. As a result other reports started to flow in. There were preachers of all denominations and from various countries. Reports started to flow in from countries around the globe.

Christ was coming on January 19th.

Everyone started to claim that Christ was coming to their church. Donations were sought to make their churches worthy of the coming of Christ. Newer bigger halls were built to accommodate the crowd. Some reserved the biggest public halls in town to seat thousands of people.

The press was having a heyday.

But now there was credibility to the story. The only question remained as to where Christ would come. Some very important theological councils were held. The clergy decided that it was certain that Christ would come on January 19. The proof was overwhelming. The visions of preachers in Korea, Iran and Poland were viewed as incredulous.

Soon rational structure was provided to the council's statement. After all, America had the best communications system in the world and the message of Christ could be beamed instantly around the globe and the world could be converted to righteousness. The kingdom as in heaven would be here on earth. God works in miraculous ways. This made sense to most Americans.

It was no longer a question of if He would come. It was now a question of where in *America* would He come.

Each congregation wanted to make sure that He landed in their church. One church started a major fund raising drive to build a new sanctuary to befit the sermon of Christ. One congregation voted to update its entire choir. They hired the best musicians in the country. One church started a major fund raising drive to replace their organ because Christ would not tolerate music from their old piano. One church had their front lawn dug up to replace their zoysia grass with fescue grass because zoysia was not going to be green enough in January. Another congregation got together and repainted their church. The board of another church took a trip to Hawaii to ponder how best to plan for the event.

There was a great amount of enthusiasm in the air. Church attendance rose dramatically. Churches had to create new and enlarged welcoming committees. Churches had to request volunteers to come and count the money flowing in.

On January 19, mothers woke up their children early. Children jumped out of bed on the first call. Most had not even been able to sleep. That night there were special television and radio shows. There were singing marathons, lock-ins, midnight services and many other activities. The air was electric.

Each one dressed in their best clothes. There had been commercials in the media suggesting that people avoid baths and instead take just showers. Jingles about the virtues of 2 minute showers were all over the waves. Even the first lady could repeat the jingle on television. Different times were allotted for showers and use of toilets, based on the alphabets of their last names. “Can you imagine if everyone in the nation was to flush the toilet at the same time?”, the honorable Vice President said during his interview on a famous show.

The morning of January 19 was a cold, foggy morning. A poor wretched man sat on the sidewalk over a stone bridge over a canal. He sat with his knees drawn to his chest and his head buried between his knees; his crumbled hat indicating where his head was. The man who looked way beyond his real age was huddled in sparse clothes. He was obviously cold and hungry but few, if any, noticed him as they passed him on the way to their church.

One child had a quarter to give to Christ when he came that day, but decided to give to the poor homeless man instead. The father gave him a sermon on the virtues of hard work. Some gave their children the sermon on the ills of liquor as they passed the old man. Others chose to look away. But most did not notice at all. They were too engrossed in the greatest happening of all time. The traffic was heavy and people had to be extremely careful when crossing streets.

A woman was walking to work at a food pantry for the poor. She stopped and invited the poor man for a meal at the pantry. As they walked, the poor hungry man asked the lady why she was not in church. Did she not know Christ was coming today? She was surprised. She had somehow missed all the news. She was also ignorant of all the theology in the world. As the story goes, the services on January 19 continued until late at night. Preachers had the best sermons they ever gave. The choirs were at their best. Fellowship continued that day till late at night. People did not leave their churches till they were ready to fall down with fatigue. But alas! Christ did not show at any of those churches.

The media had a heyday again. The membership of the churches started to fall faster than before. News about coming of Christ was never to be taken seriously again.

Somehow no one found out about the little lady who serves food at the pantry. She still believes that Christ comes there every day.

Balbir Mathur

Founder, Trees for Life

www.treesforlife.org

ACKNOWLEDGEMENTS

My heart holds gratitude beyond words to Adonai, Gabriel, the Commander, Jade-Su, Zoron, and all the Angels, Lightbeings, Avatars, and Teachers. I am just a vessel for you; therefore "my" work is truly yours.

To Patrick McManus and the entire Lightworkers Healing Method team—Jen Alexander, Pauline Baker, Luci Belknap, Diane Brennick, Kristen Coury, Joan Kershaw, Doreen LaFrancois, Dawn Mammone, Mary Anne Pogan, Mary Rice, Mercedes Smith, Donna Wylly, and Nick Exarhou—*thank you* for sharing both the Glorious adventure and the physical dimension efforts. Big hugs, much love!

To David Hancock, Founder and CEO of Morgan James Publishing—thanks for taking the chance and for being such a pleasure to work with. To Sylvia Reischke, our dedicated editor—a fond thank you for your loving precision. And look, here's an entire page without a colon. To Joan Kershaw, the most heart-centered proofreader I know—bless you for your unmatched level of lovingly mindful focus. To the rest of the early readers—Jen Alexander, Luci Belknap, Elissa Bentsen, Kathryn Hynds, Scott Osborne, and Cindy Readnower—equal thanks for your eagle eyes and your encouragement.

To the entire Lightworkers Healing Method community—thank you for courageously living your own soul plan, and for being part of the wave. As we each do our part, the world transforms.

INTRODUCTION

LIVING IN THE LIGHT

My dear friend, I know you. We may not have met in these bodies, but you have chosen this book for some reason, so I know some aspects of your way of being. First, you are not a mainstream thinker. You may have felt you didn't fit in for a long time now. Second, you are probably a spiritual seeker. Maybe you are just beginning this journey, or maybe you have been searching for a long time for something that feels true to you. Perhaps you are quite seriously on the path of awakening. Third, you might even feel a longing to awaken or expand your latent healing capacity.

No matter where you are in your journey of awakening, you can use this book as a "how-to" manual to help you be whom you came to Earth to be, to live the life your soul has planned, and to help others do the same. Step by step, higher-dimension Teachers will lead you lovingly and gently through the Lightworkers Healing Method™ (LHM), a system of healing, learning, and growth.

Don't let terminology trip you up. Whether we call them Guardian Angels, Saints, Spirit Guides, higher-dimension Teachers or something else doesn't matter. Whether we call it God, Source, Spirit, Allah, Krishna, Buddha, Christ,

Tao, or Nature, there is only one Divine Universal Heart. One Source of Life and Love. Just as we English-speakers call Ellada "Greece" and Deutschland "Germany," we use different names for Truth. Please, my friend, let's move beyond our superficial differences to find the universal truths of Spirit.

Throughout the chapters to follow, you may notice words being capitalized in a way that grammatical rules would label "wrong." If you notice this you have discovered a God Code embedded in this book: all those capitalized words are different names for God. Actually, my friend, we could capitalize the entire book. There is nothing that is *not* God, including your Virus-Ridden Computer.

If you are sensitive to Energy and struggling with that, this is a way to get your life back. Have you been diagnosed with environmental or food sensitivities or allergies? Do you have a chronic physical dis-ease such as fibromyalgia, migraines, or digestive disorders? What about depression, phobias, bipolar disorder, schizophrenia, autism, or another emotional/mental malaise? All of these are classic manifestations of unsupported Energy sensitivity. Read on, my friend. As you learn to manage your Energy body you too can return to a full, vibrant life.

If you are a spiritual seeker, this is a way to transform your own life. Your Angels and Guides know exactly what your soul needs to progress along its path. There is no need for you to follow "one size fits all" instructions. Your Guides have a personally tailored growth plan already laid out for you. Through LHM, you have access to that plan and the energetic support to implement it. This system acts as a powerful accelerator of your natural spiritual development. Be prepared for your life to transform itself for your soul's highest and best good.

If you want to awaken your healing skills, this is the perfect entry into that arena. Your Angels and Guides will lead you precisely to the best expression of your inherent healing gifts. Perhaps they will suggest you seek other training, which can serve as a complement to LHM. Perhaps this Divine healing method itself will be exactly what your soul has been waiting to express. You won't have to guess. You will know what path is yours to take. More importantly, you will receive energetic support for the journey.

If you are already a healer, this is a way to enhance your existing practice. Psychotherapists, Chiropractors, Doctors of Traditional Chinese Medicine (DOM's), Hypnotherapists, Practitioners of Energy Medicine, Shamanic Practitioners, Pranic Healers, Reconnective Healers, Therapeutic Touch and Body Talk Practitioners, Reiki Masters, and practitioners of other healing modalities use LHM to move into a higher expression of their own healing art.

LHM has an exceptional goal for an Energy healing modality: To align with the soul's life purpose. Our soul plans include life challenges, but also the expectation that we will emerge from the difficulties as victors, not victims. LHM improves the present by working with both past and future lives as well as higher-dimension Guides, Angels, and Lightbeings in a unique and powerful process. This creates miraculous healing in all arenas of life: physical, mental, emotional, spiritual, financial, and interpersonal. The full power of the Universe is revealed and is available to us in this multi-dimensional healing method. Nothing is off limits.

This book arose from LHM's core curriculum workshops, which have been honed through years of repetition and consistently produce capable healers. My students regularly report how their lives have been transformed through learning LHM. They truly do learn to be whom they came to Earth to be, live the life their souls came here to live, and help others do the same.

I am now convinced this is something that *anyone* can learn to do; it is a skill, not a gift. This method is not for the gifted few, but for the world. As we bring a critical mass of individuals into alignment with their individual souls' life purposes, LHM will do its part to draw our entire world into alignment with the Divine Plan.

We are all eternal beings on an eternal growth path. Since I learn something new every single day even after twenty-two years of working with LHM, I am absolutely sure that there is always more to be learned. LHM is presented here as clearly as I am able to convey at this particular juncture of space-time. I encourage you to continue on beyond where I am right now. Keep going. Build on this; take it farther, higher and clearer than I am able to present today. You can do it. There is no doubt.

My dear friend, LHM is both a healing system and a spiritual growth vehicle. Through this method it is possible to learn to live in the Light so that Joy is always present regardless of life circumstances. It can lead you into the space inside of yourself where no matter what happens, you are not only fine but actually thriving, living with Peace and Joy as your default setting. Beauty and wonder will manifest throughout your entire life, filling you with bliss as you realize you are truly One with the Universe. Relax into this process. Let it unfold within and around you. Let it lift you up, strengthen you, and bring you Peace. You are not alone.

CHAPTER ONE

SCARED BY A GHOST

The Essence of Desire

I did not have to ask my heart what it wanted,
because of all the desires I have ever known just one did I cling to
for it was the essence of all desire:
to hold beauty in my soul's arms.
St. John of the Cross
From Love Poems From God, shared with thanks to Daniel Ladinsky

"You're just missing it! You're missing the whole thing," exclaimed my exasperated brother as he turned sideways and disappeared. Dead people can do those things. With his departure the space behind him came into focus: an impossibly huge room with a ceiling and floor, but no walls. Small clumps of people scattered about, as far as I could see. In each group, only one or two people seemed alert and self-possessed, and the rest looked—how can I say this nicely? Dazed. Out of it. Confused. In other words, like me.

As I wandered around this strange place, mouth agape, I saw two tall people dressed in what looked like white gowns smiling benevolently and beckoning to me. Moving closer, I could see an enormous pile of books behind them. They gestured for me to sit on one of the cushions in front of them. Once we were all seated, one of them reached behind his back, drew out a smallish book, and opened it to the first page. I thought, "This might take a while." I was shocked when he smiled and nodded, telling me, "We are ready for that." I hadn't *sent* him that thought, as I did with my brother. He had seen it inside my mind. Something was obviously different about this guy. Wait a minute, was he even a *guy?* When I looked at him—her—whatever—again, she-he seemed like a woman. Her smile got bigger, watching my confusion... and suddenly he was a man again. Giving up, I thought, "What *are* you?" at him-her. The answer: "A GUIDE."

Ah.

Suddenly the logjam burst in my mind. Questions I had stored up for months (or was it decades?) came tumbling out, faster than I could even focus on them. I could simply *feel* the waterfall of questions flowing at him/her. S/he laughed, holding up her hands. "One at a time, one at a time. First things first: call me Jade-Su, and that is Zoron to my left. Second, you may call this place the Plane of the Guides. Third, we are here because it is as close as we come to Earth before the static overwhelms our voices."

With that, my formal education in the healing arts began. Or perhaps it had begun 15 months earlier, in my laundry room. You see, my brother Allen had been sick for a long time before he died. He had even had a death/revival experience during which he realized that *he* wasn't dead even though his body seemed to be. After that event, we both knew he might not survive his situation. He promised me then: If he died, if there was something after death, and if he could come back and tell me about it, he would.

Allen died on January 17, 1990, just three days after his 29th birthday. Three weeks later I was engaged in that (ahem) deeply spiritual activity of tossing out the junk mail. I walked into the laundry room, junk mail in hand, and there he was standing right outside of the window, about six feet away. He had a big goofy grin on his face, clearly very pleased to have once again played a really good practical joke on me, as he had done all his life.

Dropping the junk mail all over the floor, I ran top speed down the hall to my baby's room with vague ideas of grabbing him and fleeing the scene. Sprinting down the short hall, I could feel Allen zipping around the outside of the house three times faster. As I was opening the door to my baby's room Allen was coming in through the window, heading right toward me.

AAAAAAHHHH!

This time I bolted across the house to my husband, who was in our bedroom. "What's wrong? You look like you've seen a ghost."

"I have! Allen's here!" All this time I could feel Allen laughing his non-existent head off. This was the best prank he'd pulled on me yet! Allen sat down on the floor of my baby's room and waited patiently for me to calm down, get a grip, and come talk to him. Unfortunately I was much too panicked for that. There was no *way* I was going back in there. Gradually his humor turned to hurt, and then—ping—he was gone. My immediate reaction: "Thank God."

A few hours later when my heart rate had returned to normal, I could have kicked myself: he had given me a chance to talk to him and I blew it! Luckily for me, it was the beginning but not the end of that stage of our relationship. He now had my attention, and a profound process started which I did not understand at the time. The sentence, "I did not understand this at the time" can be inserted into almost every stage of my story. This state of affairs is probably true for you too. It can take a while to process what goes on in our lives, and that's completely normal.

In hindsight, I can see that Allen was leading me up the spiral staircase to the higher dimensions. The first time he showed up, he had come all the way down to Earth and was visible to the naked eye. The next time he showed up, he only came down far enough for me to see him if I was looking carefully. By "carefully," I mean using the same level of still, quiet attention needed to spot a tiny bird in a treetop. Knowing that he might be there, I *was* now quietly and intently looking for him, and there he would be one step higher up. As time went on, he made a shorter and shorter descent to meet me, insisting that I figure out how to ascend the stairs and meet him on an ever-higher dimension. Through the bond of Love, I reached up farther and farther in my efforts to stay in contact to him.

During this process I remained oblivious to the grand scheme of things. Although I was learning to access the higher realms, in my mind I was simply maintaining my connection with my brother, whom I Loved dearly. I missed him so much, and we were having great conversations. It was clear he had a deeper perspective on what was going on in my life than I did, so I developed the habit of asking him for advice concerning its challenges. "What do I do with this? What do I do with that? How should I handle so and so?" It wasn't as good as being able to hug him, but he was there for me whenever I needed him and was definitely more insightful than he had been during his life. 15 months went by and I was once again having one of those details-of-life conversations with him, when Allen's mounting frustration pushed him to exclaim, "You're just missing it! You're missing the whole thing." And just like that, he turned sideways and disappeared.

So there I was, somewhere above the astral planes with Jade-Su and Zoron, sitting on these plush cushions and beginning my training. We started with Chapter One, page one, of that first tiny book. At that time, I had no idea that they were teaching me the Lightworkers Healing Method.

THE LIGHTWORKERS HEALING METHOD™

What it boils down to is this: When we come into our bodies we have a plan. Our soul has a plan for the life we are currently living. This probably isn't news to you. Our

plan includes challenges (again, not a surprise). As souls we know life is going to be full of challenges, but while we are in our non-physical state we're sure that we can meet those challenges head-on and win. Then we incarnate into physical form, and suddenly life seems a lot harder than we thought it would be. The challenges can start to wear us down.

This is never the plan when we embark on our lives. We mean to experience challenges, but we also intend to succeed; to be the victor over, not the victim of, life's circumstances. Through this method of Divine Energy Healing we learn to become conduits for Divine Energy; to help people come into alignment with their soul's life purpose; to meet those challenges and succeed. To have a story of triumph.

The Lightworkers Healing Method applies to all arenas of life—physical, mental, emotional, spiritual, financial, interpersonal. Nothing is off limits. Every aspect of life can be optimized through this healing art.

The key to this system is working with the higher dimension beings: the Guides, Angels, Lightbeings, Avatars, and of course pure Divine Source Energy itself. Each of us brings our personal gifts to the table, but there's so much more available to us than our minds can comprehend. The full power of the Universe is truly open to us when we learn to work as a conduit for the higher dimension beings.

With the Lightworkers Healing Method (LHM), we follow the Guides' instructions, step by step, to bring an individual's vibration into harmony with his or her life purpose. LHM can also be described by the various processes it can include: releasing baggage from an earlier

time in this life or from past lives, retrieving lost soul Energy and helping it to reintegrate, healing life paths and soul contracts, connecting with future lives to draw their healing and wisdom into the present moment, and more.

Don't let terminology trip you up. Whether we call them Guardian Angels, Spirit Guides, or something else doesn't matter. We are all connected to wise, loving beings who have been with to us for eons. They know everything about us, including our soul's plans and what we need in order to achieve those plans. These powerful beings are always here for us, always intent on helping us move forward in our plan. They continually advise and protect us. Whether or not we follow their lead is up to us. Moment by moment we chose to follow or to ignore the signals life hands us; that's the "free will" part of this dance of life.

Warning: This is *not* a surface-level Energy cleanse. This is *not* about maintaining your Energy body. This is about getting to the root issues of the dysfunctions in your life and shifting them at the core. This is deep cleaning. Expect your life to change, and be open to the changes. Know they are good.

As the years passed, Jade-Su and Zoron led me through every step of the learning process. Again, I didn't understand what was going on at the time. I simply knew that I became aware of issues in my life, in the lives of my family, in our home, and in my business. Accompanying or shortly following the issue recognition would come an awareness of what I could do energetically to help.

By 1994, my Guides had begun their refrain of "You're not doing the work that you're supposed to be doing on Earth. You are supposed to be doing something different." One could best describe my reaction as "resistant." I had poured my life into my career and had become the established professional my parents wanted me to be. I was successful; I earned a very comfortable living; people respected me. My self-image was directly connected to my career. It fed my confidence. How could I walk away? To do what, precisely? When I asked that question, I could *not* hear the response. Resistance can do that. We just don't hear the guidance we are not open to. However, my Guides were insistent.

I would like the record to show that I never said, "No." I simply stalled. "Yes, yes. I'll sell my practice. As soon as we finish next tax season, I will. As soon as I find the right person to step into my shoes, I really will. As soon as I build it up so I can get what I need for my retirement fund, I'm definitely outta here. I promise." By resisting my life plan for five years, I created a series of business challenges and a period of extreme stress in my life that culminated in a debilitating illness. I was literally disabled for two years with chronic fatigue and fibromyalgia. My doctors averted their eyes when I asked how long it would take to heal, and mumbled things about "incurable" and "learning to live with it." At that point I knew I had to leave the security of western medicine and venture into the unknown to have a chance at healing. I got progressively less mainstream in my exploration: psychotherapy, chiropractic, acupuncture, massage, yoga, raw foods, juicing, fasting, therapeutic touch, body talk, reiki, rolfing, herbal supplements, homeopathy, flower essences, essential oils, and so forth.

And then one day I got it. As a part of my healing journey I had to seriously apply the lessons in the Lightworkers Healing Method that my Guides had shared with me. I had to stop dabbling. There was no other way for me to get from where I was (which was down and out) back to health other than through this doorway. It truly was the only door open to me. Now I understood. For the first time in my life, I started to follow Jade-Su's directions with real focus.

Six months later, my life was moving forward again. Not racing, perhaps only limping, but still moving forward. It was an amazing improvement. Then the oddest thing happened (as if this story has been completely normal up to now). Bizarrely, insights started popping into my head about people I knew, ran into, or was standing behind in line at the grocery store. I knew what was wrong with them, and I knew I could help them resolve their issues. I just didn't have the courage to offer that assistance.

My friend Jane's ankle pain broke the logjam. As she talked about it, I kept seeing over and over again how it all started from a fatal snakebite in a prior life. Finally I just couldn't keep quiet any more, and I blurted out "I think I can help you with that." Bless her open-mindedness. She plopped down on my couch and let me have at it. Thirty minutes later, with ankle pain gone and eyes as wide as goose eggs, she gasped, "Wow! Where did you learn to do *that*?"

Yeah, like I'm going to tell, I thought. *They'd lock me up in the nuthouse for that.*

Undeterred, Jane told someone else, who told someone else, who told someone else. Without realizing what was happening, I was developing a healing practice. When the fifth complete stranger called, I wondered, *was this what Jade-Su had been talking about for six years?* Jade-Su's response: "Of course, silly!"

The next few years of working with strangers and their ills—physical, mental, emotional, spiritual, financial, and interpersonal—brought me a wealth of new understanding. My belief in the Lightworkers Healing Method process skyrocketed as the phone calls came flooding in: "My migraines are GONE!" "That back pain from an injury that supposedly needed surgery to be fixed? It's GONE!" "My business went from flat to booming right after our healing session." "After a year with no buyers, our house sold right away!" "I was so depressed that I didn't think I could ever be happy again, but I feel GREAT!" "Finally I feel like my life has purpose and meaning." "I was ready to walk out of my marriage, but now we are making real progress." "My lupus is gone. Now my doctor calls it a mis-diagnosis." That's my personal favorite: the mis-diagnosis. Since I began my practice it's also been applied to several forms of cancer, arthritis, endometriosis, torn tendons, and more.

Sharing the Gift

Jump ahead to 2007, 17 years after Allen scared me in the laundry room. I had been learning and practicing this healing method for 16 years; for eight years it had been my "day job." I was happy; I loved my work and my life, which was transformed beyond recognition into a healthier, more abundant, more loving and peaceful reality. I felt I was dealing with the true matters of life on a daily basis: helping people to be healthy and happy by healing their core issues. What more could I possibly ask for?

But once again that familiar prodding at my back began. "*What? Are you joking? I thought you said this was my life's work!*" was my fairly resistant reaction. Jade-Su and Zoron were undeterred; there was more to it than I understood. "We didn't spend all this time and effort just for you," they smilingly responded. God bless them. Guides can be brutally honest, but their messages are delivered with so much Love that the hard news can become acceptable and eventually even uplifting. I finally realized that they wanted me to teach others how to facilitate these healing sessions. That was not a conversation that went well. I argued with Zoron, "Is this really a transferrable skill set?" His response: "Hellooo, we taught it to you!"

Touché. He had an excellent point. It convinced me to gather up the courage to begin teaching. It was a very scary step and I wasn't sure how to transfer the information. I wasn't a Guide. I didn't even consider myself to be someone with credibility. My certifications weren't in this arena; I didn't have a PhD in psychology or anything else that was backing me up. It was just me standing there on the freaky fringe. Who would listen to me? I begged to be given time to go back to school and put some more initials after my name—but no. "No more delays. The time is *now,"* Zoron insisted.

Gulp. Okay. I'd already learned what happens with resistance. It was time to pull up my big girl pants and get to work.

To my utter astonishment, my initial handpicked crop of apprentices "got it." After two years of teaching one-on-one I risked a formal class, and those students also "got it." As it turns out, the Lightworkers Healing Method *is* a teachable, transmittable skill set. After three years of leading full classes through the basic curriculum, I am completely convinced. We can *all* do this. It's a skill, not a gift. We have to put in the effort, but we can all do it. *All of us.* We begin wherever we are in the process, and the curriculum draws us forward into mastery. Kudos to the Avatars and true Teachers of the Lightworkers Healing Method. It is brilliant!

LIGHTWORKERS HEALING METHOD™ AND THE BEAUTIFUL PARADOX OF INTENTION

You might be reading this for your own spiritual growth and your own life healing, with no intention of practicing this art on others. If that's the case, consider this: as humans, we are often blind to our own "problem" areas, where growth is most needed. It's much easier to observe dysfunctions in others (i.e. in our subjects) than in ourselves. This is as true in the energetic arenas as it is in the physical dimensions of life. By turning the focus outward and working to heal others through LHM, we ourselves are healed of the same issues. We don't need to be aware that we have a matching dysfunction. Simply by facilitating an LHM healing process for another, we too can be healed in that arena of life.

In LHM, we merge our Energy with the Energy of our healing subject. We bring our shared vibration to the desired frequency. In so doing, we ourselves are also lifted up and healed. This does not reduce the benefit to our subject in any way. There is no limitation of Divine Flow; it is eternal and abundant. Simultaneous improvement is not only possible, but is actually in the interests of the greater good.

Students who have learned other healing modalities often have a hesitation or even a fear about merging Energy with their subject. They have been taught to protect themselves, that their subject's issues can "contaminate" them. In LHM the first step is aligning fully with the River of Divine Love; it protects us. As it pours through and around us, we can experience anything and everything in perfect safety. Spirit is with us; nothing will go wrong. Trust. Merge. Heal both your subject and yourself. When the session is complete, you will fully separate again. The only lasting effects will be positive ones; the process will improve your health and your life.

The phenomenon of simultaneous healing applies to all issues: physical, mental, emotional, financial, interpersonal, and spiritual. Let's take the example of a deep desire for spiritual growth. If you work as an LHM healer to help others who share this desire for spiritual development, over time you will discover that your own spiritual growth accelerates tremendously.

The Universe supports this fascinating paradox of healing by bringing the perfect healing subjects to you. As you merge your Energy with theirs (not holding yourself separate), you too are healed of whatever matching vibrations your Energy body holds. This process brings the understanding, at the deepest levels, that we truly are all One.

Pema Chodron is a wonderful American-born teacher in the Shambhala school of Tibetan Buddhism. Her lineage views courage as an essential element in the quest for spiritual growth. Pema teaches of three types of courage. There is the courage of the King or Queen, in which we must help ourselves first in order to help others. Then there is the courage of the Shepherd or Shepherdess, in which we must help others first in order to help ourselves. Lastly, there is the courage of the Boatman or

Boatwoman, in which we help others and ourselves simultaneously, since we are all in the same boat.

In the Lightworkers Healing Method, we immerse ourselves in the courage of the Boatman or Boatwoman. We merge our Energy into the Energy of our healing subject, not holding ourselves separate. In this way, we are both healed simultaneously. This is the meaning of the full name of the system: the Lightworkers Healing Method for Self and Others. By healing others, we heal ourselves. It is the beautiful paradox of intention. We are all truly in the same boat anyway; we truly are all One. Giving in to that reality rather than fighting against it allows for the fastest healing for everyone involved, ourselves included.

At this point in the classes, often the question arises, "Don't you then feel your subject's pain if you merge with him?" Yes, I do feel it. I feel what's going on for him, but it's a beautiful gift to me as a human being because I get to detach from pain over and over again. In the healing sessions it becomes easy to recognize that pain is just pain. I don't have any attachment or aversion to it, because it's not "my pain." It comes, and I know it will go. After practicing LHM for some years, I noticed I no longer had attachment and aversion to pain in my own life either. Pain comes and goes in all our lives. Have you noticed? It comes and goes. So, yes, I do feel it. Absolutely, I do. And it goes.

This book exists so you can learn how to apply this system of healing in your own life, in the lives of the people around you, and therefore in the world. Even if your intention is solely for self-healing and personal growth, I highly recommend you practice this with and for others, so that you can heal yourself of the issues you are blind to. Therefore, this book is written as if you will be learning to facilitate healing for other people. We are all surrounded by people who are desperate for help in at least one arena of life. Take advantage of that opportunity. By working with a variety of subjects who have a variety of challenges, your own life can come into perfect harmony in each of those areas.

Give it Time

Learning this method is a process, not an event. If you truly work with this book in the way I hope you will, you will come to master the basics of the Lightworkers Healing Method. There is much more to this. There is an entire series of higher-level classes covering a variety of more advanced topics. Don't worry about those yet. All that can come later. For now, learning the basics is the most important project.

The first step in learning this system is absorbing the energetic transmissions. Fundamentally, these transmissions are powerful calls for Divine Help. In certain circles they would be called prayers on steroids. These powerful prayers open the connections to the Divine, to Guides and Angels, and to your innate healing gifts. They make you a vessel for Spirit to use to heal yourself and the world around you. Recipients of these transmissions feel the effects physically, mentally, emotionally, and spiritually.

Our website (www.lightworkersmethod.com) includes recordings of the energetic transmissions that you would receive, were you to participate in the actual classes. Because the vibration of the transmission comes through better in audio recordings, they are not written out in the book. You have to go to the website to hear them. As you listen to those transmissions, the activations will occur within you. Before you read each of the next chapters, experience the related transmission recording. This is a substitute for what occurs in the classes. It's possible listening to the transmissions in this fashion is not as powerful as being present for them in person. However, you can listen to them over and over, and therefore receive cumulative benefit. If you use the recordings properly, you should be able to recreate the full benefit of the transmissions for yourself.

I'm going to talk you through this, but keep one thing in mind. I am not the true Teacher of the Lightworkers Healing Method. I am simply the Teaching Channel, the conduit through which the true Teachers work. *They* are with you, right there where you are reading this exact word. The true Teachers and your Guides know how this new information fits into your life path. They know what you are already capable of, and what you still need to learn or gain access to. They are there with you, supporting you through this process. They are always with you.

I don't know whether or not you're ready to walk this walk. That is up to you; it is your choice to make. If you are, this will change your life and the lives of others at the deepest levels. If the idea of trying to learn this healing art both inspires and terrifies you, that's your soul's way of letting you know it's exactly what you need to do. Congratulations on your open-mindedness and courage, my friend—and welcome.

LEVEL ONE

THE FOUNDATION

CHAPTER TWO

BEGIN THE BEGUINE

This Ecstasy *(an excerpt)*

If you listen, not to the pages or preachers
but to the smallest flower growing from a crack in your heart,
you will hear a great song moving across a wide ocean whose water is
the music connecting all the islands of the Universe together,
and touching all you will feel it touching you around you…
embracing you with its Light.
It is in the Light that everything lives and will always be alive.
John Squadra
Shared with thanks to Heron Dance

Living in the Light. If I had to limit the definition of Joy to four words, that is how I'd do it. In the Lightworkers Healing Method, as we learn to become an effective link for Divine Flow to reach the physical dimension, we also discover the Joy of living in the Light. Witnessing another person coming into vibrational alignment with her life purpose expands the experience of bliss exponentially. There's nothing like being in the front row for a show of multidimensional healing to create trust in Life. Joining in that process through the paradox of simultaneous healing is a miraculous gift of grace.

Friends, the first step in this entire healing art is opening up to become effective channels for Divine Energy to flow through us to reach the physical dimension. We use an Opening Process that has been defined for us by the real Teachers of the Lightworkers Healing Method, and that has proven to work over and over again for thousands of people.

The primary goal for **Level One** is for you to begin the beguine of becoming an effective channel for Divine Energy, in the way that is right for you as an individual. This may be the only slice of the pie you want, the one section that you are here for. On the other hand, you might be here for the whole pie. Participate at whatever level you feel called to. There's no "wrong" way to relate to this method, just as there is no "should" in this conversation. Trust your soul. Trust your Guides and Angels. Trust life.

In **Chapter Two – Begin the Beguine** we begin with a basic explanation of the Lightworkers Healing Method, using the acronym of A-COAT. After a brief explanation of Energy body structures, we explain the Opening Process of creating sacred space. We have the right to live our lives in sacred space, but very few of us know how to create and maintain it. Chapter Two covers this essential life and healing skill step-by-step. Knowing not only what to do, but why you are doing it, brings power and strength into the process. The chapter ends with a walk-through of the Opening Process that you will use throughout the rest of the book. Well before you close the cover, you can be comfortable using its power to transform your life, the lives of others, and, if you wish, the world.

Chapter Three – Meet the Guides contains exercises to help you open up to sense the subtle Energies. This may be a whole new part of life for you. If it's old hat, don't worry; wherever you are in the experience of developing your subtle senses, there's always more. You have the chance to take it to the next level, whatever that is for you. Then you'll be ready for the pivotal step: learning to take those intuitive sensing processes and shift them *up* to connect with the Divine Realms. You see, without that adjustment you can be "getting your messages," but from what source? If your messages are coming to you from Divine Sources, i.e. from your Guides and Angels, you can trust they are in your highest and best good. We always want to go with the highest level of messages available.

Remember how I pestered my dead brother for advice on life and how frustrated he got with me? It was obvious his perspective was higher than mine, and at the time my analysis stopped there. I wanted *him* to tell me what to do. However, he knew I should be going for a higher source of input than he could provide to me. This is why he pointed me on to the Guides. This is also my goal for you in this chapter: to make contact with your Guides and begin to learn how to receive their messages. These messages can give direction to your own life, and can also lead you through a healing session for yourself or for someone else. Since we are never the "deciders" in this healing art we must learn to follow the Guides' instructions.

In **Chapter Four – Sacred Space, Part Two** important details of creating and maintaining sacred space are added to the mix. We follow this with teaching how to create a sacred seal on a healing session so the outcome is Divinely perfect. After a walk-through that will allow you to practice these essential skills, we close with end-of-the-day practices to support your well-being as a healer.

As the last chapter of Level One, **Chapter Five – Ticket to Success: Foundations of Self-Care** is devoted to lifestyle changes you can make to raise your vibrations and as a result improve your subtle Energy sensing and entire life. The higher our personal vibrations are, the easier it is to maintain clear contact with the Guides and Angels. Our vibrations are simply the result of the choices we have made and continue to make in our daily lives. Good news: each moment provides us with the opportunity to make a different choice. Each moment gives us a chance to raise our vibrations. A discussion of beliefs, diet, and other habits wraps up this segment of our conversation.

Keep in mind the purpose of the Lightworkers Healing Method: To help people come into alignment with their soul's plan for the life that they are living right now. The life plan almost always includes challenges, but it almost never includes being taken down by those challenges. When we are discarnate souls planning our incarnate lives, everything seems so possible. We think, "I'll have these challenges happen in my life, and it'll be fine." That's the vibration we connect to through this system: the place where the challenges of life feel absolutely right. That is the purpose of this healing method, and it applies to all arenas of life: physical, interpersonal, financial, mental, emotional, and spiritual.

At the basic level mapped out in Level One you will open up to higher-dimension heavenly beings. Most people call these beings Angels; in Chapter Eleven we explain the terminology we use and why we use it. Again, don't let labels confuse you. For now, you can think of Lightbeings as a type of Angels. These beings have a deep desire to help and are looking for appropriate people to work through. We encourage this by bringing ourselves into alignment with Divine Flow, to see if they will be willing to work through us. This relationship isn't something that we can force any more than we can force someone to Love us, but it occurs naturally when we do our part. It just happens: Guides, Angels and Lightbeings begin to work through us. This section is about you learning how to do your part and then allowing the Divine to take over.

A DIVINE COAT

At this foundational level we're going to begin with a simple five-step process. To help remember these steps, think of the letters A-COAT. In this process, we:

- **Align** with Divine Energy,
- **Connect** to, or more precisely merge with, the other person's Energy (if we are working with a subject other than ourselves) and ask for permission,
- Turn the intuitive channels up and ask the Guides to **Open** the channels,
- **Ask** for help on behalf of the subject and notice the changes that occur, then
- **Trust** that the outcome is perfect, however it turns out, detaching from results and separating from your subject.

A-COAT: Align

The first step in this entire healing art is to align with Divine Energy. Working to help someone else's soul (or your own soul, for that matter) come into alignment with the Divine Plan without first being aligned with Divine Energy is tough going because then you're just working with your own tools. By immediately aligning with Divine Energy, the power to create the change is coming from Divine Flow, not from us. Once aligned with the Divine, you are ready to connect with the Energy of the other person.

Because this first step of the process is critical, we will go over it step by step in the very next section of this chapter, the section entitled **Creating Sacred Space**. For now, it's enough to acknowledge its importance and understand why it matters.

A-COAT: Connect or Merge

In the cases in which we are working to help someone else, it is essential to be energetically merged with him/her. In the Lightworkers Healing Method we do not attempt to maintain or even establish a barrier between the healer and the subject, which are common practices in many other Energy healing methods. Quite the contrary: we purposefully merge our Energy bodies as fully as we are able. We dive in, we become truly One with our subject. This engages the paradox of simultaneous healing, so we too receive benefit from every healing session.

Don't be afraid of being "contaminated by the subject." That is a human idea; while it is common to have that concern, you can let it go and trust Spirit. You will already be aligned with the Divine Flow; that Love will be flowing through you and around you. You will be quite safe. What's more, it is through this Energy merge that the miracle of simultaneous healing occurs. When the healing session is complete, you will fully separate your Energy once again. Only the healing benefit will remain.

This step of connecting to your subject is where your subtle Energy awareness first comes into play. Don't panic; we'll work with that. The very next chapter is devoted to developing these skills. You can do it; it's a skill, not a gift. While some are naturally more capable than others, we can all learn it. Every single one of us has the ability. This could be taught in preschool; it's that natural.

After connecting, we ask the subject's higher soul for permission to work in her Energy body and with her Guides. She will give us whatever level of access she chooses to give, and it is not for us to argue with her. It is her right to set boundaries. If our subject's higher self gives only surface level access, then we work on the surface level of the Energy body. If instead the subject's higher soul says, "Have at it, baby. Clear my slate," then fabulous—but this is not for us to decide. We simply connect with her and ask for permission. Whatever access she gives, that is the access we work within. Once we have that permission, we are ready to proceed.

A-COAT: Open the Channels

Actually opening the channels of healing, support, and communication is not our work; it's up to the Guides, Angels and Lightbeings. We do, however, have a part in this step. We must point our intuitive channels up to them, and ask the Guides to open the channels. We do our preparation, we declare our willingness to be the vehicle, and we wait. We can't force any of this, you understand. We don't force the other person to give us access, and we certainly can't force the Guides to connect—but if we're doing our part and have the right attitude, it just happens.

The moment the channels open is tangible and unmistakable: the wave of Love washing over and through us often brings tears to our eyes. Other common body responses to the tremendous Energy shift include coughing or yawning.

A-COAT: Ask

This is when the miracles begin. We have our open channel from the Guides and Angels; they are powerful amplifiers in the channels of connection between Source and us. There we are in the Divine Flow, merged with our subject and connected with her Guides. Now we can start to ask for help with whatever topics are important to the subject. Anything is worthy of Divine Help, be it physical healing, emotional healing, mental healing, financial healing, spiritual healing, interpersonal healing—it's all on the table. Her entire life is on the table. It doesn't matter what arena needs assistance; help will come.

At the foundational level, the "asking" step is simple. We present the subject's first request, out loud, to her Guides. Speaking the requests out loud adds power to your voice. Whispering silently or just thinking the requests lacks courage. "Please help Susan with her knee. It's painful and doesn't work well." "Please help Karen with her business project. She feels it is stuck and not moving forward." "Please help David's marriage. That relationship needs healing."

Using our subtle Energy awareness, we then act as the witness to what happens. Again: this is not about giving an intuitive reading. This is about asking for Divine Help and feeling, watching, or hearing it happen right in front of our subtle senses. Using the power of repetition, we present the same request several times until the energetic shifts stabilize. It can help to re-word the request and try again. If you are working with a sensitive subject, she may feel the changes happening in a variety of ways. Encourage her to interact with you, to let you know what is going on in her internal world. Speaking her truth is her part of allowing the healing.

When the first request seems to have been addressed as much as Spirit is willing at that moment, move on to your subject's second request for healing and once again present the request, out loud. "Please help Susan with her endometriosis." "Please help Karen with her sadness." "Please help David move forward spiritually." Be the subtle Energy witness, elicit your subject's reactions ("what's happening for you?"), and collaborate with your subject to repeat and re-word the requests for improved effectiveness. Once again when the energetic shifts feel like they have stabilized, then that request is also done.

A-COAT: Trust

Trust buttons up the Divine Coat, keeping it on so that grace and healing can flow through us. We must specifically trust the subtle signals that emerge throughout the process, and also generally trust that the healing session is going to turn out for the highest and best good of everyone involved. Learning to trust opens the channels to the Guides and higher dimensions even more, so that greater blessings can occur.

Those of us who have a hard time trusting ourselves will often struggle to trust subtle signals. Fortunately, the art of trust can be learned, as can all other parts of the LHM process. Building trust is a natural process. If it is exercised, trust can become the strong muscle; doubt will weaken and fade away. One way to build trust is to use your powerful intention. When an unwanted situation happens in your life, remember that everything happens for a reason. Prove it to yourself: discover what the reasons are for that situation. As you search for and find the gifts in your life challenge, doubt fades and trust builds.

Visualization exercises can also be useful in building trust. Feel free to come up with your own, or try this. Imagine a beautiful inner room deep inside of yourself, where nothing exists except trust. The room itself and even the air inside it are made of fresh, pure trust. Become aware of the

Glorious golden glow the entire room has: the glow of trust. Not only the walls, but also the air itself glows beautifully. As you breathe in, you inhale this golden trust substance. When you are there, it is impossible to doubt, since you are surrounded by and breathing in complete trust. You can go to this trusting center whenever you wish to, and be replenished with trust. As you breathe in trust like oxygen, the doubt exhales like carbon dioxide and is immediately whisked away. Only trust remains.

If you find yourself needing continual encouragement from others, then doubt is an issue for you. No worries, doubt and trust are both equally accessible in every moment. You have simply been heading toward doubt, rather than toward trust. Work with the Chapter Five section on Beliefs to change course toward trust. Build trust in Life by practicing trust-building exercises daily, by training your subconscious mind as you will learn in Chapter Five, and by asking your Guides to give you more trust. As you practice the LHM processes and notice the results, you will naturally build trust in LHM. Very quickly you will notice a profound difference in your healing capabilities and in your life.

Within the context of a healing session as well as in life, once we have asked Spirit for help, we must detach from the specifics of the result. Sometimes what our conscious mind wants is not what our souls have in mind. I did not consciously want to become an Energy healer. I just wanted to be healthy again, without changing anything else about my life. I still wanted to be respected for my professional career and stay married to my husband. Since that wasn't in my soul plan, no matter what I did to heal I wasn't getting better as long as I held onto those goals. By releasing my death grip on maintaining the status quo, by surrendering to Spirit, I could heal my body and my life.

We have to accept that maybe what our subject's soul plan includes for this life is not what her personality wants right now. Perhaps her personality wants life to be pleasant and easy, and her soul wants her to break through barriers. If we don't detach from creating results, what we are actually doing is using our own Energy to pull the subject off her soul plan by giving her what she thinks she wants, rather than just letting the plan be what it is. That is the antithesis of this method. That is forcing our own agenda and assuming we know what is needed in the situation. That is thinking we know better than Source.

As Max Ehrmann wrote in *Desiderata*, "Whether or not it's apparent to us, no doubt the Universe is unfolding as it should." Trusting that might be the most important part of the entire healing process. Like most keys to a happy life, detachment is simple but definitely not easy. When life is "going horribly wrong," it's tough to trust that it is in fact unfolding exactly as we need it to, in the most perfect timing. Even when healing sessions "don't work" for a particular subject, we can trust that this is what is needed. Even when our business falls apart, we get sick, or our spouse leaves us, this is what is needed. Even when Loved ones die, this is what is needed. This isn't about our being punished for our evil ways. Not at all! These moments are in our lives for us to heal, learn, and grow. The instant we are truly ready for life to be different, it is.

Separating from our healing subject is the last part of the process, and part of trusting. We must trust that Spirit is now handling the situation, and call our involvement in the healing complete. We call back our Energy, fully separate from our subject, and place a sacred seal on the healing session. All this is covered in detail in Chapter Four, Sacred Space Part Two.

A-COAT

Now we are there, with A-COAT. We **Align** with Divine Flow, **Connect/merge** with the subject's Energy and ask for permission, **Open** to her Guides and trust that they respond, **Ask** for help and observe the result, and **Trust** that what comes is Divinely perfect. It's a Divine Coat that we put on. The Divine Coat is what creates the healing, you see. We're willing to put the Coat on, and that is our part. The healing happens by Divine Will.

Without this Divine Coat, miracles don't happen. This is why I emphasize this foundation so much. It may sound as though there's not much going on here, but there isn't any point in rushing into the fancy techniques without this bedrock foundation locked into place. The truth is that we don't actually have to know in our conscious minds how to accomplish any healing. We just need to be able to connect to the Divine, and follow instructions.

Comments on the Basic Method

At this basic level we can simply be the link for Divine Flow, and then follow whatever instructions come from the Guides. If our intuitive channels are pointed up, the messages and energetic changes we receive are coming from some element of the Divine and are therefore trustworthy. We can ask for our mistakes and omissions to be corrected, and thereby include the element of grace.

When we are facilitating this work for someone else, we bring to bear the power of the witness. We are the witness for the other person's transformation. Being the observer solidifies and supports the energetic shifts she experiences, and in that way we facilitate the healing changes. Quantum physics has proven that the expectation of the observer modifies the results of the experiment. When we observe Energy with the expectation that it is coming into alignment with the Divine Plan, the act of observing actually makes a difference. This is one reason why it is so useful to develop our subtle Energy awareness: so we can incorporate the power of the witness into energetic healing techniques. In the next chapter you will develop or improve your subtle Energy awareness; for now, simply know there is great value to it.

Effective Asking – Bonus Tips

First, experiment with what the Guides call the power of repetition. Let's say someone has asked you to help him with a health issue. Begin with the foundational technique of "A-COAT": align, connect/merge, open, ask, and trust. In the "ask" segment, you would perhaps ask for his physical body to be healed. As the witness, you would then observe the changes in the subtle Energy. Don't stop there, however. Play with this: ask again for the body to be healed. Ask again. Then ask again. As you become more attuned to subtle Energy, you'll notice that every time you ask, something is still changing. There is a cumulative effect. The blessings eventually stabilize, but you can wring a lot more healing out of one request than you'd expect simply by repeating it several times.

Second, play with rewording the request. How we phrase the question makes all the difference in the response. To continue the example of a subject with health issues, after you ask repeatedly for his physical body to be healed, you might then get more specific. For instance, if his issue is in the pancreas you might then ask for the pancreas to be healed. As you repeat that request several times, it will also reach the point where not much Energy is shifting. By continuing to modify the request, you can continue to help.

In this example, you might try: "release any blocks to healing," "draw in healing Energy," "heal anything that contributes to this issue," "heal emotional factors of this dis-ease," "heal mental factors of this illness," "heal inherited factors of this illness," "release past life influences in this situation," and so on.

Think of it this way: there is a house with many rooms. All of the rooms are filled with smoke; all the rooms have separate doors. If you only open one door (i.e. only ask the question one way) you only release that room full of smoke. If you open all the doors, the entire house clears. By rewording the request, we can accomplish much more than asking in only one way.

Finally, there is a magic question: "Is there more that we can do right now?" If the Guides' answer is "Yes," then play with rewording the request some more, or with repeating, or with some of the other techniques that will follow. Sometimes the Guides' answer will be "No." In this case there is an important follow-up inquiry: "Is there more we can do later on?" If the Guides' response is "Yes," then narrow down the time frame of when more help is available: "Today? This week? This month? This year?"

In the next chapter we will work with discerning "Yes" from "No" in the guidance. For now, just remember how helpful it can be to know when you are complete.

Take the Pressure Off

The wonderful and blessed thing about this work is that we never have to decide anything. The only decision we make is to engage in the process: to align with Divine Flow, merge with the healing subject, open to the Guides, and follow instructions. From there the Guides are in the driver's seat. We don't call the shots. Who are we to judge what a soul needs in order for it to come back into harmony? Who are we to play God? That isn't our role. Our role is to create sacred space, make the connection, ask for assistance, observe the assistance being given, and to trust or believe it is truly occurring. That's all. The rest is up to the Divine, in all its wonderful manifestations.

THE ENERGY BODY AND ITS SIGNIFICANCE

This brief overview of a human Energy body will give you enough information to successfully carry out the exercises in the next chapters. Chapter Eight includes a more thorough description of Energy bodies; feel free to preview that if you wish.

As incarnate beings, it can be tempting to consider our physical bodies as the most important aspects of ourselves. In reality, the physical body is a small segment of our full being. Most of that which we consist of is outside of the physical form.

Think of the intricate systems involved in a physical body: circulatory, nervous, digestive, endocrine, immune, lymphatic, muscular, reproductive, respiratory, skeletal, and urinary. An Energy body has as much complexity as the physical body. Happily, you don't need to understand everything about it in order to improve it. For now, we will focus on two major components: the vertical structure of the Energy body and the chakra system.

A healthy, well-developed Energy body for an incarnating being includes a Pillar of Light stretching from the center of the Universe to the center of the planet, in this case Earth. This Pillar of Light has vertical channels, including intuitive channels and kundalini channels, which are in various stages of straightening out and lengthening. Untended channels may not initially be pointed vertically, but with our intention we can properly straighten them until our Pillar of Light looks like a tightly packed fiber-optic cable stretching from Earth's center up to Source. No matter what condition our Energy body is in, we simply begin where we are and work to lengthen and straighten our vertical channels. The more we do this, the wider, denser, clearer, and more stable our Pillar of Light grows. This is an eternal process. We will never be "done." There will always be more we can do to improve our Pillar of Light.

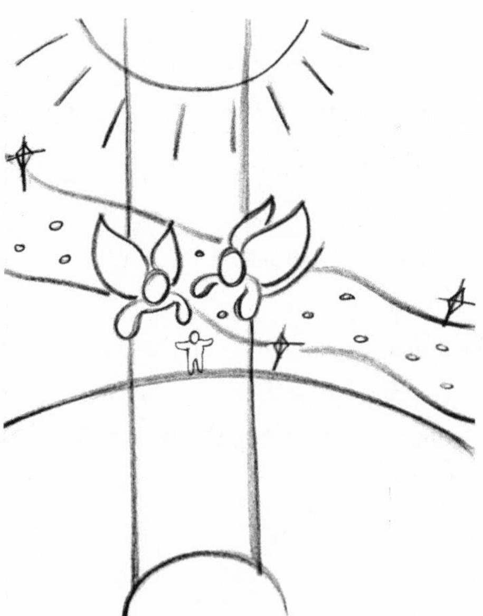

Figure One: Pillar of Light, Far View

This Pillar of Light is peppered with chakras. Generally speaking, chakras are areas running through the Pillar of Light where an Energy exchange occurs between the living being and the rest of the Universe. This is not a new idea; chakras have been discussed for thousands of years all over the Eastern world. You might think of them as openings in the Energy body, or as energetic input/output devices. There are three zones of chakras: Earth chakras occur below the physical body; Sky chakras occur above the physical body, and Body chakras run through the physical body itself. Most chakras run perpendicular to the vertical channels of the Energy body; in other words, in a standing human they are horizontal.

There are many different systems that explain chakras in many different ways. Widely known systems include the Traditional Chinese Medicine system of three major chakras or dantien, the Vedic system of seven major chakras, and the Egyptian system of nine major chakras. You might be familiar with one or another of these systems. Simply knowing this diversity of viewpoints exists will help you to be more flexible in your own thinking about Energy bodies and chakras. Consider that there might be more to learn about this foundational topic. Be open to new ideas.

The Energy body is lovingly supported by Source and by the planet through the vertical channels. It inhales and exhales prana/chi/life force through the chakras. When the Energy body is functioning well, the living being is functioning well. Difficulties arise when either vertical channels or chakras are constricted, bent, blocked, or twisted, or when imbalances are present. These challenges can be physical, mental, emotional, spiritual, financial, or interpersonal.

Most pictures of chakras depict them as grapefruit sized or even smaller. As a result, many people tend to think of them as being that size. Since Energy follows thought, when people with that belief practice chakra clearing, they will clean an area the size of a grapefruit, or smaller.

It's possible there are people out there whose chakras really are that small, but I have not worked with them. All my clients and students have chakras larger than a grapefruit. When you consider your heart chakra in the Opening Process (below), start with the idea that it might be about the size of a hula-hoop in diameter. See if you can connect to that.

Figure Two: Chakras

My friend, this is not where it stops. Your chakras and your Pillar of Light grow over time as you tend your Energy body. If your heart chakra and Pillar of Light are hula-hoop sized now, expect them to grow until they reach from outstretched fingertip to fingertip like Leonardo DaVinci's drawing of the *Vitruvian* man. From there, you can continue on until your heart chakra and Pillar of Light reach from wall to wall of the room you are in right now. And so on, and so on. There is no limit to our growth. We are eternal beings.

"What's the big deal," you may be asking yourself. "So what if my Energy body is small, off kilter, or clogged? How does this affect my life?" Think of yourself as a spiritual being, in other words an Energy-being, having a human experience. You are still your Energy-being self, simply in human form. By focusing on your Energy-being self, you can help the human-being self. You can affect every single aspect of your life by modifying your Energy-being.

A healthy Energy body looks like a completely balanced vertical Pillar of Light, with completely balanced and open chakras. This healthy Pillar of Light is wide enough that it is impossible for your physical body to reach outside of it, and stretches from the center of the planet to the center of the Universe.

Figure Three: Pillar of Light Close-Up

An unhealthy Energy body creates challenges in the life experience. Take the common example of an Energy body that is thicker in front than it is in back. This configuration creates a life of hard work, because there's no wind at our backs to push us forward. We have to create all our forward motion by ourselves. We haven't learned how to ride the Divine Energy-Currents. It's all us, baby. Another typical imbalance in metaphysical circles is an Energy body that is top-heavy, indicating a lack of grounding and therefore a lack of stability. This contributes to a life that alternates between blissful meditative experiences and struggles with money, relationships, and other physical-dimension life "details." Other imbalances have other effects, none of them good.

As we learn to focus on the back of the aura, thickening and strengthening that part, we notice that we're being lovingly propelled forward through life. Events miraculously fall into place. Divine Forces are in play. Life becomes much more effortless when our Energy fields are properly balanced. As we learn to ground more fully, we are able to maintain the Peace and Joy of meditative states throughout our lives. Life is more joyful, more peaceful, and more effective with an optimally balanced Energy body. Repeatedly engaging in the Opening Process of creating sacred space gradually brings our Energy bodies into optimal alignment and balance.

CREATING SACRED SPACE

Getting comfortable with creating sacred space inside and around us is huge. I have had students who master only this one step out of everything that is included in the entire Lightworkers Healing Method. It alone has been enough to change their lives in powerful, significant ways. Don't rush this part. Take the time you need to become proficient in creating sacred space.

When my Guides taught me the following technique, I understood this was how they wished me to begin an LHM session: by creating an environment conducive to healing. However, over the years it has become apparent that this technique can accomplish much more than that. This is fundamentally a process of creating sacred space. You can create it for a healing session, for your entire life, or for anything in between (or beyond) the two situations. Each time you repeat this Opening Process, you are drawing your Energy body toward its optimal alignment. Over time your Energy body not only aligns, but firms up in that optimal configuration.

In Energy-speak this means: *repeating this process of creating sacred space over time draws you closer to your life purpose.*

You may notice as we go through the Opening Process of creating sacred space that much of the Divine Coat is encapsulated in it. The first three steps are there: *aligning* ourselves with Divine Flow, *connecting/merging* with the subject and asking for his permission, and *opening* to his Guides. We will go through this Opening Process step-by-step. First we will break it down into its component parts, and follow up with a walk-through exercise at the end of this chapter. A recording of the Opening Process is available on our website. There's also an outline in Appendix One to lead you through this Opening Process as you begin to practice LHM.

Reading through this next section might give you the impression that the Opening Process takes a half hour to complete, and therefore you might be tempted to just skip the whole technique. Luckily this procedure can be completed in five minutes once you get the hang of it. It is quick and effective.

The short version:

Clear your Energy body horizontally and vertically. Open an Energy cross that intersects at the chest. By building a critical mass of Love at the intersection, you stimulate the birth of a bubble of sacred space. Once the bubble is formed, you call in Guides, Angels and Lightbeings. You will awaken a Vortex of Divine Light and a waterfall of Divine Love around and through the bubble. Ask for permission, and you are off to the races.

I'll explain this Opening Process step by step, so you have a framework of understanding to build upon. We follow this with a walk-through, to lead you through the process without all the clarifications. Remember that Appendix One provides the steps distilled into bullet points. Keep in mind that you also have the online recordings and you can follow along with them until the Process comes alive for you and you truly own it.

Ready? Here we go, step by step.

Breathe

The very first thing to do in creating sacred space is simply to breathe. Notice your breathing to get some indication of your Energy body's shape, and to bring body and mind together. This can be easier with your eyes closed, so if you feel comfortable doing that, I recommend closing your eyes.

As you notice your breath, if you are like most Westerners, you will notice you are breathing very shallowly in your chest. You're probably breathing primarily in the front top quadrant of your lungs. News flash: if this is so, it isn't only your breathing that is out of balance. Your Energy body mimics what is happening in your breath. For almost all of us Westerners, our Energy bodies are skewed to the front and top just like our breathing is.

Good news: in order to balance our Energy bodies we can use our breathing. Once you have connected to the breath, begin to breathe with focus. Intentionally breathe down the backs of your lungs and all the way down to the bottom of the lungs. Lungs go surprisingly far down into the torso. Pull your breath all the way down to the bottom of your lungs. As your belly begins to rise and fall, check to see if you are breathing only into the belly or if you are also breathing into your lower back. Belly breathing is excellent, but breathing into the lower back helps to balance your Energy body even more.

As your breath becomes deeper and more balanced front to back, check to see if you are breathing equally into your left and right lungs. Here again there is often an imbalance. Use your intention to balance this aspect of your breathing as well. In so doing, you help your Energy body reconfigure. As you focus on your breath, fairly quickly you will feel calmer and more centered.

Often at this stage of the Opening Process your body will speak to you. Translation: you may notice pain, tightness, pressure, or discomfort. "Ugh, I didn't notice until just now that my neck was sore. Now my wrist is hurting. There's a twitch in my ankle."

Those are messages that possibly have been there for at least a half an hour, and maybe for five years or more. Pain is simply a messenger. It just wants to deliver the message so it can move on. If we will listen to the message, it will stop. The typical reaction to pain is to push it away, to try to ignore it or at least to feel it less. This is counter-productive and causes the pain to have to hang around, perhaps becoming more insistent, until we are forced to focus on it.

Try this instead: Pay attention to the pain. How? Breathe into the pain with Love instead of trying to push it away. Imagine the pain is a hurt puppy or frightened baby, and hold it lovingly to your heart. Often that's all that you need to do to change the pain; breathe into it with Love, and it will shift. Sometimes it will migrate. Sometimes the pain will diminish or even disappear. Simply follow the pain with loving intention and curiosity, breathing directly into the center of it. For example, a pain might begin in a wrist; as you breathe into it, it can migrate up to the elbow, and then... *hmmm!* Where did it go?

For messages that are really entrenched and that you've been ignoring for a long time, it might not be that easy—but sometimes it *is* just that easy. Try it for yourself. This can open a door to you so that you can start to work with the messages of your body.

Sometimes the pain wants more from you. If it wants more, promise it that you'll pay attention to it and pick a time to do that; when you're done with this section, at lunch, before bed. Make a date with your body and then keep your promise. Your body will trust you until you lie to it, so it's a bad idea to lie to your body. Telling it the truth, consistently, gives you access to healing it. Lying to it strangles that ability.

We will go into working with pain messages in a later chapter, but for now, it's enough to know you can begin to experiment with breathing into pains. Bottom line: don't overlook these little (or big) aches and pains. They mean something, like everything in life does. There are messages in the discomfort, and you can work with them to transform your life.

Connect and Merge With Your Subject

If you are working with another person as your subject, think of him now. You can do this with your eyes either closed or open. This thought will create a link between the two of you. Simply with your intention of connecting, you will find his Energy body. There is a Glorious moment when the connection between the two of you opens up. Move into that opening with the intention of becoming one with him. As you continue to merge with your subject, you will feel the Energy change from that of "me" to that of "we."

Once you have fully merged your two Energy bodies into one, the rest of the Opening Process is identical whether you are working on yourself or with someone else. Your Energy body will merge with the Energy body of the other person, and you will function as one being.

Clear the Combined Heart Chakra

All the chakra systems I'm aware of agree that there is a heart chakra. In most systems it is agreed the heart chakra reaches through the body at the level of the chest from front to back like a hollow tube. While many systems depict this chakra as being grapefruit-sized, I suggest you consider the possibility that this chakra may be at least as big around as a hula-hoop. In many systems there is also an awareness of the vertical channels that run through the body from head to feet or vice-versa. More on those vertical channels later. We will discuss them in the section that follows the heart chakra clearing. First things first: clear the heart.

With your breathing calm and deep and the connection to your subject in place, draw your focus to his heart chakra, which is also your heart chakra, which is in fact the combined heart chakra of the two of you. Start to notice its shape, its size, its texture. Notice how it feels to you.

Become aware of the state of your combined heart chakra. Simply notice it, however it is right now. Have the intention to open it up to Divine Love, to Divine Light. Divine Presence is beaming Light and Love at us 24 hours a day, 7 days a week, 365 days a year, world without end. Spirit doesn't ever stop loving us. Our job is to open up to let the Love in. Simply begin to draw Light and Love from Divine Presence into the front of the combined hula-hoop of a heart chakra with your intent to do so.

Fill the chakra with so much Love that it actually has to expand to hold all that Love, until finally the Love exhales out the back in a River of Love. Now there is a River of Love flowing in the front of your heart chakra and out the back in a hula-hoop (or larger) sized current. This will feel fabulous: calming, supportive, healing, and loving. Let the River of Love flow. Coughing, yawning, tears and other bodily responses are common; don't suppress them. Let the body do what it needs to do to adjust to this volume of Love. When the feelings stabilize, you are ready for the next step.

Draw your focus out the back of the mutual heart chakra and connect to that element of Divine Presence that you are most personally comfortable with. You might draw in Christ Consciousness, Buddha nature, Divine Mother frequencies, Krishna Energy, or something else entirely. You might not know what to draw in, and that's also fine. Simply have the intention to draw that most comfortable Divine Vibration into the back of the combined heart chakra. Once again fill the chakra to the expansion point with Love and then allow the Love to exhale out the front. Now the River of Love is flowing through your hula-hoop in the opposite direction, into the back and out the front.

Think of it this way: if you're cleaning a clogged pipe, you can flush water in one way and it will clean a lot of the gunk out. If you then turn the pipe over and run the water in the other side, a lot more of the dirt will release because you've reversed the flow. That's why, after we first draw universal Love into the front and out the back, we then reverse directions and start drawing universal presence in the back and out the front. Coming at it from a different angle makes a difference.

I would invite you to consider that chakras can open from side to side as well as from front to back. When you're finished clearing the heart chakra back to front and front to back, why not flush it out right to left and left to right? If you've been clearing your chakras front to back (or back to front) for years, the first time you do a side-to-side clearing you'll be amazed at how much that can release, simply because it's a new angle of focus.

As that feels complete, start to swish the Energy back and forth through the heart chakra to create a cleansing turbulence. Once again, remember pipe cleaning? As you swish Divine Love back and forth through your combined chakra, remaining blockages clear more easily.

When that also feels complete, have the intention to run both Rivers of Divine Love (back to front *and* front to back) full force, simultaneously. This doubles the amount of Love present in the chakra. You will feel your merged heart chakra pop into its optimal configuration. It's a tangible sensation when the heart chakra comes into perfect alignment. Note that if you are working with another person, you are sharing the experience with him. Your combined heart chakra has just optimized.

Now that the heart chakra is at its best for the time being, shift your focus from the horizontal Energy flow to the vertical Energy flow.

Clear the Combined Vertical Energy Channels

There are Energy channels that run through and around our physical bodies, from the center of the planet through our feet, up to our head and beyond, to the center of the Universe from which Love continually flows. Visualize a fiber optic cable at least the size of a hula-hoop in diameter. The fibers represent the Energy channels that run through us and around us.

At first your vertical Energy channels (or those of your subject) might be bent or twisted. Don't worry; that's normal. Over time as you draw up Divine Earth Energy, the channels will straighten out and look more and more like the perfectly aligned fiber optic cable we intend to be. As our Energy bodies become straight and true, we can hold space so that only Divine Will comes to pass in our lives. Not our will, but not anyone else's either; just Divine Will.

Know that the Earth itself is a living being and a very powerful one. I once had a belief, shared by many people, about the Earth being wounded. Does this sound familiar? Wounded Earth. I can't tell you the number of times I have asked the Guides about this issue, both for myself and on behalf of many other people holding the same belief. Every single time without exception, no matter whose Guide is responding, the answer is this: the Earth is a powerful living being. It might have the equivalent of a bad skin rash, but it is healthy and strong just under the skin.

The Guides go on to explain that we are cells in the body, in the biosphere, that is Earth. It is us. We are it. There isn't a meaningful line of demarcation between us and Earth, any more than there is an important difference between the cells of our skin and of our bone marrow, where red blood cells are formed. We are part of the living being that contains all of Earth. It is only our perception that creates a sensation of separateness. Therefore we can freely and fully drink in Earth Energy, without any guilt about taking from a wounded, separate, being. We ARE Earth. We, the skin cells, can draw in support from the bone marrow. We are supposed to do that. It is how the system is designed. Let go of the guilt.

Let's continue with the Opening Process. After clearing the combined heart chakra, bring your focus down through the feet and into the center of the planet. Have the intention to connect to Divine Earth Energies, to both Father Earth and Mother Earth Energy. Do you notice a qualitative difference between the two forms of Earth Energy? Both are wonderful, both are necessary. Yin and yang are both equally important. Now draw in those Divine Earth Energies, as if you were a plant drawing water into your roots. Feel the Earth Energy rising through your entire shared vertical fiber optic cable. Feel the Energy flowing in through your feet, up through your body, and out the crown of your head going toward the center of the Universe. Feel the Energy flowing through and around you like an upward-rising River of Love.

If you wish, you can shift your attention to your subject to see that the Energy is flowing Earth to Sky through her body as well. You will discover that it is the same for her as for you, since you are merged. Whether you use yourself as the primary focus or use her as the focus, the result is the same. You are one.

Remember that many people's vertical channels are not nearly as well maintained as their horizontal chakras. Your and/or your subject's vertical channels might be that way. If you start to clear the vertical channels and you notice they are bent or twisted, don't worry. They will become straight over time. Have the intention to straighten the bent channels as you draw Earth Energy through them. Let them point to Source as they have truly always wanted to do. Eventually you will have the shiny straight look of a fiber optic cable running from the center of the planet to the center of the Universe. You will BE a Pillar of Light.

Sometimes in this process people find themselves yawning, or even coughing or sneezing. This is perfectly fine. It's a sign that you are opening up to more Energy, more Divine Flow. Don't suppress the yawns and coughs. Let your Energy body expand. If you know a dog, think of the behavior pattern the dog has. When you give her attention you thereby increase her Energy flow, and very often the dog will yawn. It is the same for us: when our Energy flow increases, we might yawn. This doesn't mean we are tired. It means we have a lot of Energy running through us, more than we are used to. If yawning happens for you, simply allow your crown chakra to expand to let that extra Energy roll on through. With your intention, send the extra Energy out to fill your entire hula-hoop sized (or larger) Pillar of Light. The overwhelmed feeling should dissipate immediately.

Now, move back to drawing up Divine Father Earth and Mother Earth Energies in a Pillar of Light. There will come a moment when it feels like the flow is fairly stable. When you reach that point, you are ready for the next step in optimizing your vertical Energy flow.

Bring your focus upward, all the way through your crown chakra. Reach for the center of the Universe with your attention and intention. Have the intention to connect to Source Energy and to the full spectrum or rainbow of healing frequencies.

It can be easiest to begin by connecting with all the healing frequencies you currently have access to. Perhaps you are already a practitioner in another healing tradition: Reiki, Yoga, Traditional Chinese Medicine, and so on. If so, begin by connecting to those familiar frequencies. Perhaps you have not yet consciously experienced energy healing. If not, no worries, your conscious mind doesn't need to know what these healing frequencies are. They are still there and accessible to you. Simply have the intention to connect to the healing frequencies that you are already linked to, and begin to draw those healing frequencies into your combined Pillar of Light for you and your subject, through your shared crown. You will feel the downward flow of Divine Healing Energy as you draw it into you.

As the familiar healing vibrations begin to flow through and around you, expand your intention. If you are reading this book, I doubt this is the first lifetime you have worked with healing arts. Include all the healing frequencies you have ever had access to in any lifetime. Use that past life experience. Access it. Claim it. You don't have to make yourself crazy trying to figure out how to do this. You can do this simply with intention. Just try, and notice how the Energy flow changes. It works.

Continue to expand the intention to include all the healing frequencies you will ever have access to in any lifetime to come. Know that you are an eternal being in an eternal process of growth. Therefore over time you will come in contact with ALL healing frequencies. This is the only thought that makes any sense once you come to accept the concept of reincarnation. Anything else denies the eternal nature of the growth process. In this way you can expand your access to include the whole rainbow of healing frequencies, the entire spectrum of healing vibrations. Don't take my word for it. Try it for yourself and notice the difference.

In Chapter Seven, we will open up the doors to other lifetimes. This is a normal, natural process. If you approach it as I did without preconceived ideas of what is and isn't possible, you will discover the truth for yourself. Your soul has lived before, and you can access those memories. For now, it's enough to know those lifetimes are there, and to have the intention to connect to all the healing vibrations that exist, all the healing frequencies you've ever had access to or will ever have access to. Since you are an eternal being on an eternal growth path, by definition this means you will be linked to *all* the healing vibrations with this intention.

Continue to draw these Divine Healing Frequencies from the center of the Universe into the top of your merged Pillar of Light, through the merged crown, through and around your bodies as if they were one body, in a unified Pillar of Light flowing straight to the center of the planet. Gradually the downward flow will stabilize.

As that feels complete, start to swish the Energy back and forth through your vertical channels. Once again, remember pipe cleaning? As you swish Divine Love top to bottom and bottom to top through your Pillar of Light, remaining blockages clear more easily. Now you have your Pillar of Light really flowing, because the upward rising Divine Earth Energy is met by the downward flowing Divine Healing Frequencies.

Finally, have the intention to allow both Rivers of Love to flow full force, simultaneously. Top to bottom, and bottom to top. Notice how this doubles the amount of Love present in your combined Energy body. You might even feel your Pillar of Light pop into its perfect optimal alignment. Now your vertical channels are complete, and you are ready to move to the next step of the Opening Process.

Notice that we begin with Earth Energy and then reach upward for Divine Healing Frequencies. Why? For two reasons. First, the more strongly we're grounded, the more Divine Light we can pull in and hold. If we're ungrounded our vertical channels are not fully open, which limits our capacity to receive. What's more, grounding provides a foundation beneath us in which to anchor the Light. Second, if we were to begin by drawing Source down with those channels still bent or twisted, Source Love would wash around them but not through them. When we begin with drawing our channels up to Source, engaging in the eternal process of straightening these upward-rising channels, the Love of Source begins to flow through them, strengthening from within.

Form the Bubble

By now you have a River of Divine Love and Light flowing top to bottom and bottom to top, and another River of Divine Light and Love flowing back to front and front to back. It forms a cross of Divine Energy. This is not a religious symbol; it's an effective geometric shape.

If you have taken a long time on the vertical channels, take a moment to refresh the flow of Energy through the horizontal channels of the combined heart chakra of you and your subject. Notice that Divine Love flowing back to front and front to back through your hula-hoop of a heart chakra.

Now bring your focus to that intersection of heart chakra and vertical channels. It will be at least as large as a sphere with the diameter of a hula-hoop. Focus on the intersection. Since Energy follows thought, your focus draws Divine Love to that area. The intention is to pack so much Light and Love in there that an explosion of Light happens. In healing sessions I call it an expansion so as not to scare the subject, but what it really looks like to me is an explosion of Love and Light. You don't make that explosion happen. All you do is focus on the intersection of the Rivers of Love with an intention of building a critical mass of Love.

When critical mass is reached, POP you have a giant bubble of Love and Light, surrounding you and your subject, if you are working with someone else. You can feel it with your subtle senses. It's tangible. The first sensation might be one of Peace, and of being blessed. Let yourself notice that. When you feel ready, put your attention on the exterior of the bubble. As you notice the exterior of the bubble, become aware of how strong and resilient, how light and bright it is. Notice the exterior is crackling with Energy. I think of it as being electrified.

At this point you must make a statement, a decision. You must claim the bubble as private, sacred, safe, healing space. By your definition, by your word, you make it so. "This is safe, sacred, private, healing space. Only beings that I invite in can join us. All others can just pass around on their own way to the Light." We are all on our way to the Light. It doesn't matter how "bad" we think people are. They're still on their way, just as you and I are. They might be confused or distorted or lost, but nonetheless they are on their way to the Light. They can, however, go around us. They don't have to come through this bubble. We have the right to clear space. We have the right to live our lives in clear space. By claiming that right, we make it so.

Filling the Bubble

Here we are in safe, sacred, private, healing space. Now what? The very first thing we want to do is call on our own Guides and Angels. Remember, they are the go-to people for all our questions. We might be doing healing work for another person, but we need to do it well and safely. Therefore, we call for our own Guides and Angels, as well as the healing Lightbeings, to join us in the bubble. You will feel a very tangible shift in Energy as these Divine Beings enter. Often students describe it as a wave of Love, Peace, and strength.

Once your Guides, Angels, and the Lightbeings are present, the first item on the agenda is to ask your Guides for permission to engage in the healing work you intend to do right then. This is a real question, not a rhetorical one. "Do I have permission to do this healing work with this person right now?" Usually the answer is "Yes," but not always.

Almost invariably if your Guide refuses to give you permission to work with that particular subject on that particular day, you'll realize you already knew you weren't supposed to. "I knew it this morning. I knew it yesterday.

I even knew it last week and darn it, I didn't listen. Now here we are, and the Guides just said, 'No.'"

In that position, you have a decision to make. Are you going to press on or are you going to tell your subject, "I'm sorry, I don't have permission"? My friend, let me tell you, if you press on it is ugly. That makes for a bad hour or 90 minutes in your life. The messages don't come; you just can't get clarity. You bumble and stumble. Nothing happens when you try to shift the Energy. As my daughter would say, that healing session will be a struggle-fest. Nothing will go well. Nothing you try will work. No matter how embarrassing it may be to tell your subject you don't have permission, it is the most graceful way out of the situation.

Now, if you are like me, you'll have to experiment with that concept ten times or so before you come to believe it. Feel free to make yourself miserable with this one; I did. Or (here's a thought) you can feel free to try it once and then surrender to Divine Guidance.

Part of surrendering to the guidance means trusting that when the Guides say "No," there is a good reason. We don't need to add a story about what the reason is. It isn't anything bad about us and it isn't anything bad about the other person either. It's simply not right for us to do this work with this person at this particular time.

If you find yourself in the awkward position of receiving a "No" when you ask for permission, it can sometimes help to ask: "Is it 'No' forever?" If it isn't a forever "No," then you can ask more details: "Will you tell me when it will be okay?" If you receive a "Yes," then you can ask for yes versus no guidance on time frames (next week, next month, next year) until you pin down a better time to work with that person. If it IS a forever "No," then it's accurate to tell the person something along the lines of "I am not the right person to work with you on this issue," and refer them on to someone else.

Here's the bottom line on having your Guide's permission. Since this healing method is based on acting as a conduit for Divine Beings to create healing, we can only be effective when the Divine Beings deem it appropriate. We can't force matters.

Ever.

Period.

In the next chapter you'll have a chance to practice discerning "Yes" and "No" in the guidance. That is an essential skill in this work; you really have to get this, but don't worry. Because it takes practice, it might not happen for you the first time, but you will get it. We can all get it. This is a natural process that should be taught in kindergarten. If your kindergarten class skipped over this art like mine did, no worries. We'll go through it later on in this chapter. "Yes" or "No"? That's the essential question, and it's natural to receive the answers.

Let's go back to the moment in the Opening Process of asking for permission. Let's just assume for purposes of this conversation that you have been given a thumbs up. The next request is to ask your own Guides and Angels for guidance, support, and protection in the process. Why? Three reasons. First, even though the subject's Guides will be the ones primarily directing the healing session, our Guides know us best. They know how to communicate with us. Therefore having them help with the interpretation is both wonderful and beneficial. Second, they also know best what we need in terms of support, in order to do our best. The other Guides can help too, but our Guides know our Achilles' heels, and the weak links in our chains. Finally, having our Guides protecting us in the work is also quite helpful. It is possible to make mistakes that would be uncomfortable without that protection. Once again, while the subject's Guides are also there and don't wish for us to be hurt, their focus is on the subject. Our personal Guides care about us more than anyone else does; their focus is on us. They will keep us safe better than anyone else will.

With your Guides present, call in a Vortex of Divine Light. This looks like a white tornado, and it runs around the inside boundaries of the bubble. What good is it? A Vortex creates a continual updraft, a continual cleansing of the sacred-space healing bubble. As Energy is released, it is immediately sucked up into the Vortex and taken away to be recycled into clean, fresh Energy. How do you do this? You call in the Vortex with your intention to do so. Later on we will discuss how to create these Vortices. For now, simply know you can call for one and it will come to you. As with everything else, the Vortex is tangible. Once you are attuned to subtle Energy, you feel it immediately when it enters the bubble.

As the Vortex spins, call in the River of Love and Light, which the Guides call "the Living Waters." This flows down through the very center of the Vortex into the bubble. It looks like a waterfall of sparkly hair gel: it's a viscous, shiny, sparkly liquid. When these started appearing for me, I didn't know what they were. I called it the Dippity Doo waterfall. Classy name, right? Finally I got it: it's liquid Love, Divine Love. If we call for the Living Waters, they will flow continually into the bubble. This creates a foundation of Love that supports healing. When we feel Loved, we feel safe. When we feel safe, we relax. When we relax, our Energy bodies become more open. When our Energy bodies are more open, it's easier to heal.

Once you have your own Guides backing you up in the bubble full of liquid Love and surrounded by a Vortex, turn your focus once again to the subject. This time you are not focusing on his incarnate self, but rather on his higher soul. Even though his incarnate self has already given you permission to work with his Energy body, it is important to also ask his higher soul for permission. The phrasing that rolls off my tongue at this point is: "I'm asking your higher self, your soul self, for permission to work in your Energy body and with your Guides. Feel free to place any limitations you want on that, and know those limits will be honored." In this way, he can relax into the healing opportunity and not stay continually on guard to keep you away from any topics he wishes to keep private.

The higher self may define the permissible access differently than the incarnate self does, and that's fine. By asking both aspects of your subject, the incarnate self and the higher self, you will determine what the true access is. Only when both levels of permission are granted do you truly have permission to work. Sometimes people think they are more open to change than they really are. In those cases, the higher self will grant smaller access than the physical voice does. Alternately, the higher self might give more access than the incarnate self. It's proper to ask both the physical dimension person and the higher soul for permission, and go with the smaller, more limited access. Anything else can feel like a violation to your subject, as if you are imposing your own will on him.

Having the intention to work only within complete access can make it so. Your conscious mind does not have to be able to figure this out on its own. With experience you will come to know the feel of full access. Until then, your Guides will help you if your intention is pure.

At this point in the classes, invariably someone will ask: "What about a Loved one who is struggling and doesn't know to ask me for help? What do I do then?" In those situations, you can simply ask the Divine Guides, Angels and Lightbeings to help that person with whatever he needs, to bring him into accordance with his life path, and to help him come into alignment with the Divine Plan. In other words, pray for him rather than taking an active, directed role in his healing. Unless you have been given permission, it isn't right to make that choice for your Loved one. Stepping over that line could definitely be interpreted as a violation of boundaries and lead to troubles in your relationship.

As you become comfortable with this healing art, there is a huge temptation to help Loved ones without permission. Think about it... someone you Love is struggling and is so lost and confused that he doesn't even want your help when you can be an open channel for Divine Assistance to flow through! That's just stupid, right? It's oh-so-tempting to think that you know what your Loved one needs better than he does, and barrel on without being asked for help. I am not trying to be offensive with the language here, but rather to make a very clear point: that would be energetic rape. You would be imposing your will on him without permission. Please don't do that. Whatever gains you make on his behalf will evaporate like water in the Sun anyway. There won't be anything to anchor it into the physical dimension. All that will be left of your unsolicited help is his resentment of you, which he probably won't understand and therefore will have a hard time releasing. In the end, the choice to "heal" without obtaining permission hurts both you and your relationship with your Loved one.

Let's continue with the Opening Process. At this point you will have both the incarnate subject's permission and the higher soul's permission at whatever level they determine. If the access is wide open, wonderful. If the access is small, so be it. This is not for us to question. A common impression of the approved access is one of a door opening. In your mind, move through the door and into the space of the access. This is where you have permission to work. You might perceive the access this way or you might perceive it in a completely different way. However you perceive it is fine. Simply notice the access and move into it.

Once inside the access, ask the subject's own Guides and Angels to join you in the bubble. It can be helpful to make sure your intuitive channels are pointed straight up (we will get to this in a moment) as you call the higher-dimension beings in. There is a tangible shift of Energy as the Guides and Angels enter the bubble. There can be a feeling of Peace, of Love, of grace, that suddenly comes over you. It can bring tears to your eyes. These higher beings definitely know how to make an entrance!

In the presence of the subject's Guides and Angels, ask those Divine Beings to open the channels of communication and assistance wide. This is, of course, their choice. They will open the channels to you if, in their judgment, it is a good idea. I have not found a way to force the Guides to open channels, and I've been pretty pushy in these explorations. The Guides open the linkages the way they want to, when they want to. This is up to them.

Ready to Roll

Now you have it. You have created sacred space. You've created a healing connection to your subject. You have Guides present for you and for him. The doors to the Angels and the Lightbeings are open. Now you are ready to be a vehicle to bring Divine Energy to Earth to help your subject's soul plan align, which means helping him heal his life.

It is enormously helpful to literally talk our way through the Opening Process, to verbalize the steps as we go through them. There are multiple reasons for this. First, it helps us to be precise in our thinking. If we are running through the steps silently, there is a tendency to slur the process, to be sloppy in our focus. Speaking each step out loud causes us to sharpen our mental gaze.

Second, it adds power to the process. If we are too shy to speak the words out loud, we are creating sacred space at that uncertain level. If, on the other hand, we are boldly claiming the truth of creating sacred space, we are using the power of the spoken word. I've watched people with beautiful Energy trying to create sacred space silently. Unfortunately, going through the process just in their minds lacks power. We have to claim it, to own it, to give it strength.

Finally, narrating the process for our subject lets him know what we are doing so that he can learn this life skill for himself. What a beautiful gift that is, to know how to create sacred space in which to live!

The downside of talking our way through the Opening Process in front of a subject is that we can come to think we are talking him through the steps, telling him how to create the space. "Now pull that Love through your heart back to front and front to back." This is, however, our job. As practitioners of this healing art, more than half of our part in the process is to create the space in which healing can occur. We aren't just telling the subject what to do to create the space. While he can and sometimes should join in the process, we're doing it with and for him. It's the healer's responsibility to create the sacred space. Now you know how to do that, and all you need is some practice.

OPENING PROCESS WALK-THROUGH

I'll talk you through this process now, without all the explanations and digressions. This will be something you will want to practice many times until you come to own the system of creating sacred space. If you have not already gone to www.lightworkersmethod.com for the very first transmission entitled *Open to Guides, Angels, and Lightbeings,* now is a good time to do that. This infusion of Divine Energy will help you open up, to be who you truly are, and to create sacred space. After you have absorbed the first transmission, find a quiet space. Settle in to practice allowing the River of Love to flow through and around you.

While this process can be completed in less than five minutes once you are comfortable with it, you will need more time as you are learning. If this is your first walk-through, give yourself 30 minutes of undisturbed time. For the first walk-through it can be ideal to practice this alone, but working with a willing subject will allow a huge improvement, so don't wait too long. The subject doesn't have to be a human. Pets Love this. Plants Love this. All living beings Love this. I will instruct you as if you are with your subject. If you are working alone in the very first run-through, just ignore that part. Ready? Let's go.

Notice Yourself

Whether you are working on yourself or with another subject, begin with an internal focus. Close your eyes if that helps you to calm and center, and draw your focus to yourself. Notice your breathing. If it's shallow, start to breathe more deeply. If the breath is primarily happening in the front of your lungs, breathe into the backs of your lungs, all the way to the bottom. Breathe equally into your left and right lungs. Balance your breathing and know your Energy body is also balancing as you do so.

Notice your body. If there's any pain, tightness, pressure or discomfort, just breathe into it. Don't try to push it away. Acknowledge it without judgment, decision, blame, or commentary. Sometimes that's all it needs in order to release. Sometimes it wants more. If it wants more, promise it that you'll pay attention to it and pick a time to do that: when you're done with this session, at lunch, before bed. Make a date with your body and then keep your promise. For now, simply promise the pain you'll get back to it, and move beyond it. It can stay there; you can move on.

Merge With Your Subject

Think of your subject. By thinking of her, you connect with her. Feel the link open, or simply know it is opening with the thought. Know you are becoming one with your subject. Feel the merging begin to happen, or simply know it is happening. Notice how joyful it feels to connect deeply with another living being.

Horizontal Rivers of Love

Knowing that you and your subject are one being, bring your focus into your mutual heart chakra. Bringing your focus into your own heart chakra while knowing that this is also her heart chakra makes it so. You can move your focus back and forth in the combined heart chakra from "your" heart chakra to "hers" and feel the truth of this for yourself.

Have the intention to draw your combined heart chakra into alignment with the Universal heart of Life and Love. Open your mutual heart chakra wide to this Universal presence. Have the intention to open the entire front of your merged heart chakra, hula-hoop or larger, to Divine Presence.

Very powerfully now, draw Light and Love from Universal presence right into the front of your combined heart chakra. Fill the chakra so full of Love that the chakra itself has to expand to hold all that Love. It's a giant inhale of Divine Love. When the chakra needs to exhale, let it exhale out the back so there's a River of Love flowing in the front and out the back, in the front and out the back. If coughing happens, let it happen. Don't suppress anything your body needs to do right now: move, cough, sneeze, and yawn.

Continue to draw that Love in the front of the heart chakra and out the back, in the front and out the back. Know that this is happening for you and your subject. Confirm this for yourself by looking at her, by switching your focus to her heart chakra. As you do so, focus on drawing the Divine Love into the front of the combined heart chakra. You will notice it doesn't feel any different than it did drawing the Love in through the doorway of your own chakra. "Hey, it *is* the same!" Very good.

As that River of Love flows through you, when it feels right, move your focus through the combined heart chakra to the back. Reach out the hula-hoop-size back of your mutual heart chakra and connect to that element of Divine Presence that you're most personally comfortable with. You don't have to know what or who it is, and you don't have to know what it is for your subject either. Simply draw in that most perfect, comfortable element of Divine Presence, named or unnamed, into the back of this combined heart chakra. Once again, this is a giant inhale of Love, filling your chakra again to that expansion point. When the exhale of Love happens, let it happen out the front this time. Now the River of Love is flowing in the back and out the front, in the back and out the front. Let the River of Love continue to flow back to front until it settles down a little bit. Very good.

Swish the Rivers of Love back to front and front to back through this combined heart chakra. You might even feel the chakra healing and blockages releasing as you do so. When that feels complete for now, have the intention to run both Rivers full strength simultaneously, back to front and front to back. Feel the amount of Love present in the system double. Feel the chakra firmly expand, feel it pop into a straight, firm shape. Excellent.

Vertical Rivers of Love

Gently bring your focus through your feet and into the planet. Notice your feet. Notice the planet. Start to draw Divine Father Earth Energies up from the center of the planet and into your feet. Do this with your intention; know it is happening for you and your subject. Continue to draw Father Earth Energies up through that entire vertical Pillar of Light, which is both you and your subject. Do this for the combined two of you: draw Father Earth Energies up through the vertical channels, through and around the feet in that hula-hoop sized Pillar, through and around the body, and out the crown headed straight to Source. Let that upward-rising River of Love flow from Earth to Sky, through and around you. Let the Father Earth Love flow through and around your combined Energy body in a Pillar of Light.

Change your focus to Mother Earth Energies. Calling Mother Earth Energies now, have the intention to draw Mother Earth Energies up into the feet and the entire Pillar of Light and out to Source. Let that River of Divine Mother-Love flow into and around the feet, through the hula-hoop-sized Pillar of Light through all these vertical channels headed straight to Source for you and your friend.

Have the intention to draw both Father and Mother Earth Energies up through your Pillar of Light. Let that Divine Energy flow upward in a River through and around you, Earth to Sky. If you wish, you can place your attention on your subject's body, to see that the Energy is flowing Earth to Sky through her body as well. You will discover that it is the same for her as for you, since you are merged. Whether you use yourself as the primary focus or use her as the focus, the result is the same. You are one.

Now draw your focus up to your crown and through your crown. Bring your focus straight to Source with your intention to do so. Connect to the rainbow of all the healing frequencies that exist in Source. Have the

intention to call in the healing frequencies that you're most personally connected to right now. You might know what those are, and you might not; it doesn't matter. Draw in these precise healing frequencies into the combined crown, through these same vertical channels. Call these healing frequencies through the Pillar of Light that is big as a hula-hoop, headed straight to the center of the planet. Feel the healing vibrations flush downward through these vertical channels.

Expand your intention to include all the healing frequencies you have ever had access to in any lifetime, knowing that this is not your first life as a healer. Draw in all the healing frequencies you have ever had access to. Very good. Feel the stabilizing effect these vibrations have on you and your subject. Feel the River of healing Love running through your entire vertical system headed straight for the center of the planet, through and around you and your subject.

Now have the intention to draw in all the healing frequencies you will ever have access to in any lifetime, through you and your subject in a vertical Pillar of Light. Let that River of healing vibrations flow Sky to Earth through and around you. Notice how full, stable, and complete this River of Divine Healing Love feels. Isn't it wonderful?

Swish the Divine Love top to bottom and bottom to top through your Pillar of Light. Feel your vertical channels healing; feel blockages releasing. When that feels complete for now, double it up. Call in both Rivers of Love to run full force simultaneously: Earth to Sky and Sky to Earth. Feel the amount of Love in your system double. Feel how

this expands the Pillar of Light, how your Pillar pops into a stable, strong formation.

Form the Bubble

Bring your focus into the intersection of heart chakra and vertical channels. Notice how big it is – a sphere of Light at least as large around in all directions as a hula-hoop. If it feels right, refresh the flow of Love through the heart chakra by focusing there; feel the Rivers of Love flowing back to front and front to back. Now once again focus on the intersection area. With your focus, you're pulling Divine Light into that intersection. Let a critical mass of Love build. Wait for it to pop into a bubble of Light and Love, large enough to surround you and your subject very comfortably.

When the bubble forms, simply notice how it feels inside of it: sacred, peaceful, loving, and supportive. Now notice the outside of that bubble. Knowing the bubble is going to be big enough for the two of you to fit inside, don't look too small. Place your attention on the exterior of the bubble. Notice how strong and bright it is; notice it's electrified. It is alive and buzzing with Divine Love. It can give you a shivery feeling as you connect to it. You can press on it with your focus and notice it presses back. It is real, you see. You can feel it. Very good.

Permission and Access

Claim the inside of the bubble. Declare it private, sacred, safe, healing space. It is so. By your word, you claim it. Into this bubble call your own Guides, the Angels, and the Lightbeings. Notice the wave of Love as they enter.

Ask your Guides, "Do I have permission to do this exercise with this subject right now?" Wait just a moment for the response, and know it will be subtle. If you have waited more than 30 seconds, you've missed the response. Answers are immediate. You can assume it's a "Yes" for now. If it isn't, that will become obvious. Soon you will know how to get the answer; you won't have to make the assumption. For now, assume permission is present and proceed.

Have the intention to connect with your subject's higher soul. Notice the energetic shift that indicates a connection. Again, this will happen right away. Ask the higher soul for permission to work in her Energy body and with her Guides. Tell her, "Any limitations you wish to place on this access will be honored" so she can relax her guard and accept the healing that is available.

Feel the access opening. If you're not aware of it yet, don't worry. That's what all the subtle Energy awareness exercises will be for. We will be covering them right after this section. Just know there's an opening, a doorway, at the level your subject is comfortable with. With intention, move into the access.

Ask your subject's Guides and Angels to join you in the bubble. Feel them, or simply know they will be there. Ask them to open the channels wide. Feel for the wave of Love. Notice it.

That's as far as we're going to go right now in this exercise. This is the first step of the healing process: creating sacred space. You have done it! Feel good!

Close It Down

Very quickly, friends, we will now run through the Closing Process. We will explain it in greater detail later, but for now just follow along and know the true Teachers of the Lightworkers Healing Method will make this happen for you.

Draw your focus into your feet. Reach through your feet and into the planet. Perhaps visualize you are a tree with giant roots; reach into those roots. Have the intention to ground. Feel yourself coming firmly back to the physical dimension. Notice this is happening for your subject too.

Have the intention to separate your Energy from your subject. Call your Energy back to you. Send her Energy back to her. You can say it out loud: "My Energy back to me. Your Energy back to you. My Energy back to me. Your Energy back to you." You will feel it shifting. You can even use your hands to push her Energy to her, and to pull your Energy back to you. Continue your mantra: "My Energy back to me. Your Energy back to you. My Energy back to me. Your Energy back to you."

Take that bubble of Light that you just created. With your intention expand it a thousand times over. Split it into two bubbles, one for you and one for your subject. Now each of you is individually encased in Light – so much Light. With your intent to do so, you ground those bubbles down to their own right place in the Divine Plan. Just ground the bubbles down, and know you have Divine Help to do that.

Phew. Very good. You are done. Excellent work! Feel good!

CHAPTER THREE

MEET THE GUIDES

From Taoist wisdom:

The only way to align with the Tao is to defer to its authority.
In order to do that, a person has to become:
Quiet and receptive enough to feel its presence,
Sensitive and adaptable enough to follow its direction,
Spontaneous enough to move with its flow
whenever it unexpectedly changes course,
Modest enough to realize that the individual mind cannot fathom
the vast workings of the universal Tao mind, and
Trusting enough to know that wherever its currents lead,
the Tao is ultimately acting in everyone's best interests.
*Modified from **The Tao of Equus** by **Linda Kohanov***
Shared with thanks to Linda Kohanov

When we announce the "subtle Energy awareness" segment in our classes, some faces silently shout, "I can't do this. This game's already over for me." My friend, if this is you, I can relate. Do you remember the career that I was so attached to that it took me five years to listen to my Guides and get out of there? I was a CPA, a Certified Public Accountant—for 20 years. Yes, twenty *years*! That's a long-term commitment to a career. When my Guides told me to give it up, I was a partner in a CPA firm. I loved the challenges of the business game. My clients were businesses and business owners who were playing the game to win. This was not a mellow environment. I was wrapped pretty tight, with a history of allergies, headaches, insomnia, ulcers, heart palpitations, and panic attacks. I was not a daydream believer. It was hard for me to imagine all the people living life in peace.

As if that's not bad enough, accounting was not my first major in college. Before my switch to accounting, I spent two-and-a-half years as a chemistry major, taking a total of six chemistry classes at the college level. During that time I also took three calculus classes, two physics classes, three biology classes and two statistics classes. I had a solid education in math and science. That's pretty hardcore, left brained, linear thinking, wouldn't you agree?

There's more, friend. I come from a scientific family. My dad was a western medical doctor, an eye surgeon to be exact. My mother was a mathematician and a computer systems analyst. She taught math at the college level and calculated rocket trajectories for NASA. My older sister has her Ph.D. in neurophysiology. She did basic research on the cerebellum and taught brain structure at the University of Toronto Medical School. When he died, my brother was working toward his Ph.D. in Ecology, and intensive care nursing was my younger sister's career choice.

Are you starting to form an impression of the type of person I'm describing—raised in a scientific and medical family, with a scientific education, a business background, and a partner in a CPA firm? Would you think this type of person could *sense subtle Energy*? No! That was certainly true in the beginning. However, I did learn to do this. Can you learn to do it? *Absolutely.* We can *all* do this. In fact, it's our natural way of being; this is how we are when we're out of our physical bodies. Right now, we happen to be in a body, but that doesn't stop us from being able to experience subtle Energy. We can overcome that limitation. Once again, if this were taught in kindergarten the world would be a better place; since most schools skip over this life skill, you can begin today. It's just a process. We start where we are, and we get better every single day.

On the other end of the spectrum, there's the "ho-hum, I already know this" person. If you're in that camp, simply consider that we are eternally growing and expanding beings. There is always more to learn, more to master. I've been working with this for 22 years now, and I still learn something new every single day. Set a goal of deepening your abilities in the arena of subtle Energy awareness. We can all improve these life-changing skills.

CHI DECATHLON: SENSING SUBTLE ENERGY

Subtle Energy is—ahem—subtle. You will have to be reasonably calm and centered to play these games. Don't expect dramatics; expect subtlety. Pay close attention. Notice faint sensations when they happen. Also do this, my friend: hold the attitude of "I can do this, this is natural," throughout these subtle Energy exercises. You will achieve much more when you know you can succeed than if you are only willing to "try." Don't try—do. You *can* do it.

First things first, especially if you are unsure of your abilities. Let's get some Divine Help. Put the book down, go online to www.lightworkersmethod.com, and absorb the Energy transmission entitled *Become a Healing Vessel*. This will support you as you move forward through the process. Feel free to repeat the transmission as many times as is necessary until you feel ready to proceed.

Let the Games Begin

These exercises are much more fun with a human partner, so don't hesitate to try them with a friend. However, if you are antsy to get going and the only one around is your cat or dog or just yourself, you can make do. Simply adjust the descriptions accordingly.

Chi Patty-Cake

Take yourself back to childhood. Remember patty-cake, clapping your hands against your friend's hands? We're going to play a modified version of that game. In this version, you won't actually touch your friend's hands; you will stop two to three inches short of that. Subtle Energy, or chi, will build in the space between your almost-touching hands to the point that you will be able to feel it.

Before you begin, you can rub your own palms together briskly to alert them that it's game time. Your hands may tingle a bit as the Energy flow amps up. You can begin with the Opening Process (page 53) to clear your Energy body. If you are practicing with a partner, this will also form the connection between the two of you. Bring your focus to the corners of your mouth and draw them upward. Better, yes?

Now bring your hands about a foot away from hers. Slowly bring your hands toward hers, almost touching your friend's palms with yours, but not quite. Leave a few inches between them. Slowly move your hands away and then toward each other, repeatedly. "Patty cake, patty cake, baker's man, bake me a cake as fast as you can." As you do so, put your focus in your hands. Notice when you can feel something pushing back. You might think it's simply wind resistance, or perhaps your imagination. All of that thinking is coming from your conscious mind. Our minds are not the friends we think they are. Just let those thoughts go, and come back into the moment of chi patty-cake. Continue to let the Energy build between your hands as you play patty-cake, until you can actually feel the chi of your friend's hands pushing against your own chi.

If you are playing with an animal or plant friend rather than a human one, repeatedly bring your hands close to her body and then farther away again, just as above. She will not press her body back toward you, but her chi will press against your palms just the same. If you are playing solitaire chi patty-cake, repeatedly bring your palms toward each other and then farther away again.

As you continue, you may start to lose your awareness of the chi sensations. If so, shake your body like a dog after a bath to reset your Energy field and release the doubt. Massage your hands again and give it a second go. Know there is Energy there to sense. Know that everyone can do this, which certainly includes you. Practice again, and trust that what you are feeling is real.

If this is your first experience with sensing subtle Energy, congratulations! The door has opened for you. From here on out it's simply a matter of improving and expanding your abilities. You have just had your breakthrough. Take a moment to savor your success! Be happy!

Pass the Chi-Ball

After your chi patty-cake accomplishments, you're ready to move on to the next event in this Energy decathlon. Once again, sit facing your friend. Hold your own hands three to six inches apart from each other, palms facing together, and bounce them toward one another repeatedly. As you do so, focus on the space between your hands. It is as if you are compressing the air between your hands to form a ball out of it. This is identical to solitaire chi patty-cake. The longer you compress the air between your hands, the easier it is to feel the Energy, the chi, in that space. Continue until the chi-ball is very tangible for you.

When you and your game partner each have a tangible chi-ball, both of you can form the intention that your chi ball now becomes a perfect ball of Joy and Love. If you are very sensitive you might feel the vibration of the chi-ball shift as you do so. Your heart chakra might open up a little. Some people find their eyes spring leaks about now. Whatever happens, don't suppress your natural reaction; simply let it be. When you and your friend each have a Glorious chi-ball formed, share the gift. Pour the chi-ball of Joy and Love that you have just made into the lap of your friend, as she pours her chi-ball of Joy and Love into your lap. If you are practicing solo, draw your chi-ball into your own torso. Either way, how does that feel? Isn't it delightful to receive a gift of Joy and Love? Thank your friend for the gift; gratitude counts!

After you have been practicing with this a bit, you might need to reset your Energy body. Think of it as cleansing your palate between glasses at a wine tasting. Get up, move around, bend and stretch. Have a drink of water. Go outside and find something to appreciate: the sky, the trees, or the architecture. Do something practical: sweep the entryway or pull some weeds. This not only gets the job done, it helps you get grounded again. Then, if you wish to experience more, repeat the Opening Process. This re-establishes your own Energy body in a strong alignment, and re-opens the connection with your game partner.

Feel the Field

Let me be absolutely clear about this exploration: you do *not* physically touch your game partner. That is another game entirely. In this game your intention is to develop a sense of what an Energy body or an aura feels like. This is a hands-off adventure.

If you have taken a break between Chi-Ball Creation and Feel the Field, repeat the Opening Process (page 53). Next, briskly rub your own hands together and massage them to re-energize them. Your eyes can actually be either very slightly open or fully closed. Experiment with that to discover what you like best.

First, bend your elbows and face your palms toward your own chest or belly. Holding your hands three to six inches away from yourself, gently bounce your hands toward your body. Keep your focus on your palms. As you repeat this, once again you will begin to feel something pressing against your hands. Slowly switch your focus between your hands and your torso. Perhaps you will also feel a slight pressure against your torso.

Now slowly draw your focus back into your palms and once again notice how your own aura feels.

When you and your friend are both satisfied with this step, slowly rotate your hands until the palms face your friend. Just as you did with your own aura, gently bounce your hands three to six inches toward and away from her torso. Focus on your hands; notice the pressure as it builds against your palms. There it is; you are now feeling someone else's Energy body, someone else's aura.

If you are very sensitive, you will notice a qualitative difference between the way her Energy body feels as compared to your own Energy body. Everyone has her own vibrational fingerprint. Everyone "feels" a different way. By slowly rotating your hands to face first you and then her, you might begin to notice these delicate differences.

When you are ready for more, slowly move your hands around your friend, never touching her physical form, but continually feeling for her Energy body. This is the classic Feel the Field Energy exploration. Become aware of fluctuations in the aura. It is very rare to find an aura without any variations. You might feel lumps or bumps in her Energy body, concave or convex areas. There may also be places that feel stronger and other places that feel emptier. Perhaps you will notice differences in temperature, warmth in one area and coolness in another. Some areas might feel smooth while others are rougher. Simply notice what you perceive.

Practice sensing around her head; as with the torso, your hands can stay three to six inches away, so no worries about the hairdo. You can even try to feel the Pillar of Light itself as it extends above her body. If your friend is lying down, you can also sense it below her feet. Take your time as you practice sensing an aura.

Isn't it fun? Feel good! You have done it! Now that you have one method of subtle Energy observation, you are firmly in the game. From this point on, it is simply a matter of adding more tools to your second-sense kit.

THE INVISIBLE GORILLA

Humans place a lot of emphasis on sight. For many of us, it is the sense we trust the most. Our society has phrases like "I see," "see here," "see it to believe it," and even the nonsensical "can you see what I am saying?" Our belief in the power of sight is even institutionalized into the legal system, which places a lot of faith in eyewitnesses. All of this stresses the point that we like to be able to see things. In subtle Energy sensing, clairvoyance (clear viewing) is something many people are interested in mastering. Actually using our clairvoyance is not at all difficult. The challenge is to believe we can do this. If we don't think we can see Energy, we won't be able to. If we know we can see it, there it is.

Let's review some scholarly literature on a topic called inattentional blindness. Dr. Daniel Simons of the University of Illinois at Urbana-Champaign is currently an expert in this area. He and his colleagues from Harvard University paired together to conduct an experiment. Test subjects were asked to count basketball passes by players wearing white shirts and ignore passes made by players wearing black. Approximately 50% of these observers failed to notice when a person wearing a gorilla suit entered the display, stopped and faced the camera, thumped his chest, and exited on the far side. To half of the test subjects, the gorilla was effectively invisible.

A lot of additional research has been done on this topic, both before and after this classic test. The conclusion is that it's hard for us to see unexpected things. In other words, it's harder to see something we don't know to look for.

Clairvoyance is the same. There is a gorilla sitting right there in front of you: the Energy body of your friend. If you know the gorilla is there, then you will look for it. If you don't know to look for the gorilla, it's harder to see. So know this: there are energetic messages there that are visible to your subtle Energy eyes.

The first trick to activating second sight is the transmission; the second trick is to know to look for something unexpected. In other words, be open to whatever comes; don't judge it. The third trick, of course, is to expect to be able to see. *Know* you will be able to do this, and move forward with that attitude.

Scholarpedia (the peer-reviewed open access encyclopedia written by scholars) has a nice article on this phenomenon. You can view it at www.scholarpedia.org/article/Inattentional_blindness. You can also try Dr. Simons' tests for yourself by visiting his website at www.simonslab.com.

Claim your full potential for yourself. We can all do this. It is natural. With practice, everyone can learn to understand a foreign language, yes? This is exactly the same. Seeing, or perhaps more accurately visualizing, is available for you. You see, when we shut our physical eyes it can be easier to pay attention to our subtle eyes.

Second Sightings

Sit facing your practice partner. Refresh your Energy body and your connection with your friend by repeating the Opening Process. Now close your eyes, and gently massage your face and head to alert it: game time!

While keeping your focus on your partner, notice what visual images come to mind. If you are not strongly visual, these will be more like ideas of images than actual images, and that's fine. The key is to be immediately aware of any impressions you receive. You might get an impression of a fountain, a soccer field, a forest path, a schoolroom, the color blue, a scythe, springtime, falling down a tunnel, brightly colored tents, or something else entirely. In other words, it could be anything at all. Don't have preconceived ideas of what you will see; that's like looking for the white-shirted basketball passes and missing the gorilla. Simply watch in your minds' eye for anything. Be open to the unexpected.

The next key is this: trust your first impressions, your very first impressions. Trust them even if they don't make sense right away. They are coming to you from your soul and your Guides, and they will become clear if you play along with them. If a questioning thought occurs like,

"Did I imagine that? Was that real?" acknowledge that it's coming from your conscious mind and simply move past it. While your conscious mind very much wants to help, the best it can do is to get out of the way. All attempts to "think your way through this" will short-circuit the process. Those analytical thoughts are showstoppers. This is not a question of thinking; it is a question of perceiving. Ask your conscious mind to step aside and allow your soul and your Guides to lead you.

Think of this process as a virtual slide show: once you accept the first slide, a second one appears. If you stop to question the first slide, the second one won't come. If you accept the first image that comes to you, a second one will come. If your first ideas are wrong, they will soon correct themselves as subsequent information flows in. If, on the other hand, you immediately question the first image, your car has stalled out. It's a lot easier to steer a moving car than to start a stalled one, yes? Relax! This isn't the real deal; it's just a game. It's your very first practice attempt, so you can be wrong and it doesn't matter. Keep going. Simply use the first impression as a clue and move on. You can correct yourself as you go.

Many people, perhaps most, see it as "wrong" when things don't go perfectly, and develop a habit of wanting everything to go "right." Unfortunately, this habit slows our own growth tremendously. When something "goes wrong," it is simply a learning experience. At each stage of the journey, we can ask for the right number of things to "go wrong." Not so much going wrong that it's overwhelming, but enough so that we can grow and learn. Then when things "go wrong," we don't freak out but instead figure out what the message is, make the adjustment, and move forward.

There is no "wrong" with this experience. The images you receive don't necessarily have to make sense to the other person at this stage of the learning process. When they do, that's wonderful confirmation, but just because your friend doesn't immediately recognize the situation doesn't mean the images are wrong. Consider your partner has almost certainly lived many lives before this one. She might not remember all of those lives yet. That goat might have been really important to her when she lived in Turkey in the year 1200 CE, even though she doesn't remember it now. Keep going. Don't let that stop you. Later on, you will need to achieve a higher standard of understanding, but for now, simply accept what is.

My friend, I do *not* mean, "make up a story." This is *not* about imagining. Imagining has creative Energy; this way of being has *receptive* Energy. This is about quietly observing what is already present in your partner's Energy body. This is about catching the thought-ball the Guides toss to you, not throwing a thought-ball of your own.

The final key is to realize how subtle these visual stimuli can be. There can be a brief, muted flash of a visual impression, and that's it. Our job is to notice that faint signal and also to be open to the ones that follow. Try it: refresh your Energy, rub your face and head, and with closed eyes take a look at your friend.

How to Improve

If you have had visual success already, feel good! Take a moment to savor your breakthrough! If not, don't make this mean anything. Truly, we can all master this. Clairvoyance is a learnable skill, not a gift you either have or don't have. You might be thinking, "Fine, so what's my next step?" There are four potential doors to go through; at least one of them will apply to you. As you apply the solutions, you will have your moment of discovery. It will come. The four doors are explained below. The first door is the most commonly applicable; the last one is the most atypical.

The first door is simply to re-set your Energy body to improve its current state of being. Hydrate yourself; the more water you have in your system, the easier it is to sense subtle Energy. Shake yourself like a dog after a bath. Rub your face and body. Take three deep breaths. If you have access to Energy clearing sprays, healing tuning forks, or essential oils, use their vibrations to reset your own.

If that doesn't do it, take a break. Re-establish your Energy flow by doing whatever it is that naturally helps you to feel good. This might be going outside, it might be listening to uplifting music, it might be exercising, or it might be something else. Pay attention to yourself: what feels like a great idea to you right now? As you follow your internal wisdom, you will begin to feel more yourself.

When you feel fully present, see if you want to try again today to experience this breakthrough, or wait. It is possible that you may have already spent your psychic Energy supply today, and tomorrow might be a better choice—but that's not always true. Sometimes right now is the perfect time. Be aware of the human tendency to put things off that we don't think we can accomplish. Trying again right now is a thousand times better than intending to try tomorrow and never coming back to the project again. If now is the time, then repeat the Opening Process (page 53) and go for another round.

If you have gone through door number one and still feel you haven't "got it," then go through the second doorway: change your expectations. Consider that you might in fact be receiving the subtle visuals, and you are not recognizing them. Remember the definition of "subtle": "delicate or faint." These images will *not* be a flashing neon Light the size of a billboard directly in the center of your mind's eye. Think along these lines: in a dim room, out the corner of your eye you catch a glimpse of the tip of a cat's tail just as he leaves the room. Be alert for impressions happening at that level. Trust your very first impressions, even if they don't make sense right away. Keep going, moving forward in trust. If this is hard for you, re-read the section on Trust in Chapter Two and repeat those trust-building exercises.

If you have been at this for a while, give yourself the gift of an overnight. Don't do any more today. Your psychic gas tank might be empty. You might need to sleep to recharge yourself. You might also wish to listen to the transmissions on the website again. Try again later: maybe tomorrow, maybe this weekend. Each time you work with these exercises, it will get easier. Think of the process of creating these linkages with the following analogy: you are hacking a path to the Light through the jungles of your mind with a machete. Every stroke creates progress. As you continue on, you will approach the end of the jungle and the Light will start to shine down the path to reach you. Keep going; tomorrow could be the day you reach the open meadow.

When you have adjusted your expectations and refueled your tank, try again with that attitude. Very often, this is exactly what is needed. If this is you, congratulations on your breakthrough!

Now, my friend, it is possible you have followed all of the instructions above to the letter, and still haven't had the experience of breakthrough. You might still be feeling "Why not ME? Why hasn't this worked yet for ME?" There are two more possibilities, one much more likely than the other.

The third door is to change some habits to clear your Energy body. Fewer internal clouds make it easier to receive these impressions. Skip ahead to the segment entitled "A Diet For Success" that comes later on in Chapter Five; it is written for you. This is another aspect of improving your Energy body and therefore your clairvoyance. It doesn't take long for new habits to yield results; a week of clean living makes a huge difference in subtle Energy skills. Give your body seven days of A Diet For Success, and then try again.

Door number four, the least likely possibility, is that it's not good for you, right now, to receive these messages visually. Therefore you are being protected from something that would slow your own personal growth and evolution. This does not mean "never." It simply means "not right now." Keep on your spiritual growth path, gratefully use the subtle sensing tools you already have access to, continue to work to develop these other tools, and move forward.

Don't judge yourself as flawed because of this, my friend. I did not have physical-dimension clairvoyance in the early years of my process; I could only see clearly when I was looking directly up to the higher dimensions. Eventually I realized I didn't need to see the Energy of my clients directly to be able to help them. By focusing on their Guides I was led precisely to their needs. I could simply use the psychic software that was available to me rather than pining for the upgrade I wanted. It wasn't until I detached from ever being able to see Earthly subtle Energy clearly that full clairvoyance dropped into my lap. Be thankful for what you have, and move on. That might be exactly what you need to do, in order to have more. Gratitude matters so much more than we expect it to.

Listening for the Light

The final subtle sense we will work with right now is clairaudience, or hearing the subtle messages. As with second sight, it is rare to actually hear an audible voice, although that does happen. The more common way clairaudience presents itself is with the ideas of words or sounds: a bird's song or angelic music can confirm you are on the right track. The screech of brakes or clanging bells can be a warning to "STOP. There is trouble ahead." Thoughts of words flit through the mind; if you are "in the zone"—if you have created sacred space and your channels are pointed up—those might be verbal messages from the Guides.

As with the previous Energy exercises, begin by refreshing your Energy body. Sit facing your game partner and direct your attention to him. Eliminate visual distractions by closing your eyes, still keeping your focus on him. Now simply become receptive to whatever wishes to present itself to you. Be alert to sounds or words, or thoughts of sounds or words. Trust your first impressions even if they don't make sense right away. Follow the bouncing ball of "sound-thoughts." They will explain themselves as you go through the process. Keep moving.

It can help if you narrate the flow of thought-messages out loud. Don't be thrown if what you're verbalizing doesn't make sense to your game partner right away, although that certainly can happen. More often than not, it will make sense to one or both of you later. Give the "aha" moment time to bubble up. Have fun with it; this is only a game! You are free to make as many mistakes as possible. Be willing to sound like a complete idiot if that's what it takes to open this channel. Giving up what your game partner thinks of you is the most helpful step you can take to advance. Don't make up anything; simply let what comes, come. If nothing comes, that's okay. Over time and with practice, it will.

Naturally Multisensory

If you wish to practice with other techniques before you move on, you can. We can sense our world subtly in all the ways we can sense it physically: through smell and taste, with empathy, and with our inner knowing or felt sense. Practice any of these methods with your friend. Try to smell the Energy. Try to taste the Energy. Don't lick your friend, just open to the ideas or sensations of taste appearing for you. Pay attention to your friend and consider how she is feeling right now. See what comes to you through the doorway of empathy. Physical, emotional, mental or spiritual sensations might appear inside yourself that reflect how she is feeling right now. Become aware of your inner knowing, your felt sense. Consider you already have the answers fully formed inside of you.

You only need one means of sensing subtle Energy before you advance to the next stage. If you have at least one method turned on, from my perspective you are ready. If you aren't sure, just go for it. Take a chance and discover what happens. There is so much grace. Your Guides *Love* you. They *want* you to succeed. They will help you through this and you can do it, with their help. Flash your learner's permit and move forward!

POINT THOSE CHANNELS UP!

My friend, up to this point you have been opening and expanding your intuitive channels horizontally, because you are practicing with someone else who is currently in a physical body. We begin this way because it's easiest, but opening up psychically on the lower dimensions is definitely not the goal in this method. With LHM you are merged with your subject. In essence, you become them. You don't need to scan them. Instead, you will learn to take that open channel and focus it straight UP. You will learn to move above the heavier/lower dimensions and vibrations, and stretch for the top reaches of your range. Your goal is opening to the highest possible frequencies or vibrations, raising your vibrations as high as they will go while simultaneously maintaining your grounding. In this way you can be the bridge from the Divine to the physical dimension.

This step is crucial in making contact with the higher dimensions. Point those intuitive channels UP to the higher dimensions where the Guides, Angels, Lightbeings and Ultimate Source are waiting. Your powerful intention does this. In order to help your mind focus on the higher dimensions, you might turn your eyes up in your head, turn your palms to face up, and perhaps even hold your arms up. All of this helps, but the real key is your intention to point your intuitive sensing channels to the higher dimensions.

My friend, your Guides have been waiting for this moment for a long time. Know they are there, right above you, and they want to get your attention as much as you want to feel them. Are you ready? Let's begin.

First decide which sensing method you feel most comfortable with, and alert that sense you are getting ready to notice it. Most people find it easiest to work with their hands at first, so I will word the instructions that way. If you are working with another sense, modify accordingly.

If you have taken a break between the previous exercises and this section, refresh your sacred space by repeating the Opening Process (page 53). Rub your hands to alert them to turn on. Hold them, palms up. Turn your eyes upward behind closed eyelids. Ask your Guides to step on your hands, to press on them, to give you some kind of signal that you can feel in your hands.

Some sensation will occur. Perhaps your palms will tingle. Perhaps you will feel subtle pressure on your hands. As this occurs, your conscious mind might chime in; "Did I really feel that?" Remember, today is a day to trust yourself. Breathe. How does your heart feel? Trust your heart. It knows.

If you just aren't sure whether or not you feel something, there are a couple of things that I would like to say to you. First, practice makes perfect, and over time this will get easier and more clear. Second, often the hang-up at this stage is a question of whether or not your Guides and Angels are even there with you. Honey, they *are* there. They are *always* there with you. There is absolutely no privacy. It's like the Santa Claus song: They see you when you're sleeping. They know when you're awake. They're always there for and with you. Are they trying to reach for you? Absolutely and without a doubt. Their greatest Joy will be to have you recognize them.

Now, simply try again, knowing that every single time you do this it gets easier and easier. It's like learning to ride a bicycle. The first time you tried to ride, did you fall down? I did. That's how it goes. We try again and try again and try again. Ouch. Then one day we are riding our bicycles and all is well. It is the same with this. Point your palms up and ask your Guides to press on them, sit on them, or stand on them. Notice the sensations.

Sometimes at this point in the classes, someone gets a bit of pressure in her head. She might even say, "Nothing's happening except I have a headache." If this is your experience, consider the possibility that the sensation you are experiencing could in fact be your Guides knocking on your crown chakra. Open your crown and let them in.

If you are still unsure, practice a bit more with the subtle sensory exercises of the Chi Decathlon. Develop more confidence with your subtle Energy skills. Read the segment entitled "A Diet for Success" in Chapter Five, and put it into practice in your life. Then try again: point those channels up. Success is inevitable. This is a natural way of being. We've all been dead before, and we're all going to be dead again. When our bodies are dead, only our subtle essence remains, so of course we are fully sensory with subtle Energy while in dead mode. Therefore, in the here and now it's just a matter of remembering what you already know. You can do this while in a body, just as well as you can when dead. It's simply a matter of practice.

Making Contact

By this point, you will have one favorite method of subtle sensing you are working with. You will have felt confirmation that your Guides are present. Now is the time to flush open the channels of connection between you and your Guides. As with all skills, practice makes perfect. Simply begin wherever you are right now, and know you will improve. The second time through will be easier than the first. This is an exercise you may want to repeat many times, until these channels are flowing freely. After that, it may never call to you again—or it may. You will know. Follow the call if and when it comes.

In a moment, I will walk you through the exercise of making contact. It begins with the Opening Process to refresh your sacred space, and then moves into firming up your grounding to create a solid base for your Pillar of Light. The more firmly you are grounded, the higher you can fly. Next you will point your intuitive channels up to your Guides and Angels, locking the top of your Pillar into position.

As your Pillar of Light stabilizes, you will energetically shoot up inside the Pillar as high as you can, repeatedly. In this way you will rise above the physical dimension's static as far as possible. When you are at the apex of your reach, you will call for your Guides to meet you at that level. They will come. They always do. They have been waiting all your life for this moment.

If you are truly at the top of your range, this will not be a sustainable vibration for you, and very quickly you will feel yourself falling back into heavier dimensions. No worries; don't fight it. It is in the very process of moving up and down that you open the channels. Allow yourself to settle back to the physical dimension. We will "rinse and repeat"—or in this case, ground and repeat.

Since you will be in the higher dimensions, you will have expanded access to Divine Assistance. Don't waste the chance. Have a list ready of requests for help with the significant challenges of your life. While in the presence of your Guides, present your requests. You will have come into a powerful state, and the desires you express in this state will be answered powerfully.

Ready? Let's go, my friend!

MEET YOUR GUIDES

To prepare, think of the predominant challenge in your life right now. Be sure it is written at the top of the list you just prepared, because in the moment it can be hard to think clearly. Be careful with your wording. There's a tendency to entreat, "Tell me what to do with this challenge." While information is helpful, you're limiting the Divine. You're telling the Divine, "Help me by telling me what to do." It's ever so much better to simply say, "Help me in whatever way is most appropriate." That might include instructing you, and it might include simply an Energy boost to blast through whatever is tripping you up right now. This makes sense, yes? Do you have your request ready to go?

Begin by sitting comfortably and bringing body and mind together once more. Bring your focus inside. Repeat the Opening Process (page 53). Notice the Energy flowing through the fullness of your heart chakra, the entire hula-hoop, back to front and front to back, back to front and front to back. Refresh your Energy body top to bottom and bottom to top. Be that hula-hoop sized Pillar of Light. Very good. Bring the focus to the intersection of heart chakra and vertical channels, allowing the critical mass of Love to build until it pops into a bubble of sacred space. Claim the sacred space; declare it so.

Bring your focus more deeply into the Earth. Drink fully of the Divine Earth essence. Ground yourself as fully and intensely as you can in this moment. As that stabilizes, have the intention to point your intuitive channels straight up. Ask your Guides and the Lightbeings to draw these channels firmly into place. Ask that your grounding also be locked into position. Intend that your entire Pillar of Light become as straight and true as it is able to be, right now. Ask your Guides for help to make that be so; trust this help is instantly given.

Now begin to bounce up and down inside of your Pillar of Light, as if forming a concentration of Light inside the Pillar. Dip into the Earth a little bit deeper each time, and shoot out of your head a little bit higher with each bounce. As you do this, it widens your range and flushes out your Energy channels. Reach down lower; jump up higher. In a moment, on the count of three you will shoot up through your crown and head straight for Source, and therefore to the Guides. It can help to exhale forcefully as you shoot up. It can also help to visualize yourself as being rocket-powered. It's takeoff time, my friend. Ready?

One, two three: GO. Exhale, jump, rocket boost, to the very top of your range. Quickly repeat again: one, two, three: GO—doubling the height. Repeat again: one, two three: GO—twice as far this time. Repeat again: one, two, three: GO—doubling the height again. The final push: one, two, three: GO—doubling again, into the fifth dimension.

Quickly present your behest to your Guides. If you are truly as high as you can go, you don't have long here. Get that request onto the table, and then simply allow yourself to BE.

Soon you will feel yourself falling back to the physical dimension. Let that happen, and when you feel ready to repeat the process, intentionally dive down through your Pillar of Light and into the planet. Reconnect with Earth Energy. Draw it in deeply, firming up the base of your Pillar. Notice how you are able to ground more deeply than you could, just a few moments ago. When you feel grounded and stable once again, point your intuitive channels directly up and notice how they reach farther into Source than they did before. Once again ask the Lightbeings to draw your Pillar as straight as it will go.

Begin to bounce up and down inside your Pillar of Light, as if you are mentally bouncing on your toes. When you feel ready, on the count of three, take off. One, two three: GO. Exhale, jump, rocket boost, to the very top of your range. Quickly repeat again: one, two, three: GO—doubling the height. Repeat again: one, two three: GO—twice as far this time. Repeat again: one, two, three: GO—doubling the height again. The final push: one, two, three: GO—doubling again, into the fifth dimension.

Quickly read that same behest for help with your central life challenge to your Guides. There is power in repetition, and you are in a more powerful place than you were just moments ago. When the request is on the table once more, simply allow yourself to BE.

As you notice yourself falling back to the physical dimension, know you are flushing the channels even more clear. Repeat this process until you feel complete with it. As that feeling of "done for now" rises up, honor it. Allow yourself to reach all the way down through your Pillar of Light. Ground yourself by focusing through your feet and into the planet. Connect once again to Divine Planetary Energies. Draw in Father Earth and Mother Earth Energies. Feel how they support and strengthen you. Focus on your roots, your connection to the planet. Feel your oneness with the Earth.

If you feel headachy, open your crown more. Holding your crown in its old, smaller configuration creates pressure and therefore pain. Expand both horizontally as if stretching your hat to a larger size, and vertically as if pulling the top of your hat up like a stovepipe. If you feel nauseous, dizzy, or just strange, ground more fully. This exercise is fundamentally an expansion of the channels between you and the Divine. That stretching of the Energy arteries can leave you ungrounded, so continue to draw your focus down. Notice your feet. Bend and flex your ankles. Circle your feet around, first one way and then the other. Then start to move your knees like you're marching while sitting down. Now wiggle around, still seated. Get your shoulders into the action. Moving, moving in the chair.

When you feel ready, take a sip of water, move around, and possibly go outside. Give yourself plenty of time to process this exercise. Put the book down. Drink plenty of water; moving Energy uses water molecules and can dehydrate you. Replace that lost fluid now. Maximize the benefit. You did it; congratulations!

ONE ESSENTIAL SKILL: DISCERNING YES VERSUS NO

My friend, this is what you have been working toward. Being able to get clear guidance is a Big Deal. Clarity is essential for a Lightworkers Healing Method practitioner. From my perspective, it's also extraordinarily helpful, if not essential, for living a fulfilling life. Our Guides and Angels are continually showering us with directions. The good news: they are always exactly correct. Their advice is perfect because it is Divinely Wise and Loving. The tougher news is that it can be difficult to understand the guidance. Our challenge in the moment is to sense the directions accurately. Over time, the challenge is also to have the courage to follow the guidance.

Disclaimer: this does *not* mean following your Guide's advice will keep you comfortable in the short run. Sometimes our life purpose, our soul's deepest desire, does not match the superficial wishes of our personality in the moment. We might wish to stay in a situation of marginal comfort, when the soul plan calls for us to jump out of the nest and fly. It's scary and decidedly uncomfortable to take that leap. However, in the long run following the guidance leads to the most Joy, fulfillment, Peace, and Love.

Be forewarned that clarity comes more easily for questions with less emotional content. It's ever so much easier to have clarity about what a stranger should do in his life, than what you or a Loved one should do. If your goal is for self-healing and personal growth, give yourself time to practice the exercises below before you ask your Guides whether or not to move, quit your job, leave your spouse, or have a child. By beginning with easier questions, you will allow yourself to get comfortable with the ways in which your Guides transmit "Yes" and "No" to you. Work with this enough that you are confident, before you move on to big life questions. Also remember that you are your own most difficult subject, and improve your skills by practicing with others.

As a healing practitioner, you will be amazed at what you can accomplish if you can distinguish "Yes" from "No" in the guidance.

You will have to ask meaningful questions, of course—but clearly recognizing the answer can make the difference between right action and struggle.

Having just been through the "Meet the Guides" exercise, you have begun to flush the channels clear. Because you've been through that exercise, it's going to be easier for you to sense "Yes" and "No" than it was just 20 minutes ago. Don't think you have to jump up and down like that every time you want to work with the Guides. It's effective and you can do it, but it takes a lot of Energy. It's not necessary to go hopping up and down between dimensions every day. All you need is a connection, a working inter-dimensional phone line. Our goal now is to test the phone lines.

Let's begin with a basic question of black and white—literally. If you have a white ceiling or wall nearby, that will do. If not, find a piece of white paper. The first question will literally be: "Is this paper/ceiling/ wall white?" You probably will not have a huge amount of emotional attachment to the answer. It will be easy for you to sense the response. If you are a very precise person, part of you might be arguing about the definition of "white." "What if I have an off-white ceiling?" If this thought has occurred to you, simply choose something you can agree is close enough to white to be called white. Widen your definition of "white." For purposes of this discussion, I will assume you have chosen a white piece of paper. If you are using another option, simply adjust the wording and continue.

As always in working with subtle Energy, it's quite helpful to begin with the Opening Process (see page 53 or Appendix One). This clears your Energy body and surrounds you with sacred space. As you complete that, acknowledge to your Guides that you will now practice discerning "Yes" from "No" in their guidance. If you wish, you can ask them to use your favorite sensory method: pushing on your hands, giving you auditory or visual impressions, or whatever you prefer. You can also leave it up to your Guides to determine which method they will use, and trust they will choose wisely.

If you have chosen a particular sensory method, alert it to turn on: rub your hands, your face and head, your ears, and intend they be "on." For purposes of this discussion I will assume you have chosen tactile sensing, i.e. your hands. If you have made another choice, trust yourself and go with it. I am not implying you should be using your hands; it's simply a common choice. If you are using another sense, merely adjust the wording and continue.

Draw your focus to yourself; turn your palms to face your torso and bounce them gently toward and away from yourself. In this way you can be sure your sensing is "on," because you will feel your own Energy. Now turn your palms to face up, as you did when you initially made contact. With this motion, draw your focus to your Guides, and ask them to confirm the connection by pressing on your hands. If nothing comes right away, bounce your hands gently up and down until you can feel your Guides' Energy pressing back at you.

Once you have felt contact, present the question, "Is this paper white?" See what you notice. Repeat the question several times, slowly, to give your system time to build up a noticeable response. This is what "Yes" feels like. It might feel like lightness, fullness, pressure, warmth, tingling, or something entirely different. It might be in one hand or both hands. Everyone feels this differently; there isn't a right or wrong way, there is simply your way. Just notice what is happening; this is how your Guides are choosing to communicate "Yes" to you, right now.

Rub your hands together to clear the Energy. You can also tap your sternum or your crown to reset your Energy body. Now change the question to, "Is this paper black?" Once again, repeat the question several times, slowly. Notice the change in the sensations. There might be a feeling of cold, emptiness, heaviness, feelings of being closed, or something entirely different. There isn't a correct response; there is simply what your

Guides are using. This is how your Guides are communicating the thought of "No" to you.

Rub your hands together to clear the Energy, and go back to, "Is this paper white?" Repeat the entire process several times, noticing the difference in the response between "Yes" and "No" with this very basic exercise.

If you have been using your hands up to this point, start to expand your horizons. Tap your sternum or crown and rub your eyes to reset your Energy. Now repeat the white/black exercise with the intent to receive images, or thoughts of images. Common signals are green versus red lights, thumbs up versus thumbs down, a hand beckoning versus a hand held up to stop you.

Again tap your sternum or crown and rub your ears. Repeat the exercise with the intent to receive words, or thoughts of words. Typically, "Yes" and "No" are used, but many Guides have a real gift of humor and might use other words that suggest "Yes" or "No" to you. Be open to what comes.

Tap your sternum or crown and rub your heart chakra and solar plexus. These are typical locations of what the Guides label the "truth meter": that area of a body that communicates "Yes" versus "No" guidance. Now repeat the white/black exercise and notice how your body feels, especially in those areas. Some people literally feel a pain when it's "No" and a feeling of well-being when it's "Yes." Feeling happy, relaxed, or peaceful can mean "Yes;" feeling irritated, upset, or anxious can mean "No." For some people, their bodies literally get pulled forward with "Yes" and pushed back with "No." For others, their breath feels free and easy when it's "Yes," tight and closed when it's "No." The point is that there's wide variability; however your Guides communicate with you is perfect.

My friend, there is one critical point to make when it comes to using our emotions as guidance. ***Fear is often misinterpreted as a "No" signal.*** Because our souls plan for life to have challenges, events that can trigger fear are built into the system. This does not mean we are supposed to run away from the challenges. Whatever simultaneously inspires and terrifies us is *exactly* what our souls want us to do. It's tough to be fearless, but easy to learn that fears can be irrelevant. We can learn to feel the fear and move forward anyway. As we do so, we stop weaving from side to side in our life paths and simply move forward.

As you come to know how your body reacts when the guidance is "Yes" as opposed to when it's "No," another beautiful gift will arise. Have you noticed that people don't always tell the truth? Once you master this art, no one will be able to slip an untruth past you. You will get a "No" signal with incoming untruths. This doesn't mean the person means to lie to you; they might be honestly confused. It is simply a way of knowing when truth is present and when it is absent. This doesn't usually mean you will know what the truth is, if it is absent. You will simply know that what is said isn't true.

Once you have experienced signals with your questions of white versus black, you can expand your horizons. Gradually expand your questions to include more emotional content. Stand at your closet in the morning and ask your Guides what to wear. "Is the item to the left? Is it to the right?" Narrow it down until you have it. When you are ready to tackle a bigger challenge, ask your Guides what it is you really want to eat. "Is it in the pantry or the fridge? Is it on this shelf? Is it on the left or right?" and so on, until the lucky snack is identified. Next step: ask your Guides what part of you feels hungry: "Is it my physical body? Is it my emotional body?" If the hunger is coming from anything other than your physical body, ask if food is really what you need, "Yes" or "No." Be open to the response.

Do you see how this can ripple through your life? Every choice becomes a Glorious game of subtle sensing. "Does this soup need more pepper?" "Do I go to the party with my friend or stay home and be peaceful?" Practice at every opportunity with the multitude of small choices in life. Through this practice you will develop an energetic muscle that will be there for you when the real life-questions present themselves:

"Do I accept this job offer, or wait for a better one?" "Is this the right home for me, or do I keep looking?" "Am I seriously ill, or is this just the flu?"

A Work in Process

My friend, remember that practice makes perfect. If you are unsure right now, don't let that discourage you. In the classes, I observe students who actually receive the "Yes" and "No" messages clearly, but feel confusion about the answers. The most common reason for this is that they have a challenge trusting themselves. Usually that means they have a hard time trusting themselves in other arenas of life, too. That may not be true for you at all, but it certainly is true for many people.

If you struggle with trusting yourself, it might be helpful to learn to work with kinesiology, or with divination tools. You might, for example, enlist the aid of a pendulum to get more clarity with your "Yes" and "No" responses. As long as you intend to be communicating with your Guides through these tools, your Guides will use them to speak to you. Be very clear about this: your intention is to access the wisdom of your Guides, not of your body, regardless of the method you use to focus on their directions. Intention counts. You want to be sure you have the inter-dimensional phone line incoming, not simply the body-wisdom phone line.

If you struggle to perceive the messages, it is possible that your Energy field is fogged. If this is your situation, first check your own alignment. Open your Energy cross. Go back to the beginning, the Opening Process, and try again. If the fog is still present, check your attitude. Are you trying to Make It Happen? Don't bully yourself or rush yourself; give your field time to become clear, calm, and quiet. Subtle Energy is subtle! That won't change, but we can learn to "listen quieter." By becoming calm, we improve our capacity to sense.

Over time, there are many things you can do to improve receptivity, in terms of diet and lifestyle habits. See "A Diet for Success" in Chapter Five for an overview. In the short term, calming yourself makes a big difference. Breathe. Relax. Refresh your Energy cross, and try again.

The bottom line is that we can all do this. It is natural for us to be able to receive messages from our Guides. We're all eventually fully multi-sensory in the subtle realms. Use whatever method opens up for you first, and know that, in time, the other systems will also start to speak to you. Simply begin where you are and know that it gets better.

CHAPTER FOUR

SACRED SPACE, PART TWO

If I had six hours to chop down a tree, I'd spend the first hour sharpening the ax.
Abraham Lincoln

In Buddhism, the concept of dependent origination is often explained as all phenomena being the result of causes and conditions. In plain language, that means everything is the result of what came before it. Apparently Abraham Lincoln knew this too. In Energy work as in life, how we prepare can make a huge difference in the end result. Therefore, properly preparing the healing space before the subject arrives can make the difference between "good work" and "Divine Work."

CALLING IN THE VORTEX AND LIVING WATERS

When my Guide Zoron first taught me to create a Vortex, I understood he wanted me to bring one to life in my healing studio. When I eventually realized the Vortex was producing sacred space, it became clear

Zoron had more in mind. Through building Vortices, sacred space can be generated anywhere. You can establish a Vortex where you sleep, throughout your home, and where you work. In other words, you can live your life in sacred space.

Zoron's instructions to me were clear and simple. He told me, "Sweep your healing studio in a counterclockwise circle. Thoroughly. Every single day." Being ignorant but willing, my response was, "I can do that." I began every day by thoroughly sweeping the physical-dimension floor of my healing studio in a counter-clockwise circle, with my physical-dimension broom.

I had no idea why I was doing this. My floor was not dirty. As the weeks went on I questioned the time investment, but Zoron was unbending. Eventually, I started to notice something pushing on my back as I swept the floor. That's when I realized there was an upward-rising Vortex spinning inside that room, and my ignorant, unintentional sweeping had created the Vortex. It hadn't been my intention to create a Vortex. I didn't know there was such a thing. I was sweeping the floor in a circle because my Guide said, "Sweep the floor in a circle."

A Vortex creates a continual energetic exhaust fan. It carries away heavy hurting Energy immediately, so your healing space can continually be energetically squeaky-clean. There is no need for salt bowls or other Earthly means of disposing of heavy Energy. The Vortex immediately sucks it up into Divine Centers of Energy Recycling to be converted into clean, fresh Energy. Over time, Vortices of Divine Light can create sacred space absolutely anywhere.

I am often asked how I perceive these Vortices. To me, a Vortex looks like a tornado of blindingly pure white Light, spinning simultaneously in both directions while sucking used energy upward and bringing Divine Love down. They vary in size; often they start out small and over time can become enormous. A full-grown Vortex reaches from the center of the Earth upward to the center of the Universe. Being inside of one feels like being in the eye of a tornado straight from Source: calm and peaceful, surrounded by a wall of Love spinning at enormous speed. There is only Light and Love inside a Vortex. Everything else is sucked up to Source.

When we discuss Vortex creation in the classes, common questions include: "How long do I need to sweep?" "Can I just sweep the room energetically with my intention?" "What about carpet?" "What about rooms where the furniture blocks my way?"

To all these questions, the response is, "Do the best you can." It is helpful to actually sweep the floor, for two reasons. First, it spreads the effort of creating the Vortex between your Energy body and your physical body; it's easier than using just your mind. Second, it's a lot easier to be thorough if you are focusing on a physical floor and broom; you can see the floor-areas you haven't yet swept much more easily than you can if you are using intention alone. If you have enough time, sweep until you feel complete or your yes/no discernment tells you you've finished. If you are rushed, one time around the room is better than none. Carpet can be swept; this is an Energy cleanse, and Energy accumulates in carpets even more than it does on hard floors. If furniture blocks your way, physically sweep where you can and reach with your intention where the broom can't go.

Many students report amazing transformations where they build and maintain Vortices. Previously troubled projects or businesses thrive; problematic customers or clients go away and are replaced with "perfect" ones. Homes transform as well: chronically angry or upset people calm down; confused people find clarity returning; relationships heal; pet misbehaviors stop; plants perk up. Don't be deceived by the simplicity of this process of creating sacred space. Try it for yourself. See what comes of intentionally sweeping your floor in a counterclockwise fashion, and creating a permanent Vortex.

In addition to tending this permanent Vortex first thing every day, it's a good idea to reinvigorate it before and after every client. If you are sweeping daily, intentionally walking in a counterclockwise fashion while pushing the air with your hands is enough to pump up the Vortex between healing sessions. If you wish to use incense, Energy-clearing sprays, sage or the like as you walk—that's fine. Belief has power. Use whatever you believe will refresh the Vortex as you walk it.

Over time your Vortex will grow. Like a baby, it will start at a perfect size and grow larger and more powerful as you continue to nourish it. One day you will notice the Vortex forms a magnificent Pillar of Light flowing from the center of the Universe to the center of the Earth.

Dippity-Do Waterfall

Do you remember Dippity-Do, the sparkly hair gel from the 80's? A few years into the process of tending my Vortex, I noticed something that looked like Dippity-Do coming down through the middle of my healing studio's ceiling. The obvious questions to my Guides: "What is that? Is it good? Is it bad? What am I supposed to do with this sparkly hair gel waterfall coming into my healing studio?" Their response: "It's the Living Waters. It's good. You'll figure it out." Like a curious cat, I dabbled in the Living Waters until it became clear what they are: pure essence of Divine Love. "Yes," I agreed, proving my capacity for understatement, "This IS good."

Over time your Vortex sanctifies the space it spins through, so inevitably the Living Waters will begin to flow right down the center of the Vortex. The pure essence of Divine Love is naturally called into any sacred space; like attracts like. You can also speed up the entire process by directly asking for the Living Waters and appreciating the result.

As they continue to run, both the Vortex and the Living Waterfall will increase in size and force. Reasonably soon, you can have a magnificent cyclone of Divine Love spinning around a huge waterfall of Divine Love that pours throughout the space and pools on the floor, creating a beautiful foundation of Love for healing. In this loving and protected sacred space, your good healing work becomes Divine Work. More importantly, your good life becomes a Divine Life.

Miraculously, you can trigger this birthing of sacred space by thoroughly and intentionally sweeping your floor daily, in a counter-clockwise circle. While doing so, appreciate how the Vortex continually cleanses the space. As you complete your sweeping, call for the Living Waters to come down through the center of the Vortex and fill your healing space with Divine Love, and give thanks.

Improving the Vessel

My friend, so much of life depends on the attitude with which we meet it. If my mindset about someone coming to me for healing is, "You're a mess. Good thing you came to me, because I have my act together," I will not be facilitating a Divine Healing that day. Since criticism and judgment are foreign concepts to the Divine Mind, the judging thoughts will separate me from Source. The attitude itself will block any Divine Healing that might otherwise have occurred.

In getting our attitudes right, it is important for us to remember for whom we are working. We are not serving the incarnate self of our healing subject, however much it may look like that. We are actually helping the higher soul of the incarnated being. When we open up to that truth we can feel the beauty of her higher soul cascading around and through us, and a healing attitude is born.

Fifteen minutes before every healing session, I turn my focus to the person I am preparing to work with. As I become aware of my subject's higher soul, I feel like I should get down on the floor and kiss her feet. It is as if Mother Theresa or Thich Nhat Hanh has asked me to help. My heart opens with gratitude for the chance to serve. Any stupid ego-personality-level ideas about the subject fly away and seem completely unimportant. There is nothing I will not do for my subject, if that is what her Guides tell me to do. Then and only then do I have an attitude that can truly facilitate Divine Healing.

Once I feel my heart open and my gratitude bubble up for the chance to help this magnificent spirit, I make a request of her Guides, "If there is anything you want to do in my Energy body to improve it so that I can help your ward who is getting ready to walk through my door, have at it." This one little step has quite possibly created more growth and healing for me than anything else. Why? Every Guide who comes through the door with their ward can see some flaw in my Energy body, because we're eternal beings with eternal potential for improvement. Very often the Guide will respond, "I'll fix that," and tweak my Energy body. What a blessing; every Guide brings a gift.

These two steps of viewing the subject's higher soul and asking her Guides to make improvements may seem like trivial details. You may be tempted to skip over them if you are pressed for time. However, they can have a huge impact on the success of your healing practice as well as on your personal growth and healing. Simply *thinking*, "I am serving the higher self of my subject" does begin the process, but it is not enough to truly open the doors to Spirit. It is the visceral experience of the glory of the subject's soul that truly makes the difference in attitude. I highly recommend you make a habit of actually experiencing yourself as a servant of the higher soul of your subject, and also of asking your subject's Guides to improve you. Try it for yourself. It's possible you'll get hooked just as I have.

TROUBLE-SHOOTING WHEN "IT'S NOT WORKING"

It's important to facilitate healing work in sacred space, with a servant's attitude. You have experienced how to create both internal and external sacred space. The Opening Process creates internal sacred space; the Vortex and Living Waters create external sacred space. At some point these internal/external lines will blur, but for now, this can be a helpful way to think about these processes: creating sacred space in and around you.

As we all know, *cleaning* is something that has to be done repeatedly. Whether we are talking about brushing our teeth, dusting a house, or maintaining sacred space, the truth remains. "Clean" is not a forever state. Occasionally during a healing session it will become clear that your sacred space is tarnishing. How might this present itself? Multiple ways. Sometimes the work becomes difficult: you can't hear or see the Guides; you can't sense the Energy changing, or perhaps you can sense that the Energy *isn't* shifting. The session feels "stuck." You might even start to feel "off," as if you're spaced-out or queasy or something else equally uncomfortable. This doesn't mean you're no good at this work. All these signals point to one issue: your sacred space needs to be refreshed.

Begin with re-establishing the external sacred space. Focus on the Vortex and nourish it until you feel it pulsing with real power. Don't be shy; get up and walk the Vortex until it pushes at your back. Explain to your subject that you are strengthening Divine Presence in the room; she will be as grateful as you are to feel the change. When the Vortex is tangible to you once more, shift your focus to the Living Waters. Can you feel them? If not, focus on the Waters, and call them into the space. Asking the Vortex and Living Waters to "pulse" or "power up" can help make the sensations more tangible, so you can be sure they are running. Your external sacred space should now be revived, making it easier to clear your internal world.

The next step is to refresh your personal Energy alignment. Chances are, it has wobbled. Begin with the quick Energy-resetting steps: shake yourself off to reset your Energy body, just as you did in the subtle Energy exercises. Tap your sternum, rub your face, hands, and arms. If you have access to Energy clearing sprays, healing tuning forks, essential oils, or other Energy-clearing tools, use them. Point your intuitive channels up; chances are they have fallen down to the physical dimension.

Unless you feel perfectly clear already, repeat steps from the Opening Process (page 53 or Appendix One) as thoroughly as feels helpful. You might begin with your grounding; draw up more Earth Energy and feel it increase your stability. Focus next on your connection to Source. Breathe through your crown to open it wider and intentionally draw in more healing Source frequencies. Now notice your entire vertical Pillar of Light; flush it top to bottom and bottom to top. Move your mindfulness to your heart chakra and flush it back to front and front to back.

Now focus again on your subject. Once again notice her higher self; your heart will open in response to that Glorious being of Light. Feel the gratitude bubble up for the chance to serve her. Once again have the intention to become one with your subject's Earthly incarnation so the two of you can be simultaneously healed of the presenting issues. Feel the Joy of the merge.

Draw your attention to the intersection of the heart chakra and vertical channels; notice the "pop" as the bubble of sacred space explodes into being around you and your subject. Notice how much better you feel as you re-establish sacred space both outside and inside of yourself.

Figure Four: Sacred Space

Once again point your intuitive channels up and call for the Guides, Lightbeings, and Angels to reconnect with you. Feel their Love and grace pouring down upon you and your subject. Take a moment to bathe in the bliss. That should do it! You should be re-established and ready to move forward again.

Notice what you are doing by going through these various steps: you are repeating the three steps of A-COAT that come before the "ask" part of the equation. You are putting yourself back in the zone so that the Divine can reach through you to the physical dimension.

Find the Trail

Now go back to the last clear message, the last point in the session you felt good about, something that occurred before you began to feel stuck. Consider that you may have taken a wrong turn after that point. Remember that we are not the "deciders" in this work; that we never impose our own ideas on the situation. Let go of your original idea of what should follow the last clear message; ask your subject's Guides for another option. If a new message comes through, follow that track instead. This should get you in motion again.

If the only message that comes from the Guides is the identical message even with your intent to let go of the original idea, this verifies you were on the right trail to begin with. You are pursuing the proper course. Therefore, there *is* a way to progress; you can let go of that doubt. With new confidence that there is a way to make it through the sticking point, having both re-set your Energy body and asked again for clarity, move forward once more. Ask your subject's Guides to help you. Flash that learners' permit and trust that you will be able to move forward. It will happen.

My friend, this is true in your LHM sessions and also in your life. When you have that "stuck" feeling in life, first reset your Energy body by recreating sacred space within and without. Then go back to the last thing you felt sure you should do with your life, and ask your Guides what you should truly be doing. Be open to a completely different message coming through—but also be open to moving forward on the original track with a new belief in place. Things "going wrong" do not necessarily mean you are headed in the wrong direction in life. If everything always went perfectly, how would you learn? Things "going wrong" give you a chance to grow. Since Life is about growth, things will regularly and consistently "go wrong." They are *supposed* to "go wrong;" that is in fact "right." These events are not inherently wrong. It is your thoughts about them that make them feel wrong. As Max Ehrmann wrote in *Desiderata*, "Whether or not it is clear to you, no doubt the Universe is unfolding as it should." Relax. Trust. And move forward.

Let's turn back to your situation with your subject. If after all of this you still have the "stuck" feeling, consider that what you are trying to accomplish might not be in accordance with the Divine Plan. Perhaps you are trying to push an earthly agenda; perhaps your subject's original intention is flawed. What to do? Give up trying to Make Something Happen. Relax into the arms of the Divine. Trust that the perfect solution has already come. Let go, let God. That is the final piece of the puzzle, the final "ahhh" moment of releasing resistance, when we realize that the response to our asking has already arrived.

SACRED SEAL ON THE SESSION

Closing an Energy healing session properly and fully is every bit as important as opening it properly. I Love the Closing Process. It is like wrapping a gift. It completes a beautiful healing session and brings it to perfection.

Make it Perfect

The first stage of the process of ending a healing session is asking for our mistakes to be corrected, our omissions to be included, our poorly done work to be done well, and our well-done work to be made Divinely perfect. This creates a Divine errors and omissions insurance policy on our healing work.

Often this request will trigger a big Energy shift. Feel this as a wonderfully supportive event, not as criticism. Thank goodness, we don't have to be perfect to achieve perfect results. As long as we are doing our best with pure intentions, the Divine will pick up the slack. It will add what we aren't able to provide.

If you do feel a large shift, you can ask the Guides if there is more you can do to help complete whatever that shift represents. It is possible you are supposed to circle back and do a bit more work in an omitted area. If so, you will continue to be guided through the "ask" portion of the healing session until once again it feels complete, at which point you will again begin the Closing Process.

This is a wonderful habit to develop both for healing sessions and for life, because we will in fact handle things poorly from time to time. Have you noticed: we make mistakes in life? Many of us have a pattern of regret when we realize we messed up. "I didn't handle that situation well at all. I wish I could go back and fix it." Good news: since all time is now, we can do exactly that. We can go back in time and mend our missteps. Sometimes it takes months or decades to realize that we goofed, but there is no limitation of space-time. We can always go back in time and correct the energetic imprint.

After asking for errors to be corrected and omissions to be included, ask for the subject's Energy body to be brought into perfect optimal alignment for right now, in this moment, in this life. We don't have to know what that perfect alignment is. The Guides know. There is almost always a very tangible Energy shift with this request. If you repeat that request several times, you'll notice the changes continue in a diminishing pattern. The first request for optimization brings a large shift, and subsequent requests bring smaller and smaller changes until it feels complete.

Not to sound overly dramatic, but this next sentence is the Key to the Kingdom.
Ask for both you and your subject to be brought into optimal alignment.

This was a big one for me. I was fine with not giving my own Energy to my clients. I knew it was right for them to receive Energy directly from Source, rather than from me. I knew it was okay for me to keep my own Energy so I could live my own life. But asking to share in the healing at the time they were receiving it? That was a bigger step. I'd think, "This is their time. This healing is for them. I don't have to benefit. After all, they are paying me for this. I really shouldn't benefit." Finally I could hear my Guides absolutely s*houting*, "Hey! What kind of twisted thinking is that? This is the Universal Abundant Flow of Source! There's no limit to how much healing can flow, right here and now! There is plenty for everyone. To think anything else is a belief in Divine limitation, in scarcity."

Oh. Right. I forgot.

"May this person be brought into perfect optimal alignment, and me, too. May we both benefit. May we both be brought into optimal alignment for this day, for this lifetime, and for all eternity. May we both receive, right now, whatever we need." Over time as you work with many different subjects, this brings your Energy body into a healthier and healthier and healthier configuration. This benefits everyone. You become a better healer, a better person, and a better influence on the world.

We have asked for errors to be corrected and omissions to be included, for our work to be made Divinely perfect, and for both our subjects and us to be brought into perfect optimal alignment. At this point the healing part of the session is complete. Now it's time to stabilize the Energy.

Stabilize the Healing

The first step of stabilizing is to ground the energetic changes fully into the physical body. After spending what is usually over an hour out of your bodies, it's important for both you and your subject to come back at the end of the session. Drifting blissfully feels great for the time it lasts, but that isn't the goal. Bringing that Light back into our lives is the goal. Living a joyful, fulfilled life is the goal. Unless we ground the changes into physical dimension, the healing benefit floats away.

Getting yourself and your subject back into the body may or may not be easy for you. All of us have our natural way of being. For some of us, lifting out of the body is a bit of a struggle, but coming back in is easy. For others, lifting out is very easy and natural, but coming back in requires some focus. Don't make your natural way of being "wrong," or anyone else's either. What matters is that you become aware of how your own Energy body functions, and learn what you need to focus on in order to move into balance.

Whether working only with yourself or with someone else, this step is the same. Since you are still connected with your healing subject, you can simultaneously physicalize the Energy for the two of you as easily as you can for yourself alone. With intention, draw the optimized Energy of the session into the physical bodies. Draw it into the skin, into the soft tissues of muscles, organs, and glands, and into the bones. Continue to draw the Energy both inward and downward, including the bones of the legs and feet. Pack the perfected Energy into the body until every single cell of the body is bulging with Light.

Don't stop even when every cell of the body is chock full of optimized Energy. Continue to draw the Light down through the feet and into the grounding cords, which are the energetic connections to the planet. Some people visualize these connections as roots to a giant tree. Others relate to them as beams of Light that link into the center of the planet. However you perceive them is perfect; there isn't a wrong way. Keep drawing the Energy down farther and farther into the grounding cords until the floaty feeling is gone and a calm centered quality has taken its place. That's the signal that you are sufficiently grounded to proceed to the next stage of the Closing Process.

Separating and Calling Back the Energy

When you work with someone else, you merge and become energetically one with him. Therefore at the end of the session you must re-establish boundaries to be complete with his healing session. The starting point of separating from your subject is simple: recognize that the two of you are energetically bonded because you have engaged in healing work together. Call your Energy back to you and send his Energy back to him. Speaking the words out loud: "My Energy back to me, your Energy back to you," adds more power than simply thinking the words silently inside of your head.

Think of it this way: when your Energy is fully blended with another being, it's like a big mixed up pile of rice. Some of the grains are wild rice, and some are brown rice. You want all the wild rice to form one pile and all the brown rice to move to another. Luckily you understand how to work with Energy, so you don't have to pick each grain up in order to do this. You simply call out: "Wild rice over here, brown rice over there," and the grains respond. This is exactly what we do when we separate our Energy. We don't have to pluck each quark separately. We are the callers in a subtle Energy square dance: "My Energy back to me, your Energy back to you." As with all energetic shifts, you will feel tangible changes as you separate the Energy.

Energy merging occurs not only in healing sessions but also throughout our lives. Loved ones you haven't seen in years, acquaintances you emailed last month, and even the stranger behind you in line last week might have some of your Energy, and vice-versa. Therefore, it's helpful to call Energy back from third parties for both you and your subject, and to release third party Energy from both of you. It is not usually necessary to know when or how you or your subject picked that Energy up. "My Energy to me, your Energy to you, everyone else's Energy back to them." Often these intentions create another powerful Energy shift. Continue until the separation step feels essentially "done." When that occurs it is time to move to the next step of the process.

Ask for Divine Help

It is possible you have been using primarily your intention to create the changes during the Closing Process. Now that you have done your part, it is time to ask for Divine Help. "Help us optimize, ground and stabilize, separate and set the Energy." Since repeating requests yields better results, repeat several times until this too feels complete.

Completing the Sacred Seal

At this point all that is left to work with is the bubble of Light that you formed in the Opening Process when you created sacred space. It will transform into a sacred seal on the entire healing session. With a combination of intention and asking for Divine Assistance, expand the bubble a thousand times over or more. Now there's so much Light that even though you are going to split this bubble into smaller bubbles, no one feels that they're being shortchanged. Create a bubble for you, a bubble for your subject, and a bubble for everyone else you touched in the process. You don't have to know who all those people are; simply cover them in Light with your intention. When you feel complete with this step of separating the bubble, you are ready for the final part in the Closing Process.

In the final step of the Closing Process, draw the bubbles down into the Divine Plan. Each bubble goes to its own right place in the Divine Plan. You don't have to know what or where that right place is. Simply with your intention to ground all the bubbles into their own right places, it happens. As with all steps, there is a very tangible shift of Energy as the bubbles arrive; they click into place. As with all steps, you may need to repeat this a few times until the clicks occur. It is common to experience a joyful feeling of "all's right with the world" as the bubbles lock into position.

Now you and your subject are both in your optimal Energy alignment, grounded and stabilized. Your Energy is sorted out; everyone is sealed in Divine Light, and in his or her own right place in the Divine Plan. With this, your sacred seal and your healing session are complete. Give thanks! Gratitude counts!

CLOSING PROCESS WALK-THROUGH

After all that explanation, a quick run through is the perfect way to deepen your understanding. First, create sacred space; refer to page 53 or Appendix One for the Opening Process walk-through. Then return here for the rest of the experience.

Friend, take a moment to notice how it feels to be inside sacred space with your subject. It is very nice, even wonderful, yes? Take a few minutes and use the open channel to the higher dimensions to receive Divine Help. If nothing else, you can ask for both you and your subject to be given that which you need most. Repeat your requests a few times; notice how the Energy shifts as a result. If you wish to add other requests for Divine Help and Healing, feel free to do so, remembering the power of repetition.

As the response to your requests stabilizes, start the Closing Process. Ask for any errors to be corrected; repeat that two or three times and notice how the Energy changes in response. Ask for anything that was omitted to be included; repeat the request a few times and notice the differences. Ask for poorly done work to be done well, and well-done work to be made perfect. Repeat that progression until it feels complete. Ask for your subject's Energy to be brought to its perfect vibration and alignment, and for you also to be optimized; repeat the request until the response dwindles.

Now have the intention to physicalize the Energy and to ground your mutual selves. Draw the optimized Energy

in through the skin, through the soft tissues, muscles, organs, and glands, into the bones of the body. Fill all the cells of your bodies until they bulge with Light. Continue to draw the optimized Energy in and down through the bones of the body, through the bones of the legs, through the bones of the feet, and into your grounding connections to the planet, your roots. Repeat this internalizing and grounding process until it seems complete. You should feel a sense of calm, centered well-being.

Now start the separation process. Call your Energy back to you; release your subject's Energy back to him. Call your Energy into your sides and your back as well as into your front. For both of you, call your Energy back from wherever you have left it lying around. For both of you, release others' Energy and send it back to them, whoever they are. Continue the process of separating the Energy until the changes stabilize and you feel completely yourself.

Now having done what you can do with your intention, ask for the Lightbeings to help you both to ground, stabilize, and separate. Notice after all your beautiful work, there is still more they can do. Repeat your request until once again the changes stabilize.

Take the bubble you started with and expand it a thousand times over with your intention to do so and with Divine Help. Split it into individual bubbles: one for you, one for your subject, and one for everyone who's Energy you touched. Everyone is now encased in an individual bubble of Light many times larger than the original bubble. Finally, draw all these bubbles down to their own right place in the Divine Plan. Repeat this step as many times as needed until you feel the bubbles click into place—then

give thanks to the Guides, Lightbeings, Angels and of course Source for all the loving support. Trust the process is Divinely perfect, just as it is, and declare your session complete.

Congratulations! You did it! Feel good! Acknowledge yourself!

AFTER A SESSION AND AT DAY'S END

In this entire self-care arena (and in fact in this entire book), I do not want to give you rigid rules that you must follow. Instead, I intend to encourage you to pay attention to how everything feels. Notice the things that feel right and the things that feel off, and adjust your thoughts and actions accordingly. Nonetheless, there are some guidelines and rules of thumb you might find helpful as you begin the process of noticing what needs to be handled differently.

As part of creating the sacred seal on the session, there is a process of disconnecting, grounding, stabilizing, and setting the Energy for both the subject and you. I would Love to be able to say, "Just do the Closing Process and all is well with you, my friend." However, the truth is that even if you have disconnected perfectly, that Energy connection opens up again when you talk to the subject immediately afterward. Therefore, as blessed as the sacred seal is for both you and the subject, you as the healer will need to do more to stabilize your own Energy, especially if this is your day job.

Once your subject is out the door, repeat the entire disconnect process again. "Your Energy to you, my Energy to me. Your Energy to you, my Energy to me. Your Energy to you, my Energy to me. Grounding, stabilizing, separating, and setting the Energy." Give thanks again for a complete session; gratitude has power.

In the short run, you can add more strength to the separation with various rituals of disconnection that continue the process. Rituals that combine physical action with a mental intention to separate from your subject are more powerful than using either one alone. If you like to wash your hands and wrists with salt, then wash your hands and wrists with salt. If you like drawing circles around your body using your hands, a stick of incense, or a tuning fork, then do that. Anything that you believe will help you disconnect will in fact help you disconnect. Belief is what gives ritual its power, not the ritualistic action itself—but the power is there, so use it.

In the long run the strength of your Energy body and your beliefs about living in the Light are much more important than rituals of closing and sealing. As your Energy body gets stronger, it remembers how it should be: formed through and around you in a solid Pillar of Love. Think of it as cellular memory, but at the level of the Energy body. Finally, as you come to believe it is not only possible but also that you deserve to live your entire life inside a secure space of Light and Love, the problem of draining connections is truly healed.

Let's be clear about this, my friend: it is not that we disconnect because the subject's Energy is icky. He is a wonderful person on his soul's path. Everyone on the planet, without exception, is on his or her path to some degree or another. Rather, you will send his Energy back to him because he needs it, and draw your Energy back to you because you need it. An open link between the two of you will drain one of you; most likely it will be the person who was already giving, i.e. you. Your session is over. It was perfect just as it was, the gift has been given, and your interaction is complete for now. You each need your own Energy back to live fully.

Day's End

When you live in the Light, you feel good the moment you wake up. As the day goes along and you are facilitating healing sessions, you feel better and better. By the end of a day of Energy healing, you are so full of Joy it simply overflows everywhere. That is, IF your Energy body is in the proper configuration. If something is out of alignment, you will feel "off" in one of two ways: either drained, or so full of Energy that you can't sleep, as if you just drank a cup or two of espresso.

Often, simply grounding yourself more thoroughly will solve the situation regardless of which uncomfortable extreme is presenting itself. If it's possible, go outside and do a bit of weeding or other light yard work. The combination of practicality and connection with plants and Earth can be very grounding. Exercise is also enormously grounding and has the benefit of strengthening your physical body. If you feel over-energized, consider some pleasant exercise.

Sometimes the issues go beyond a lack of grounding. Regardless of your choice of professions, you can feel drained at the end of your workday. This is true for people in all lines of work; whether you are an Energy healer or an accountant or something in between, pay attention to how you feel at the end of the day. If you feel drained, there's Energy leaking out of you somehow.

What to do? Begin by repeating the process of disconnecting from anyone you have interacted with that day. Enlist some external support; try essential oils, Energy-clearing sprays, healing tuning forks, crystal bowl recordings, or the like. If that doesn't do it, re-establish your Pillar of Light by repeating the Opening Process (page 53 or Appendix One). Follow that with asking your Guides and Angels to restore your sovereignty over your own Energy. Use the suggestions for resetting your Energy body in the "How to Improve" section found on page 72. That might be enough to set things right inside of you.

If you still feel tired, you are still leaking Energy. Don't be discouraged. You are supposed to feel good; you *will* feel good again. You simply need to do a bit more to get there. Take the next step: ask for higher-dimension help to heal the leaks. When you are learning, this will often be enough to re-establish well-being.

No worries if even after this call for help you don't feel right. This is actually good news; it means your Guides consider you to be capable of doing more than you think you can. They wish you to use your subtle

Energy skills to check yourself for leaks. It can be challenging to get clarity about your own Energy when you are inside of it, but you are ready to do this or your Guides would not ask it of you. One solution is to try this trick: imagine you are standing behind or beside or in front of yourself, preferably at a distance so you can get a nice overall view. Now assess your Energy body with your subtle Energy sensors (hands, subtle eyes, or other method of your preference).

As you find the drains, ask your Guides and Angels to remove them. If you have done your part, they will do their part. It's your job to do your best—but your Guides Love you. They won't let you flounder if you have truly done what you are able to do. Almost always, you will feel better right away. If you are still feeling drained, you haven't found all the leaks. The moment you have identified and asked for help with the very last one, you will feel absolutely fine.

If, on the other hand, you are so twitchy and full of Energy that you can't sleep, you have unprocessed Energy in your system. There's a reason that Energy is in your system. It's there for you to use; usually for the number one priority that your Guides have assigned to you. Figure out what that priority is, and send the Energy to that issue. Don't be afraid to use the trial-and-error method of arriving at the answer if needed. What does that mean? Let me give you an example.

Let's say I find myself buzzing after a day of healing or teaching. It's clear I am supposed to use the Energy for something, but I am not sure what its intended purpose is. I sit or lie in bed quietly and wait for the awareness to come. "What am I to do with this Energy?" Ideas will pop into my head; I try them out. "The back part of my field can be thin from time to time, so I'll send it there." That step helps absorb about one percent of the extra Energy, so that's not it. Next try: "My grounding can be eroded, so I'll send the extra Energy there." Eh, one percent again, so that's not it either. "I have been afraid to take that big step forward; I'll send the Energy there." Voila! That's it! When I find what I'm supposed to do with that Energy and send the Energy to that aspect, I'm no longer twitchy. Instantly all is peaceful, all is well. I've done what was mine to do, and I immediately slip into sleep.

My friend, this is true in life too: when we have truly done all that is ours to do, instantly all is peaceful, all is well. Even vague, low-level anxiety is a signal that something is "off." No worries, through this method you will be able to find your path, take the required energetic as well as physical dimension steps, and live in perfect Peace.

All this having been said, the real name of the game is "Beliefs." In the long run, our beliefs determine our experience of life. If at some deep level you believe healing sessions drain you, over-energize you, or cause you to become ungrounded, they will. If your deep beliefs are that healing sessions heal, cleanse, ground and strengthen you, they will. Amazingly so. In the next chapter we will begin with a discussion of working to master our subconscious beliefs rather than be ruled by them.

CHAPTER FIVE

TICKET TO SUCCESS: FOUNDATIONS OF SELF-CARE

If I would preserve my relation to Nature [the Divine],
I must make my life more moral, more pure and innocent.
The problem is as precise and simple as a mathematical one.
I must not live loosely, but more and more continently.
Henry David Thoreau

BELIEFS

Beliefs are really the bottom line of what creates our lives. All Energy conforms to our beliefs, be they conscious or subconscious. The Energy of our lives creates the manifested "reality" of our lives. In other words, what we accept as True About Life is eventually what happens in our lives. If we believe life drags us down, it will. Conversely, if we believe all events of life strengthen and heal us, they will.

In the absence of specific beliefs, general beliefs will rule. The conscious mind creates only the proverbial frosting on the cake of belief. The rest of the belief package, the cake itself, comes to us from other influences. The society in which we live, our families of origin, and our past experiences, both in our current bodies and in previous ones, shape our beliefs. For example, we're born into a world that believes in time and gravity, a world that believes we need to eat and sleep, and that believes germs cause disease. Do you believe these things? You may say, "Yes, but these things are True. These aren't beliefs. These are True." My friend, that IS a belief: what we think is True.

Many people work with affirmations, positive statements about life, to shift their belief patterns. If you've tried this, I suspect your experience is that sometimes affirmations work and sometimes they don't work. Affirmations work when our existing beliefs are close enough to the vibration of the affirmation that we are pulled into the affirmation's current of alignment. They don't work when our existing vibration is too far removed from the vibration to catch the affirmation's wind in our sails.

Let's use the common example of an affirmation about Love. If you truly believe, "People Love me, and I'm just having a bad year with my relationships," then affirming, "My life is full of Love" will remind you of your belief. Poof! You're there again, in alignment with feeling Loved. On the other hand if your subconscious belief pattern is, "People just want to use me, no one really cares about me, and I can't count on anyone to stick around," when you say, "My life is full of Love," your Energy body reacts with, "That is a Big Fat Lie." At best, you aren't being pulled into alignment with the affirmation. You could even increase your feelings of being unloved, because what you are truly affirming inside is, "Love is a big fat lie, big fat lie, big fat lie."

Your subconscious mind is like a powerful horse that you ride through life. In horseback riding, who's truly in charge? The horse. If the rider learns to communicate effectively with the horse, the horse will do what the rider wants it to do, but the horse is *deciding* to cooperate. The trick to changing your beliefs and therefore your life is to train your horse and change your subconscious thinking. You might be thinking,

"I already know that, but how? It's easier said than done." Actually, my friend, it is very simple when you focus on how the subconscious mind functions.

The subconscious mind does not accept statements that are too far from existing belief patterns. It only responds well to statements that are close enough to the existing beliefs that they can be accepted. It will, however, respond to questions. If you ask the subconscious a question, it will charge off to find the answer. It does not evaluate the question; it simply looks for the answer to the question. If you ask, "Why is there no Love in my life?" off your subconscious will go to find all the reasons why there's no Love in your life. Conversely, if you ask, "Why is my life so full of Love?" off it will go to find all the reasons why there IS Love in your life. As the horse of your subconscious mind looks for the answers to the questions you ask it, it pulls you in the direction of the answer. Asking the horse, "Why is my life so full of Love?" pulls you in the direction of a life full of Love.

It's human nature to continually want to improve our life situations. As a result we tend to focus on the areas that need improvement and ask ourselves, "Why isn't this working?" That sends the subconscious mind off to find all the reasons why it isn't working, firmly locking in place the not-working-ness. Just flip that around in your mind. Thinking about the identical topic, ask yourself instead, "Why is this working?" and engage the power of your subconscious mind to change your vibrations. Change the habit of questioning from negative to positive, and change your life.

"Why" is a more powerful leading question than "How." "How" calls upon the mechanics of creating good in life, and can lead us in the direction of thinking we have to create the change ourselves. "Why," on the other hand, allows us to leave the details up to the Universe to provide. We open up to Trust when we ask "Why" rather than "How."

KEY DISTINCTION:

The goal is *not* to find the answer to the leading question; the goal is to engage the power of the subconscious mind in manifesting the desired outcome.

The point of asking yourself positively worded questions is to lead your horse down the road toward the objective. As the subconscious mind pulls you in that direction, your vibrations get closer and closer to what you want. When you train your horse regularly and consistently, one day you will wake up thinking, "My God, people really DO love me."

Because this is so important, let's run through two more examples of the difference between using a statement of affirmation and using a positively worded question. Financial worries abound in this society, so let's work with that. If you are struggling with money and you affirm, "My bank account is so big," your subconscious mind will usually respond, "You liar." At best, nothing changes. Conversely, if you ask "Why is my bank account so big?" all the subconscious mind knows is that you're asking it a question. It sits up when it hears a question, and responds, "Oh, a question? That's my job. I'll take this," and off it goes to find the reasons why your bank account is so big, dragging your Energy body into alignment with abundance.

If you struggle with poor health, consider these leading questions: "Why am I so healthy? Why does my body work so well? Why am I so comfortable in my body? Why am I so vibrant? Why do I have so much Energy? Why do I feel so wonderful?"

The Great Little Book of Afformations by Noah St. John and Denise Berard is an excellent resource for positively worded questions in many arenas. Noah and Denise also have many other fine contributions in this arena of working with beliefs. If your subconscious mind is an unruly stallion dragging your life in unwanted directions, you may benefit by their line of products.

The belief-development process doesn't always rise to the level of the conscious mind. Therefore, you may or may not become aware of the answers to the leading questions. Fortunately that doesn't matter. Our lives aren't created at the level of our conscious minds. We may think they are, but that isn't so. Life happens at a deeper level, and we have to shift our definition of reality at that deeper level to have lasting change.

Remember the part of our beliefs that we personally create is just a tiny portion of the entirety of what we hold to be true. All the rest is coming from something else other than what we personally think we believe. We absorb the beliefs of the society we are born into. We inherit the beliefs of our parents and ancestors. We draw in the beliefs of our previous incarnations. Working with the subconscious through positive questioning can address all layers of beliefs. It's foundational.

Because Energy is amorphous, it shifts and changes as soon as the belief pattern changes. Therefore as Energy workers, it's crucial to pay attention to what we believe about Energy. If we believe we can be "contaminated by the bad Energy of our subject," we can actually create that unfortunate situation for ourselves. This may be a belief you have already absorbed from society, in which case it is probably manifesting into your experience. If, on the other hand, we believe we can be simultaneously healed of the same vibrations that are creating issues for our subjects—we can. Ask your subconscious, "Why do the healing sessions I facilitate also heal ME?" and notice how quickly your experiences change.

As an Energy worker, your beliefs about your own Energy body are pivotal. Becoming aware of existing beliefs is the essential first step. If you believe Energy sensitivity makes you weak, it will. On the other hand if you believe Energy sensitivity makes you strong, it will. If you believe your chakras are small, you can make them small, but it does not serve you to have small chakras. If you believe that you have no vertical Energy channels, your vertical channels wither, and it does not serve you to have no vertical channels. What serves you is to be a strong vertical Pillar of Light, with your chakras fully open in all directions.

When you start to visualize your Energy body to its potential, over time it becomes that. Energy truly does conform to thought. Working to improve the Energy body's structure is tremendously helpful in times of life challenges. In those times it is normal to have so much fear and resistance that we can't hear the guidance of what our life path is. Even when the conceptual ideas freak us out, we can always improve the Energy body's structure. As we do so, the fear and resistance ease and we can once again respond to the guidance with an open heart and mind. My friend, as your Energy body grows into its potential, so do you. You will BE who you came here to be, and be living the life you came here to live.

Changing your beliefs is a process. It usually doesn't happen in a moment. Typically reinforcement is required to weed out all the components of an unhelpful belief pattern and to establish a helpful one. It happens over the long haul, but the long haul could be three weeks or twenty years, depending on how actively you work with it. Work to heal your beliefs; meanwhile, support your well-being with physical dimension actions.

A DIET FOR SUCCESS

Many students express a desire to be able to feel, see, and hear more clearly in the subtle realms. A few lucky souls are able to maintain full clairsentience, clairvoyance, and clairaudience without any effort. For most of us, however, adjusting our lifestyles can make a big difference in our abilities to sense subtle Energy. We can shift our physical diet, our mental diet, and our emotional diet. We can develop better habits of exercise and meditation. The cleaner our life is, the clearer our sensing is. This is great news. Don't feel limited by your abilities the way they are now. We all have infinite potential. Changing your habits can help you fulfill your inherent destiny.

We're all at different points on the spectrum of psychic ability. Some are naturally such clear channels that they can watch horror movies or CNN 24 hours a day, eat only nacho chips and Big Macs, and still be extra-sensory. That would not work for me. I need to live a cleaner life.

Wherever you are on the spectrum right now is fine; no judgment. You can always improve by making physical dimension choices that support your ability to be a clear channel. If you continually put toxic substances into your mind or your body, it's going to be harder to be clear. If you live clean, it is much easier.

Let's begin with the basics of physical diet. When we have belief mastery, we can eat rocks and drink gasoline and be fine. I am serious. There are people who live without eating anything. They have belief mastery on that topic. They know physical food is not necessary for life to thrive. Jasmuheen is well known as someone who lives on Light. Google her if you wish; read her books. She hasn't eaten since 1993. I assume you have a different belief, and that's fine. I am not recommending you tackle something as ingrained as the need to eat. I'm simply providing this as an example of the power of belief mastery.

For the rest of us who are still working to master beliefs about food, it's important to support ourselves in the interim. We are what we eat, so it serves us to eat in a way that allows us to become what we wish to become. As you know, everything has a vibration. When we eat, we put the food's vibrations into our bodies. If our intention is to increase our abilities to sense subtle Energy, it's counter-productive to ingest low vibration substances.

Certain categories of substances tend to drag our vibrations down. Intoxicants and other numbing agents will trash your extra-sensory abilities faster than anything else. This is not a philosophical or moral stance. If you're working on improving your sensitivity, is it a good idea to put a numbing agent in your system? Numbing agents numb. That creates movement in the opposite direction on the spectrum of developing extra-sensory perceptions.

This is a big issue in North American society today. Numbing agents are everywhere. We can begin with alcohol, nicotine, and other recreational drugs, although this topic is much larger than that. Alcohol has been used for anesthesia in times of crisis. During the Civil War, when they ran out of anesthesia the medics would give soldiers alcohol before cutting their limbs off. Alcohol is a depressant that acts as a numbing agent on the central nervous system. Nicotine usage is a bit more complicated. In large doses it straightforwardly functions as a painkiller. In smaller doses it confuses the sensory apparatus like caffeine does, through overstimulation.

In our society this issue is much larger than recreational drug usage. Pain pills, sleeping pills, and anti-anxiety medications are wonderful examples of drugs that are designed to numb us. Those three categories of over-the-counter and prescription drugs can devastate an Energy body and make it tough to sense subtle Energy at least as much as a recreational drug can.

That having been said, having had chronic fatigue syndrome and fibromyalgia for a number of years, I know what it means to not get sleep day after day after day, how you lose your ability to function. I know what chronic pain does and how it wears you down until you can't hold your Energy body together any more and all you can do is shake and cry. As someone who experienced chronic anxiety and even panic attacks for many years, I know that fear-overload is as devastating to a system as physical pain. I know that sometimes, you just have to do something to break the "cycle of bad." When I was breaking down with pain and fatigue, I was desperate for relief. Jade-Su's advice was, "Use the tools that are available, but minimize it." If you're at the stage where you're shaking and crying and you can't hold your Energy field: take a pain pill, a sleeping pill, or an anti-anxiety pill. Break the "cycle of bad." Just don't do it on a regular basis, because you're pouring numbing agents into your system over and over again.

In addition to these categories of drugs that are intended to numb, many other drugs numb as a side effect. Antihistamines, allergy medicines, anti-depression medications, Parkinson's drugs, ADHD prescriptions, even some cholesterol medicines are recognized as creating sleepiness—in other words, numbing the brain so intensely it falls asleep. Bottom line: in many cases, pharmaceuticals are not our friends in developing our extra-sensory abilities. Remember Jade-Su's advice: use what is necessary to deal with life, but be aware that it has an effect. If your goal is to improve your subtle Energy awareness, numbing agents are counter-productive. Minimize them.

Processed foods typically cloud Energy bodies and don't have many redeeming qualities. Meats, especially red meats, have heavy Energy. As such they can be grounding and strengthening, but can also serve to reduce subtle sensitivity. Commercially raised animals are often traumatized and terrorized before they are slaughtered; that vibration is in their bodies and therefore in the meat. Think about it: do you really want to ingest that vibration? Other foods will affect you in various ways. Be aware of your needs at all levels; eat mindfully in ways that support your well-being physically and energetically.

My intention is not to create a laundry list of do's and don'ts for you to memorize. My intention is to create a sense of awareness so that you start to notice what you're doing to yourself with your actions. Notice that everything you eat, drink, smell, and put on yourself affects you. Start to make decisions, consciously and mindfully, about what you're putting into your system, or on your system.

Be aware that your emotional attachment to the answer might change your perception of the answer. Back when I was a normal member of our society, I liked a nice glass of good red wine or champagne when we went out to dinner. Giving that up was not on my list of fun things to do, but it was helpful to let that habit go. That glass of red wine wasn't worth the three days it took to get my Energy body back to prime condition. If I had two glasses, then it took six days before I felt perfectly clear and clean again. The decision became easy as the results became clear. "Am I going to drink two glasses of wine and knock myself back for a week?" That isn't worth it. It's the difference between authentic Joy and a glass of wine.

All this having been said, when we really are masters of our belief we can eat rocks and drink gasoline. At that point in time *but not before then*, we can have our commercially raised steak and glass of red wine without harming our sensitivity. But trust me, dear friend: it's a long journey to that way of being. And maybe by then, your goal won't be to have a glass of wine with dinner.

There is one substance that's fabulous to put into our bodies when we begin working with Energy, and that is water. Why? Zoron explained that moving Energy burns water molecules. When he started telling me this, I have to say that my little chemistry-major brain clicked into gear. "What do you mean by that? How does that happen, exactly? What is the mechanism? Are we breaking bonds by moving Energy?" That didn't go over well with Zoron. "We're not playing that game with you. This isn't a theoretical discussion. Try it and see for yourself the difference it makes." Of course he was right. Whether or not I like it he is always right about my life, just as your Guides are right about yours.

Water is a carrier for Energy. Energy movement burns water molecules. Therefore, the more Energy work we do, the more we're living energetically, the more water we need to drink. It's easier to sense and move Energy when we are well hydrated. In addition, drinking enough water lets our system not only tolerate the Energy work but actually be strengthened by it rather than becoming dehydrated and drained. Since being fully hydrated increases the speed of energy moving through our bodies, it increases the pace at which we are able to change our lives. If you are chronically dehydrated it is more likely that you are good and stuck in life than if you drink plenty of water.

Bottom line: drink more water. Most of us need to drink twice as much as we think we do. Drink a liter of water in the morning as you start the day, and drink a couple of more liters as you go. If you don't do that, after a day of Energy work you can be quite dehydrated, because you're moving a lot of Energy.

Mental Diet

Diet consists of more than food and drink. Our diet also includes what we put into our minds—what we read, the movies, videos, or TV we watch, and the conversations we engage in. If you want to have more clarity for subtle sensing, limit your exposure to media, and watch with whom you associate.

Mainstream media outlets, including the news media, are not generally designed to bring our minds into states of Peace and well-being. Media outlets often choose to air themes of pessimism, violence, and cruelty; that is their choice. It is our choice whether or not to pay any attention to it. "Entertainment" should cause you to feel more joyful, not more fearful. "News" should contain information that empowers you to live more effectively, not to paralyze you with fear and indecision.

Notice what you are feeding your mind, and how you feel after you have ingested it. Do you feel full of Peace, Love, and Joy, or do you have mental indigestion? Consider whether or not you really benefit from your viewing and reading choices. Ask yourself, "Did that help me or hurt me?" As you become aware of the effects your media diet has on your well-being, it will be easy to change your habits toward that which improves your life. Nothing else will make any sense.

Much of our mental diet comes through the people we associate with. When you associate with positive, loving, optimistic people, your subtle senses open up because the world seems like a safer place. If you keep company with critical, pessimistic, negative people, it becomes harder to open up because your state of being is more guarded. This does not mean they are "bad" people. They are on their growth paths too, headed toward Source just as we all are. They are doing the best they can, just as we all are. It's simply that it is not helpful to have much interaction with them.

That having been said, sometimes we find ourselves listening to someone who is thoroughly negative, because they need a loving ear and a loving heart. If you find yourself in that position, ask your Guides, "Is this for me to do?" If the answer is "No," excuse yourself from the situation as kindly as possible. If the answer is, "It *is* for you to do," consider it an opportunity for inner practice. As you listen, silently do an Opening Process for yourself to create sacred space in and around you. Focus on your Pillar of Light; hold it strong and true. As you do so, you help yourself and your companion. You will feel much less triggered by her words. You will be living in the River of Divine Love, and you will simultaneously have more compassion for your friend, and better boundaries between the two of you. Your interaction will be healthier.

Be proactive to counteract all the negativity that seems to come at us whether we want it or not. Feed your mind positive vibrations. Whatever works for you is perfect. Sing along with a joyful song; that frees the soul. Read positive and inspirational books to reset your Energy. There are hundreds of uplifting books to choose from; find ones that appeal to you. I have benefitted enormously from *The Miracle of Mindfulness*, by Thich Nhat Hanh; *The Art of Forgiveness, Lovingkindness, and Peace*, by Jack Kornfield; *Comfortable with Uncertainty*, by Pema Chodron; and *Love Poems From God,* by Daniel Ladinsky.

Say "yes" to life daily. Connect to the Divine in whatever way suits you. If it means gardening, then garden. If it means walking on the beach, walk on the beach. See a sunset. Sing a song. Pray. Meditate. Pet your dog. Do whatever lets you open your heart to the Divine, at least once a day. No matter how bad your day has been, fighting with life doesn't improve the situation. Accept what is, find the gift in it, and be grateful for what you have. Trust that it can improve. Forgive yourself and the world. Let go of fighting—with the world around you, with others, and with yourself. Let go and find Peace.

Notice the power of connecting with the Divine by meditation or prayer to improve your well-being. Labels are not important in this arena. What matters is that you set aside some quiet time each day to commune with Source. If this will be a new habit for you, start manageably: ten minutes is a thousand times better than nothing. Begin with the Opening Process to create sacred space, and then simply sit quietly, eyes closed, with your attention focused inward. Notice how you feel. Intend to open to the Divine, to release your burdens, and to accept blessings. Notice how you feel at the end of the ten minutes; compare it to how you felt when you first sat down. Almost always there is a remarkable improvement in well-being.

In short, become aware of the effects your habits have on your experience of life. Minimize exposure to violence, cruelty, and pessimism. Add generous helpings of positive thinking, seasoned with moments of Divine connection. In all arenas of life, develop the habit of finding what's right for you. Continue to give your soul what it needs, and be aware that may change over time. Your Energy body will feel safer, it will expand, and your subtle senses will bloom.

MOVE BREATH, BODY, AND ENERGY

Breath

Breath is always with us, and it has enormous power to heal physically, mentally, emotionally and spiritually. Intentional breathing supports the Yoga, the union of body-mind-spirit. Deep, full breaths help cleanse and open the Energy channels in a way that complements the benefits of physical exercise. Our Opening Process begins with conscious breathing because that helps to clear and balance the Energy body as well as the physical body. To be sure you are comfortable with that stage, consider reviewing the entire "Creating Sacred Space" section in Chapter Two.

Proper breathing can eliminate pain on many levels. Our physical bodies can give us wonderful practice with this art. If yours has pain, be aware of the tendency to avoid experiencing the sensations. Unfortunately, avoiding the experience requires it to continue. Instead, breathe into the discomfort with an openhearted, compassionate curiosity. "Lean into the sharp point," is a saying in certain Buddhist circles. Don't avoid the feeling; don't judge it as being "bad" or "wrong." Be as specific as possible in your thoughts about it: rather than labeling it "pain," discover exactly how it feels. Is it hot or icy? Sharp or heavy? Recognize it as the messenger it is; breathe right into it with loving inquiry. That may be all it needs to be able to let go, and therefore to heal. As the blockages (and therefore the pain-signals) lift, your subtle awareness improves.

Breath can also clear emotional pain. Stress, anxiety, tension, fear, and anger indicate an Energy imbalance. As with physical pain, we can wish to run away from the emotions, to *not* feel them. As with physical pain, this simply extends their presence in our lives. It can help to set aside a time to tenderly breathe into the emotions and feel them. If this idea feels overwhelming, set a time limit. Be with the grief, fear, or anger for two or three minutes with the same loving compassion you gave to your physical discomforts. Be open to the emotion moving and shifting. Sometimes that's all it needs, and then it can be gone.

Breathing into the backs of the lungs and into the bottoms of the lungs will help balance the Energy body. When we habitually breathe shallowly in our chests, our Energy bodies tend to be front-end loaded. This Energy configuration creates a life of hard work in which gains must come from our own efforts. As we increase the amount of Energy at our backs, we have Divine Wind pushing us forward. Life becomes easier; larger gains happen with less effort. Simply developing the habit of breathing into the fullness of the lungs including the back will go a long way toward creating this ease.

Body

A large part of healing happens by moving Energy, and moving Energy is easier if we move the physical body. These two aspects of our being are not nearly as separate as we might think. The physical body can affect Energy movement just as the Energy body can affect its physical counterpart. Regular, complete physical exercise is an effective way to flush the Energy channels clear. It is helpful for our physical health, our energetic health, and our ability to sense subtle Energy. Daily physical motion keeps our Energy channels open and flowing freely, not giving Energy the chance to stagnate into blockages.

Two kinds of motion are helpful: elevating the heart rate and moving the muscles and joints. Aerobic conditioning (raising the heart rate) increases the amount of chi Energy in the body. Just as with water in a hose, the more Energy there is moving through the system, the faster the Energy moves. Faster Energy flow makes it easier for our bodies to blow out Energy blockages.

Moving the specific location of a blockage is also wonderfully helpful. If there is pain in a knee, keeping the knee immobilized is not nearly as helpful as gently, lovingly bending and straightening it. The physical motions remind the body it can also move the Energy. Therefore, going through a full range of motion (moving all your muscles and joints) helps to release the blockages that might be lodged in those body parts.

As long as you include both range of motion and something to elevate the heart rate, the style of movement isn't important. Choose something that you can learn to like, and do it at least ten minutes every day to keep your Energy channels clear and clean. The more frequently and thoroughly you move your body, the less Energy stagnates, the more clear your Energy body will be, and the easier it will be for you to sense the subtle dimensions.

In addition to basic daily movement, it is very helpful to move your body before and after healing sessions and meditations. These are times of increased Energy flow, as well as times in which increased subtle awareness is possible. Moving your body in advance helps you ground, clears the healing channels, and is a signal to your Guides that you are doing your best to be a clear vessel.

During a healing session, higher vibrations flow through you. Post-session movement is almost essential for grounding the higher dimension Energies into the physical dimension. Grounding those frequencies into your physical body extends the period of time they benefit you, because the physical body is the densest part of your being and therefore holds the vibrations the longest.

In addition to its direct energetic, mental, emotional, and physical benefits, exercise has a less tangible but equally important contribution to our development. If we want to move forward in life, it is helpful to develop a habit of challenging ourselves in as many arenas as possible. When we consistently take the easy way out, we tend to stay stuck in the status quo. When we do our very best in multiple arenas of life, breakthroughs come faster. Giving your best effort in physical exercise is something that you can quantify, which helps develop a habit of stretching your limits in other areas as well. Since we all have different fitness levels, "challenge" is personally defined. Don't worry about what anyone else is doing or not doing. Whatever level demands you to stretch and grow is perfect, and will help create the habit of moving forward in life.

TUNE YOUR FOOD

My friend, every day we make choices about what we put in, on, and around our bodies. In the previous section, "A Diet for Success," we discussed choosing substances whose vibrations are already healthy. However, we can and should move beyond the idea that the world around us must hand us exactly what we want and need in order for us to thrive. We have the right to live our lives entirely in sacred space. Nevertheless, in order to achieve this we have to accept our responsibility to create it. Therefore this section discusses how to take energetic actions to create a life that supports you.

The processes of creating sacred space discussed in Chapters Two and Four work with your personal environment as a whole. Now we will focus on specific elements of your environment: your food and drink, your toiletries, clothes, jewelry, and any other objects you come into close contact with. In this way we take responsibility for improving our energetic environment and move beyond being a victim of circumstance or habit. If you suffer with allergies as I did in the first forty years of life, this section is for you. If your lifestyle doesn't agree with your well-being, this section is for you. If you wish to draw yourself forward on your spiritual growth path, this section is for you.

All substances hold a vibration. Coffee, hair color, prescription drugs, and even Burger King Chicken Minis can actually nourish your well-being *if* you put the time and effort into changing their vibrations before you put them in or on your body. Learn to tune your food to improve your well-being.

Right now, get something to practice with: a drink, a food item, a piece of jewelry, or a container of toiletries. It is ideal to find two of something. Set one aside as a control; work with the other. With those at hand, you are ready to proceed.

Begin by noticing your breathing. Either quickly or fully, repeat the Opening Process of creating inner sacred space (page 53 or Appendix One). Next, draw your focus back into your heart chakra, and notice its vibration in whatever way is right for you. Help yourself focus by holding your hands in front of your heart chakra, palms facing toward your body. How does your heart's Energy feel? Look? Taste? Smell? What does it sound like? Do the best you can today; know that as you progress your ability to notice subtle differences will improve.

While holding one palm facing your heart, shift your focus to include your practice item by turning one palm toward it. Invite it to join the vibration of your heart. Notice it will respond; the palm that faces the item will feel more and more like the palm facing your heart. Repeat the invitation a few times. Very quickly the item will feel remarkably similar to your heart's Energy.

Now draw both hands up to the level of your crown chakra, palms facing in. Focus on the frequency of your crown; sense it in as many ways as you can right now. Come to know the quality of your crown. Then shift your focus partially back to your practice item by pointing one palm toward it. Invite the practice item to now join the vibration of your crown. Once again you will notice the response. Repeat the invitation a few times until the item's pitch matches your crown.

Now extend your arms straight above you, palms facing in. Right where your hands are, there is a chakra. We call it the first sky chakra because it is the one closest to your physical body. Feel the Energy of this sky chakra; come to know its pitch. Then point one palm toward your practice item, partially shifting your focus there. Invite it to join the frequency of your sky chakra. Repeat until that is stabilized.

Now point your sky-chakra palm directly up to Source; feel the vibration. Invite the practice item to join in the frequency of Source.

I suspect you believe we are complete, yes? After all, nothing has a higher vibration than Source. Even so, take this next step with me, my friend. This is a lesson in humility. It took me a while to understand it, but you may "get it" right away. Observe.

Face both palms toward the practice object and call for Lightbeings who know exactly what to do, to improve the frequency of the object. Notice the immediate and profound shift that occurs.

How can this be? It is not that Lightbeings have a higher vibration than Source. They are extensions of Source, just as we are. It is not the comparison between Lightbeings and

***Source* that is valid. The relevant comparison is between Lightbeings and *us*. It's simple: higher-dimension beings have better access to Source than we do. Therefore, they can channel a more pure vibration of Source-flow into the object than we are able to.**

Notice your practice object. Compare it to the "control" item you set aside at the start. How do you feel about drinking, eating, or wearing your practice object now? Spirit has profoundly blessed it. It is sacred. It can draw you forward on your life path, that optimal and perfect plan for you.

As you develop the habit of raising the vibrations of everything you eat, drink, and wear, over and over you are taking responsibility to improve your life circumstances. By including the last step of asking for Lightbeing assistance, humility and reverence for the higher-dimension beings also naturally grows.

TUNE YOURSELF

An important part of this self-care section is working directly with your personal Energy to optimize it. Working with your own Energy creates a cycle of "good." As your Energy body clears, your subtle Energy awareness will improve. Similarly, you will increase your ability to move Energy by strengthening your Energy body. We can all do this. You don't have to be a master of Energy to get started. Begin where you are; work with the awareness and abilities you have, and know both will improve.

For best results, begin with the end in mind. Have the intention of eventually developing a perfectly straight, balanced Pillar of Light that flows from the Center of the Universe to the Center of the Planet, through you and around you. If you were to look at a cross-section of this Pillar of Light, it would look like a fiber-optic cable: lots of channels of Light, each laser-beam straight, tightly packed with no space in between. This

Pillar should be wide enough that you can't lunge out of it. Stretch your arms as wide as they will go. Look at the tips of your outstretched fingers, and lunge side to side while reaching out as far as you can. The space in between the farthest reach of your fingertips is a good size to work toward. Your Pillar may begin as a thread of Light that runs down through the center of you, but the goal is a Pillar so large your entire life occurs inside the space of its Divine Flow. Begin where you are and work toward the goal.

Keeping the goal in mind, one basic pattern of clearing your personal Energy body contains these basic steps:

Begin by noticing how you're actually breathing to develop mindfulness of your existing habits. Do this with curious loving focus, not criticism. Lovingly shift your breath until you are breathing deeply and equally into the bottoms of both lungs, with extra focus on breathing into the backs of the lungs and into the lung that was being lightly used to begin with.

Clear your chakras using a combination of your intention, your breath, and moving your hands in the direction you wish the Energy to move. Swish your hands front to back at the level of your heart chakra as you breathe deeply with the intention to flush that entire chakra-tube clear back to front and front to back. Repeat this process with the other chakras. Move down the chakra line from the heart to the root and on into the chakra at the feet, then come up the chakra line from the feet all the way to the crown, then work your way back down the chakra line finishing at the heart once more. Having cleared your chakras back to front, now clear them side-to-side. Flush them clear from right to left and left to right with your intention, your breath, and hand motions. The pattern of

beginning at the heart, moving down to the feet, up to the crown, and ending at the heart works best for most people.

Now improve the alignment of your chakras so that they are perfectly stacked on top of each other. Feel your column of chakras like it is a stack of giant donuts, and smooth them into a perfect column by moving your hands up and down in and around the column. It may help to imagine you are standing in front of yourself; draw your hands up and down the hologram of yourself to smooth your chakras into alignment. Your combined intention, breath, and hand motions can accomplish this easily.

Shift your focus from the horizontal chakras into your vertical channels. As in the Opening Process, draw Divine Earth Energy up from the center of the planet through your vertical channels. As an eternal being engaged in an eternal growth process, there will always be channels that are now ready to straighten up and point toward Source. Draw these channels newly straight with your intention, breath, and hands. As those channels line up perfectly, Love from Source begins to flow through them, creating a tangible feeling of being washed with Love.

Smooth and straighten your Pillar of Light by moving your hands up and down in and around the column. The natural bends, twists, and sags caused by life's events release as your Pillar of Light becomes laser-straight. Your physical body may respond by straightening up. If you have spinal issues such as scoliosis, spending extra time with this step can be very helpful in healing your physical body.

Lovingly spin your field on this vertical Pillar of Light by compressing it from each end like a child's toy. Imagine you are a child's top with a handle at the apex, and that

pressing down on the handle makes the top spin. As you compress your Pillar of Light, it spins and balances.

Finally, ask the Lightbeings and Angels to help you improve your Pillar of Light. You may feel them gently tugging you from either end. You may notice gentle vibrations as they lovingly shake you as if removing wrinkles from a sheet. Take Joy in that; notice how wonderful it feels. As their work settles into place, create a sacred seal with the Closing Process (page 105), and give thanks. Gratitude counts.

You can greatly improve the health of your Energy body and therefore of your life by repeating this simple process daily. As more Light, Joy, Peace, and Love flow through you, your Pillar expands and your life improves. The next chapter begins with a section on more structural Energy clearing techniques. Incorporate these methods into your daily routine and watch your life blossom.

My dear friend, working with our beliefs is the most important self-care project we have. Take those steps first and last. When we fully master our beliefs we can eat rocks, drink gasoline, and thrive. However until then we must work within the confines of our belief system, as it is in this particular moment. Choose your diet wisely. Work with your breath. Move your body. Raise the vibrations of all you eat, drink, and wear. Refine your Energy body; consciously engage in the eternal process of improving your Pillar of Light.

Walk in Light, live in Light, be Light.

LEVEL TWO

LETTING GO OF THE PAST

CHAPTER SIX

CLEAR THE DECKS

Excerpt: ***Interview with Balbir Mathur,*** *Heron Dance, Issue 11*

The boat I travel in is called Surrender. My two oars are instant forgiveness and gratitude—complete gratitude for the gift of life.
I am thankful for the experience of
this life, for the opportunity to dance.
I get angry, I get mad, but as soon as I remind
myself to put my oars in the water, I forgive.
I serve. I do the dance I must. I plant trees, but I am not the doer of this work. I am the facilitator, the instrument. I am one part of the symphony. I know there is an overall scheme to this symphony that I cannot understand. In some way, we are each playing our own part. It is not for me to judge or criticize the life or work of another.
All I know is that this is my dance. I would plant trees today even if I knew for a certainty that the world would end tomorrow.

Balbir Mathur, Founder of Trees for Life

Shared with thanks to both Heron Dance and Balbir Mathur

Teacher after teacher, from tradition to tradition, shares fundamentally the same message: living in the present moment, moment by moment, is the doorway to lasting happiness. Simple enough. Then it gets interesting with all the variations of how to achieve that. If you have spent any time with "living in the present moment" as the goal, you will know this is easier said than done. Memories and plans creep into the oddest moments, stealing Joy from the present.

In the Lightworkers Healing Method, clearing the baggage of the past is an important step to being fully present. Friends, you will be amazed at the transformations that occur in the lives of your healing subjects as you help them let go of their buried traumas and pain. LHM practitioners report that the feedback coming from their subjects about these treatments are enough to erase their thoughts of "am I making this up?" Doubt and many other self-inflicted wounds heal during this process.

These next two chapters present the curriculum of **Level Two – Letting Go of the Past.** After mastering the curriculum through this section, many students discover they have marketable skills to use in a healing practice.

Chapter Six – Clear the Decks opens the conversation of locating and releasing unresolved issues in your subject and clearing unhelpful Energy connections she may have with others. It introduces some structural clearing and alignment techniques, and leads you into the dance of working with Lightbeings, who are commonly referred to as "Angels." In the interests of precision we call them by their proper name, but if you are more comfortable thinking of them as Angels, they don't mind. Many students find this is a perfect transitional level between the foundational techniques of Chapters Two through Five and the higher-level techniques that follow.

Most people drag their baggage of traumas around with them, frustrating their efforts of living in the present moment. **Chapter Seven – Bread and Butter** begins with the process of locating and releasing buried traumas; through this process life circumstances transform. The soul fragment retrieval process that follows instantly creates permanent healing and goes far beyond basic shamanic techniques. An exercise to gain access to past lives ends the chapter. Don't be intimidated by this. None of us are limited to the one body we currently occupy. We are naturally a continuum of Energy that flows through time in various bodies. In many societies, it is considered normal to remember one's other lives. Relax; you too can open the doors. It's a natural process, and Chapter Seven includes some exercises to lead you through it. Go to the website, receive the related transmission, engage in the exercises, and experience it for yourself so you can help people truly heal the root causes of their dysfunctions.

LHM is fundamentally a process of helping people realign with their life purpose. Letting go of the burdens of the past is a huge part of that process. Through the paradox of simultaneous healing, your own life will also transform as you help others release and become free to live in the present.

STRUCTURAL CLEARING OVERVIEW

The first point to keep in mind about structural clearing is that issues appear in the order in which they need to be treated, so they can release. If you already have a healing practice, you know this very well. There could be thirty-seven causes of a subject's illness, but at first you might perceive only the first one, the issue on top of the pile. You may have a sense of more to come, previews of coming events, but it's rare to know all the causes at once. There would be little point, as they are not all simultaneously accessible. Healing is an unfolding process.

The second theme to remember about structural clearing is that, like all types of routine maintenance, it must be repeated. You can sweep your subject's Energy field today and the odds are good that next time you will need to sweep her field again. It's like brushing teeth or mopping floors; we need structural clearing over and over again throughout our lives. This is just part of having a clear and clean Energy body. This differs from the deeper healing techniques of Chapter Seven: once those are fully completed, you are finished with them. You can think of these deeper healing techniques as a home renovation as opposed to mopping the floors.

When you are using LHM there's always the issue of finding the balance, and this is definitely true in the arena of structural clearing. What is yours to do? What is for the Lightbeings to do? What is the subject's part to do? It's a joyful three-way dance: you, the subject, and the higher beings. As you become comfortable with the process, you will come to Love and trust it. Be patient with yourself; give yourself the repetition you need to let that trust develop.

There is a do-it-yourself method that we can use when the structural clearing is ours to do, and that is where we will begin. We will also discuss working with some Lightbeings that specialize in structural clearing, and lead you through asking them for help. Don't worry; they really are there. They really do want to help. If it is for them to do, their part of the dance, they are joyful to share the load. It's most effective when we first do our part, and then ask the Lightbeings to do their part.

Sometimes there is a huge difference between our results and what the Lightbeings accomplish. With new LHM students, the Lightbeings are usually willing to come in and clean up all the loose ends. This does not mean you "did a bad job." It is simply a function of the difference between what we are capable of, and what higher-dimension healers are able to accomplish. When we do our very best to follow the Guides' instructions step-by-step and then ask the Lightbeings to "make it right," everything works.

If you already practice another healing art that includes structural clearing techniques, feel free to use any methods that work for you. However, try these methods too, and see what the Guides prefer you to use. They know best; years of experience have convinced me that their suggestions always yield the greatest benefit. There isn't a "right" way or a "wrong" way, but there will be the ways that work best for you. Your Guides know what methods you are to use in any situation. Continually ask which method to use, and be open to the answer changing over time.

Friend, if you are new to Energy healing arts, relax! Remember, I was a CPA. It sounds like a joke: an Energy-healing accountant. Even so, I got there and so will you, since this truly is a natural process. There is an amazing amount of support from the higher dimensions when we commit to learning. Besides, this book has come to you for a reason. If you are reading these words, you can do this. Keep your focus on that thought like a beacon, take a deep breath, and continue.

SCREENS OF LIGHT

Often when the Guides say, "this Energy field needs to be cleared," they want us to start with the Screens of Light. These screens already exist in the higher dimensions. They are made of Love, of Divine Flow, of Source Energy, of Light, and are given to us as tools for healing if we ask for them. They come in various sizes; ask for a specific screen and it will come to you. We begin with the larger, stronger screens and work our way to the finer, more delicate screens. This way we clear the big chunks of Energy blockage first, and clear smaller and smaller blockages until we are complete.

Begin with a screen the size and shape of a chain link fence but made of Love. It's very strong and has a wide mesh. It is designed to pick up the biggest chunks of debris in an Energy field. Ask for one and it will come. This happens right away: when we ask, it is given. If you are sitting there waiting for it and thinking, "Where's my chain link fence?" then you have simply missed it. It came to you the moment you asked for it. Try this: hold out your hands and ask for the screen to be put in your hands. You can feel it land there when you ask for it. It has weight.

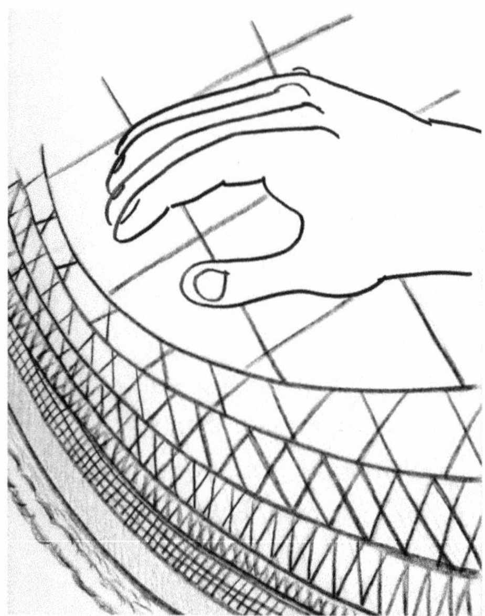

Figure Five: Screens of Light with Hand

When the chain link screen arrives, ask in what direction to sweep the subject's Energy field. This varies because there isn't a "right" or "wrong" direction; there is simply the direction that is best in this particular situation. Sometimes you'll be told to sweep the subject's field from head to toe, and sometimes from toe to head. Sometimes from the back to the front, and sometimes from the front to the back. Right to left or left to right. Every subject is different; every session is unique. You don't have to figure it out yourself. A wonderful and blessed facet of the Lightworkers Healing Method is that we never have to decide what to do. We simply create sacred space, point our intuitive channels up to the Guides, and follow their instructions.

If you are in doubt of what direction to sweep, begin with the screen beneath the subject and sweep upward. If you start working in one direction and it starts to feel off, try a different angle. It can be quite helpful to draw screens through in multiple directions, coming at the blockages from different angles and directions.

Whatever direction you are instructed to sweep in, be sure to start at least a body's length from the body. In other words, if you are working with a person who is six feet tall, start at least six feet under or above or away from her body. In this way you will sweep enough of the working part of her Energy body to really help her.

Be sure you are sweeping all the way through her field, not stopping at the skin. You are sweeping both the part of her Energy body that is outside the physical body and the part that is inside the physical body. Our skins are not the important dividing lines we think they are.

LHM practitioners usually find it easiest to move our arms and hands as we do this. This helps the mind to focus. It can be harder to sit quietly clearing an Energy body purely with mental focus than it is to enlist some physical motion in the process. If you are physically tired but have mental Energy, it's possible you'll find the reverse to be true and have an easier time using only the mind. Even so, this burns just as much Energy as physical motion does, and you're forcing the mind to do all the work. If you use your hands, you're spreading the workload around. It isn't that one way is right and the other way is wrong. Experiment with this; notice what works best for you in each situation.

Sweep the chain link screen of Light steadily through your subject's field. You might notice that it's collecting chunks of Energy as you do so. Typically, the screen gets noticeably heavier as it picks up blockages. If you are visual the chunks might look like big rocks or black tarry things. When the screen starts to feel full, draw its edges up around the payload and send the entire package, screen and all, up to Source for recycling.

You don't have to know how to transmute the old blockages into clean fresh Energy; Source knows. Simply toss the full screen as high up as you can with the intention that it go way above the astral planes and be transmuted. Declare, "I'm sending this to be recycled," and toss it way up there. Poof, off it goes. Some element of the Divine will take it off your hands. Lightbeings will take it or the Vortex will lift it up. You can feel the weight lift as it leaves.

You might have to pass a chain link fence through the Energy field two or three times until it no longer picks up debris. Each time, send the screen and its payload to Recycling as soon as it feels heavy. There is an unlimited supply of Divine chain link fences; you don't have to scrimp. Repeat the step until it feels complete. Confirm with the Guides, using your yes/no discrimination: "Am I finished with this stage?" If in doubt, screen again; when a screen passes through completely clean, it's time to move on.

Once all the truly big chunks of blockage are cleared, move to a smaller mesh Light-screen. Call for one with holes about an inch square. The mesh is a little bit finer, but it's still fairly strong and it can pick up small rocks of Energy. Now it's simply a matter of repeating the process with the smaller screen: bring the screen through the subject's field and send it to Recycling with whatever it picks up. Repeat this as many times as is needed before you move on to the next smaller size.

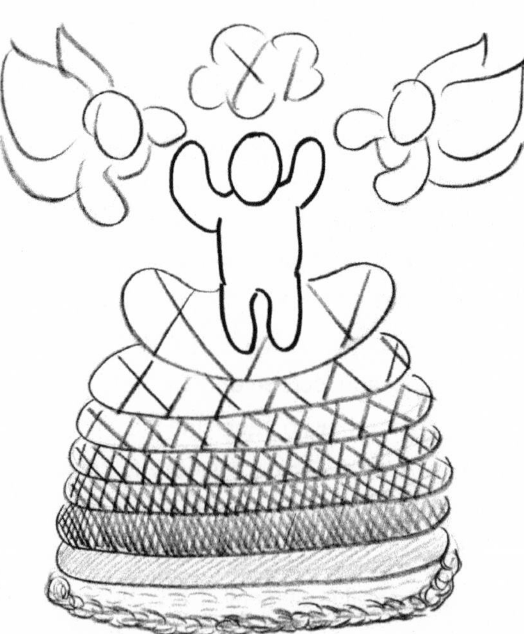

Figure Six: Screens of Light, Far View

Now ask for a screen with holes one half-inch square, and bring that mesh through in the same way, sending it to Recycling each time it fills up. Shift to half-inch screens; when a half-inch screen passes through the Energy body completely clean, move to a quarter-inch screen. Next use eighth-inch screens to get the small pebbles of Energy blockages. Each time bring the mesh through, and send it to Recycling. The screen after the eighth-inch screen looks like the screens that we put on our windows to keep the bugs out, but it's made of Light. As you bring this one through it will pick up debris the size of grains of sand. The screen that follows this has the consistency of a linen bed-sheet made of Light. Bring that through as many times as is needed, noticing how it picks up the very fine bits of blockage, and send it to Recycling.

The finest grade of these screens is like fog, but it's sticky like a spider-web. Whereas all the others feel like they're in a thin plane, this screen feels like a thick band of sticky fog. The sticky fog not only picks up the smallest bits that the bed-sheet couldn't get, it also aligns the Energy body. Like brushing or combing hair, the fog lovingly clears what it's supposed to clear while bringing the rest into alignment. As you can imagine, this feels fabulous to the subject.

That's the do-it-yourself method of clearing an Energy body with screens. It's simple but quite effective. Simply draw progressively smaller Light-screens through the Energy body, clearing roughly six feet larger than the physical body in all directions, and send the filled Light-screens to Energy Recycling. Start with chain link and use finer and finer screens, all the way down through the sticky fog.

Because this is such a straightforward technique, it is helpful not only in working with other subjects, but also in self-treatment. First, a bit of help with the thinking-mind. Our minds are often not the friends we think they are, and this process can trigger the mind. There may be a tendency to think, "If I have big chunks in me that a chain link screen can pick up, I must be a mess." This line of thinking creates a tendency to not want to see that we ourselves need the chain link fence, so we can hold on to our self-image as being "beyond that." This misunderstanding can cause us to cheat ourselves out of that deepest level of clearing. It can also lead to judgmental thoughts about our healing subject, if he has big blockages.

The truth is, every time we start a new growth cycle we begin again with new big chunks of Energy blockages. These big blockages are not an indicator of where your subject is in his *eternal* growth process. Instead, they show where he is in the growth cycle that he is *currently* in. If the big blockages are there, it's an indicator he has recently begun a new growth cycle. If there aren't many big blockages, it's a sign he is almost complete with that particular cycle. That's all it means, so there is no need to cheat either him or you out of the deep clearing the chain link can provide. If he has just begun a new challenge in his life, guess what? It's chain link fence time. Quit judging this as a sign of how advanced his spiritual development is, and see it for what it is. It is *help*.

Screenmasters

When you're finished with your best attempts at clearing an Energy field with screens, it's always a great idea to connect with the Lightbeings who work with this subject. They often introduce themselves as the Screenmasters. They Love for us to call them after we have done our best, and let them optimize or perfect our work. Their work is faster and better on every level, but we have to do our part first in order to achieve the best result. In rare circumstances they are willing to do all of the work, but that is the exception. The Screenmasters almost always want us to do our best before they step in.

How do you call them? With intention. Just form the intention of asking for the Screenmasters to join you, and then notice the Energy shift that announces their presence. The way you notice this is personal, depending on your strengths. It might be tactile, visual, auditory, emotional, olfactory, felt sense, or something else. One way isn't better than another and all ways are valid; there is simply your way.

Once you notice the Screenmasters are present, ask for them to clear the subject's field. Again, notice the Energy shifts that occur each time they do their part. These shifts happen very quickly, so if you find yourself wondering if the Screenmasters are going to do something, you've simply missed it. Ask again, and this time be ready to notice what happens almost before the words are out of your mouth.

Repeating the request yields even better results. You will notice the results eventually stabilize. After requesting their help several times, it will be time to thank the Screenmasters, and to move on to the next stage of the healing session.

By first using our own efforts and then calling for the Screenmasters, we see what we're capable of doing. We then see what they are capable of doing, after we have done our best work. This is a beautiful exercise in humility. Comparing our results to theirs keeps us in our place very effectively. It's hard to get too big for our britches in this work, because it's made brutally obvious moment-to-moment how little we're capable of doing compared to the Lightbeings. This is not to diminish our contributions, but rather to help us clearly see our place in the team of Divine Energy workers.

ENERGY CORDS

People who are familiar with Energy terminology know that this is a topic of great discussion in many schools of Energy healing. A basic explanation of an Energy cord is that it is a connection that has formed between two people, or between a person and a concept, relationship, group, or place. For now, let's just stick with the person-to-person cord for simplicity of discussion.

Often cords exist because one person wants something from the other person. She might be envious of something, or she might want the other person's help. Usually there isn't an intention to drain or harm the other person. That intent can exist, but that's beside the point. There's usually only an unconscious desire to have or be something that the other person has or is. This forms the connection, and once formed, Energy cords can drain.

This Energy drain can only happen to us if we allow it to happen. We are the creators of our experience. We create, attract, or allow everything in our lives. Over the long term, we have to work with our beliefs to change this pattern of allowing our Energy to be drained. If you are struggling with this idea consider reviewing the Beliefs segment of Chapter Five.

When an Energy cord is present, it's a connection between two people. Energy is transferring either one way or the other. Someone is getting drained. Usually neither party has conscious awareness of this situation. The "drainee" can tell cords are present because she feels exhausted. She has no Energy. Often her sleep is disrupted; it's hard to sleep with cords in place. It can be tempting to think, "She is tired because she's not sleeping," but this is a deeper exhaustion. It is there when she first wakes up in the morning, even if she has been in bed for ten hours. If you have experienced it, you know what I am referring to.

Energy cords are a huge issue for many Energy-sensitive people. Because their Energy bodies tend to be open and soft, Energy-sensitive people often have a pattern of Energy cords, and therefore of exhaustion. Looking at this from the perspective of beliefs, the real cause of the issue is an unhelpful underlying belief. One common cause of Energy cord receptivity is a belief of needing to continually give to others. Another common cause is a resistance to grounding, which typically this arises from a belief that life is more pleasant out of the physical body than in it. Again, beliefs are a larger topic than this, but this is a good example of how our beliefs affect our Energy bodies and our lives.

In my personal healing journey, I learned many different techniques for cutting or removing cords in many different schools of Energy healing. These methods all worked a little bit, or for a little while, and then the cords would be back. I'd cut all my cords or pay another Energy healer to cut them for me, and literally thirty minutes later, there would be cords again. After years of trying all the methods I could find about Energy cords, finally I asked my Guides: "What is the deal with the cords?" They said, "You're thinking about this whole topic wrong. Cords are simply a blending of Energy that isn't helpful right now. You just need to un-blend the Energy."

I still wasn't getting it, so they had me start tasting the Energy of cords. Why? Because taste is very sensitive. If I put salt in your coffee, could you look at your coffee and tell there was salt in it? Could you listen to your coffee and tell? Could you stick your finger in your coffee and tell? Could you even smell your coffee and tell? I'm thinking your honest response to all of these has to be "no." BUT—could you taste the coffee and tell I had put salt in it? Of course you could.

Being a good enough student, I started tasting the Energy cords that were draining me. Lo and behold my Energy was in every single one of them—every single one. Not a lot of it, but a little. Each cord had some of the other person, maybe a lot of the other person, but always a little bit of me. Finally I understood: it's *always* a co-creation.

Since cords are always a co-creation, we dissolve them by sorting out their Energy. Call your Energy back to you; send everyone else's Energy back to them. It's like sorting out brown rice from white rice that is all mixed in together. If you try to do it piecemeal with your conscious mind it will take you a lifetime, so forget that. Separate this simply with your intention. "Brown rice over here, white rice over there. My Energy to me, everybody else's Energies back to them."

Sometimes that general sorting request (mine to me, everyone else's back to them) will work. Sometimes a general request won't work and you have to get more specific. "My Energies to me, that certain person's Energies back to him." In this way we start to become aware who we create cords with. Patterns emerge. We can learn how our thinking and beliefs can shift to eliminate cords from our experience.

If you're afraid this is going to harm your son or daughter or other Loved one who you feel is feeding from you, then ask that they be connected directly to Source instead of to you. You don't need to form this connection to Source for them. The Guides and Angels can and will do that 20,000 times better than we ever can, so let them do it. "May my Loved one be connected to Source. May they be fed directly from Source. I call my Energy back; I quit trying to play God with them." It's not for us to do, you see? This is for the Divine to handle.

If you're working in the Energy realms, you are blending Energy with your subjects. Period. Remember that you have to repeatedly separate from your subjects, and almost certainly from other people in your life as well. If cords are an issue for you, then call your Energy back frequently and work with your beliefs.

Someone you treated five days ago might still be in your Energy field. You might have dissolved the cord once, but it may have re-formed. Since the cord was already there once, it grows back easily. Connections form with thought, you see. If the subject thinks about you, bing, that connection will open up again, and the Energy drain starts up once more. Repetition is our friend as we begin to work with our cords. At first, continually have the intention to call back your Energy and send everyone else's Energy back to them.

Over time as you become more aware of this dynamic, you will become less willing to create cord receptors. As you withdraw your Energy more and more frequently and with increasing firmness, your Energy body will begin to remember, "I don't want to do that." Cords will eventually cease to be a problem, as your Energy body will no longer have the receptors for cords to attach to. In other words, over time we can learn how to hold our Energy bodies so there is no access for cords.

Remember: this is like brushing teeth. We do it today, we're going to do it again tomorrow and we're going to do it until the fundamental underlying belief pattern shifts and it's no longer a problem. That can take a while, so we have to be consistent and patient. We're eternal beings. Anything worth having takes time to create.

One finesse point: in calling your Energy back from your cords, pay special attention to your back. Cords often attach in the back because our attention is primarily focused forward. As a result, the back is the weaker side of the field, and therefore where it's easier for the cords to attach. The time spent focusing on your backside as you call your Energy back to you can yield the best results.

The final step in this process comes after we have done the best we can. At that point we can connect to the Lightbeings who do this type of healing, the Cordmasters, and ask them to make it right. Sometimes, especially at the start of our learning process, we can go straight to the Cordmasters for help, and they will clean us off. However, as we become capable of more, more is required of us. The day will come when it won't work to go straight to the Cordmasters because we have to do what is ours to do.

We have to continually find the balance: what is for us to do and what is for the Lightbeings to do. Cordmasters know that we are capable of learning these skills for ourselves. They want us to do our best before they step in and clean up the mess. How else will we learn to do this? If they continually change our diapers for us, we'll never become self-sufficient. That having been said, if we are doing our best they will help us until one day we can do this entirely on our own.

Here is a quick summary. If you or your subject is feeling drained or exhausted, if you have no Energy today, check for cords. In almost all cases you're getting enough Energy. It's just not being used the way you want to use it. We all get our daily supply of Energy and we're spending it in some way, either with awareness or not. If our Energy is draining through cords, we're spending a lot of our Energy without awareness. The fewer cords we have, the more Energy is available to us to use with intention. Eliminating our cords and eventually our cord receptors stops this involuntary and unintended Energy loss. This allows us to move our Energy into our own life and our own focus.

To remove Energy cords simply withdraw your Energy from the cords and send the other people's Energies back to them. Continue until it feels you have done all you can do. At that point, ask the Cordmasters to improve your work, to bring it to completion. Repeat this over and over again, day after day. Over time your Energy body will become more resistant to cords, because you will have lost the habit of creating cord receptors.

One final point about cords: there is a tendency to think of the person who is benefitting from the cords as "bad" in some way. In spiritual circles, it can be quite compelling to want to think we are "beyond" creating cords. We want to think that only *other* people create cords, not us the enlightened ones! Just to set the record straight, this is an almost universal subconscious human tendency. If you doubt that, test it. Ask right now to call back all the cords you yourself have created that drain other people. Then—no judgment! It simply is what it is.

See how easy it is to be compassionate with those who create the cords when we find that we ourselves are also doing it? It's completely understandable. Big hugs all around, as we call our Energy back to ourselves and send everyone else's Energy back to them.

SPEARS

While a cord is a continuing connection between two people, a spear is a hurled blast of Energy. It is an event, and it is out of anger. Someone gets angry, and boom! There's a blast of Energy that shoots out from him and hits the other person. If he is really angry, it's a big spear. If he is mildly irritated, it might feel like pins or needles. Like cords, spears often affect our backs, simply because our Energy fields tend to be thinner and weaker in our backs.

Once again, no judgment. This is an almost universal subconscious human tendency. Let's not do a spiritual bypass and say, "I don't throw spears, enlightened beings don't do that, only bad people do it." Let me say this very clearly: we all do it. We all get irritated from time to time.

Keep in mind that the Buddha got angry; Jesus got angry. Remember the story of the moneychangers? What do you think was happening there? Jesus probably threw some hugely damaging spears at those people, given how energetically powerful he was.

Have you let go of the idea that only other people throw spears? We all do this. If you doubt it, right now ask for all the spears you've tossed at other people to come back to you harmlessly. Feel that? It's humbling and helps us be compassionate. When we come to terms with that, we can let the judgment go when it happens to us, or to a subject. "Someone threw a spear at me!" Oh, well; spears happen.

We have a choice of how to think about the spears tossed at us. We can either see them as bad events, or we can notice that someone just gave us an Energy gift. Do you ever feel you don't have enough Energy to get through all the things on your plate? Won't it be great if somebody throws some Energy at you? It is, if you're working with it properly.

Just as with cords, Energy spears are a topic of conversation in many Energy schools. Most of these schools of thought teach students to pull the spears out. Unfortunately, here's the thing about spears; they are rarely designed to come out. They are usually designed to get into their target and stick, to hurt. Remember: spears are created from anger. If the sender is really angry, the spear is big and sticky, designed to be a problem for a long time.

The more capable someone is with Energy, the more lives they've had working with Energy, the more likely it is that their spears are well designed and are tough to remove. Therefore, if you move in Energy-aware circles, this issue might affect you more than it affects someone else; you are associating with people who have big Energy bodies and lots of Energy practice over many lives. This is also why it's so important for us to grow spiritually and not just energetically: so we can handle our big Energy bodies responsibly.

If you are in a healing session and realize your subject has a spear or two stuck in him or is sporting that oh-so-attractive pincushion look, quit trying to do what doesn't work. Stop trying to pull them out; it's like pulling out a fishhook or an arrow. Good luck with that. Instead, pull them in and ball them up; it's a gift of Energy, no strings attached. It might not have felt like a gift initially, but it is a gift.

Energy is Energy is Energy. There isn't inherently "good" or "bad" Energy; it is simply Energy. When we notice a spear, the most helpful first thought is gratitude: "Thank you for the Energy." Next just pull the spear all the way inside of the subject. As you pull it in, ball it up like play-dough; now it's clear this is simply Energy. It no longer looks or feels like a spear; it simply looks and feels like a lump of Energy.

Once you have the ball of Energy at your disposal, decide how to use it. Eventually you can use it to bolster the weaker areas of the subject's Energy body. However for now, until you master transmutation, it's easiest to simply eject the Energy out of him in a helpful way. For example, throw it out his feet into the Earth if he needs more grounding. It's like compost to the planet; the planet completes the transmutation. Throw it out his crown if his connection with Source needs expansion or clearing. Source will transmute it into clean fresh Light. Throw it out the sacrum in the lower back to propel him forward on his life path. Again, Source will handle the transmutation part of the process. Bottom line: use the spear's Energy. It's a gift. "Thank you for the gift."

When you have done your best to locate and remove all spears, ask the Lightbeings who work with spears, the Spearmasters, to make it right. As always, if you do your best first, the Lightbeings will be glad to help the healing subject.

Finally, heal the hole in the aura where the spear entered. Begin by washing the Energy wound with Love and Light, and then patch it with that same Light as if spackling a nail hole. Continue until it feels you have done all you can do. Then ask the Lightbeings to heal the wound, and witness what happens.

Just as with cords, some spears will come in a general call, and some will need to be worked with individually. Sometimes the subject's Guides will show you who the spear came from, but caution you not to share that information with the subject. You are "in on the secret" so you can do your job properly.

On the other hand, sometimes the subject has to have awareness that somebody is angry with him in order to be able to release the spears that anger created. Large caution flag: this part can be extremely tricky for the subject. When you tell him who pitched the spear, there is a tendency for him to feel hurt, strike back, or react in some other way. If his Guides want him to have the realization of who is angry with him, there is a reason—but be very sure his Guides have that intention. Be very clear about this, before you speak. Err on the side of caution: assume the subject does not need to know who is angry with him. Share the information only if the Energy refuses to shift without that communication, and choose your words with extraordinary care.

Remember the Guides can show you things that are, simply so you can do a better job of facilitating. Just because his Guide shows you it's his ex-wife who tossed the spear, that doesn't mean he needs to know it. Sometimes, however, there is no way around this: the only way the spear will release is for you to identify the sender. In that case, it will be your responsibility to *use extreme care* as you word the message. Try it out in your head before you open your mouth. Repeatedly ask the Guides if you have the instructions right. Don't trigger World War III with careless words.

In these cases in which the sender has to be properly identified before the spear can release, the reason is almost always so the subject can change his thinking in some way. Often the message has to do with the subject being compassionate with the angry person, with understanding where her anger and fear come from, so he doesn't respond in kind. At this point we facilitators are usually supposed to help the subject get really clear that it's not just "bad people" doing this, that we're all tossing pins and daggers at each other until we learn not to do that.

Often the Guides will suggest an exercise to make that point. They will have the subject call back the spears he himself has thrown to the person who he is right then judging as being "bad." This mutual calling back of the damage that anger creates not only heals the situation, but also gives rise to understanding and compassion. No one is a "bad person." We are all doing our best. Spears happen.

A frequent question at this point is, "If I made spears that are designed to not come back out, how do I call them back?" Good question—but it's very simple. If you created that spear, it is a part of your Energy. We can all call our spears back, and they return to us obediently. They might be made so the recipient can't pull them out, but their creator can always pull them back. They're made with password protections, so to speak—we can remove them even though no one else can. This is good for us in multiple ways, because when we call back our spears, we're calling back Energy. Most people feel a little bit Energy deficient at some point in time. That's your Energy out there, call it back. You'll be blessed by the process.

This is another lesson in humility. Let's see what we're doing with clear eyes and not with self-criticism. All is forgiven, but let's just see what's going on here, yes? As we call our spears back, we become aware of how many there are. Then, having our Energy back, we can use it in the way that is most helpful. Energy is just Energy. No Energy is inherently "bad." These spears are just Energy that is now freed up for us to use in our lives.

One more point: we can always ask for our mistakes to be corrected. It's never too late. All time is now. Let's not get upset with all the terrible things we've done; instead, let's fix the terrible things that we've done.

Let's get completely clear about this: every human being either has done or will do really terrible and awful things at some point in her evolution as a soul. Me too. You too. No judgment. The reason souls need to do horrible things is to develop compassion for perpetrators of violence. It's easy to be compassionate for the victims of brutality; it's much harder to have compassion for the perpetrators. Until we have experienced for ourselves what happens to push souls into savagery, it's tough to understand that they are also suffering. So, my friend: no judgment.

Remember, we can always ask for our errors to be corrected. We can also ask for our omissions to be corrected. That applies in this healing art, and it also applies in the game of life.

SPINNING THE FIELD

When time is of the essence, spinning the field is a quick Energy body reset. Think of those tops that children have, in which you push the handle down and the top spins. In this analogy, you (or your healing subject) are the top. Visualize a hologram of yourself (or your healing subject) between your two palms, and compress yourself as you would the child's top. Unlike the toy, this Glorious top (which is you) spins simultaneously in both directions as you compress it from either end.

As your Energy body spins in both directions simultaneously, two things happen. First, your field is stirred so that areas with too much Energy are relieved and deficient areas are filled. Secondly, that which you no longer need is flung off, as if you were in a centrifuge. Because this technique is so effective, it can create a temporary sensation of dizziness or even nausea; this will pass in 30 seconds. If you are willing to process that, you will experience the benefit quickly. If that sensation bothers you, spin your field more slowly. It takes longer to achieve the result, but it's gentler.

PRACTICE EXERCISE WITH SCREENS, CORDS, AND SPEARS

Enough theory! Give yourself some personal experience of the process so it makes sense. First, get some Divine Help; go online to www.lightworkersmethod.com and once more absorb the second transmission entitled *Become a Healing Vessel.* Then get into a space where you won't be interrupted for at least 30 minutes. Sit in a comfortable way, and bring your focus to your breath.

Create Sacred Space

Begin with the Opening Process (Appendix One).

Screens

Now move into clearing with the screens. Choose a direction in which to draw them through you. Ask your Guides: is it best to pull them from bottom to top, from top to bottom, or in some other direction? Don't get hung up on this decision. Ask, and then take a chance and start one way. You can always adjust course.

First ask for the strongest screen, the one the consistency of a chain link fence, made of Light and Love. With your intention, know it is there for you to work with. You don't have to know how to make it; simply ask for it and know it is given. Have the intention to bring this chain link fence screen a body's length either below your feet, above your head, behind your back or in front of you, depending on which way you intend to draw it through you.

Begin to draw the screen through and around you with your intention. Draw it through your entire Pillar of Light, at least the diameter of a hula-hoop with a nice

wide overhang of screen all around, and draw the screen through that entire Pillar. Make sure you're pulling it through the back of your field as well as the front. Draw it through the left as well as the right of your field. Draw it through the interior as well as through the exterior of your field. Make sure you're cleaning your entire Energy body. When it feels like it's getting too heavy to work with, gather the edges together to make a pouch and then send it way up to Divine Recycling. Then start a fresh screen.

Often during this process people will notice their bodies coughing, sneezing, yawning, burping, and the like. This is normal. It does not mean you are tired or ill. It is a sign of Energy moving and releasing. Don't try to stifle the yawns and coughs. Let the release happen.

When the chain link screen passes through clear and easy, then move to the inch square mesh screen. Ask for it and know it is there. Start again a body's length either above or below your physical form, and draw the inch-square screens through your field. Send them to Recycling as they fill up, and repeat the process as many times as is needed until the screen passes through cleanly and easily.

When that feels complete, with your intention ask for the screens with mesh a half-inch square. Again, you don't need to know how to make these screens. They come to you from the Divine. Now pull the half-inch mesh screens through your field, sending them to Recycling as they fill. Repeat the process until it passes through you cleanly and easily.

Ask for the screens with quarter-inch mesh and repeat until it feels complete. Next move to screens with eighth-inch mesh and repeat. This screen often has a lot of work

to do. Don't let your mind make up too many stories about this. Energy is just Energy; it's not good or bad. Clear it out and let it go.

Move now to that bug screen size, still made of Light and Love. This picks up what you may think of as grains of sand of Energy. Often people who work with Energy notice a lot of Energy releasing with this size screen. Use it until it feels complete. Next call in the linen bedsheet made of Love and Light. Repeat as many times as is needed.

Finally call in the sticky fog. Most LHM practitioners *Love* the sticky fog. It feels great: very soothing and cleansing. Once again use the fog until it feels complete.

Now that we have done the best we can with this process, we can ask for Lightbeing assistance. Ask the Screenmasters now to come clean you, and know they come. Simply say, "I'm ready." Isn't this amazing? After all that cleaning you just did, notice how much of a difference the Lightbeings make. It's truly humbling. Ask the Screenmasters to clear your field perfectly and optimally. You can repeat the request a few times, until once again the benefit seems to be complete.

Cord Removal – Our Cords

Bring your focus back into the intersection of your heart chakra with your vertical channels. Take a breath or two. When you feel centered and ready, move on to cords. We'll begin with an exercise in humility and understanding, to release judgments about "people that make cords."

Form the intention right now to call back your Energy from the cords you created to others. That's right, the ones you have created. Try it with an open

mind, and experience this for yourself just as I have. At this point in the classes when I ask for a show of hands of people who notice Energy coming back, all the hands go up. We all do this. It is a natural human tendency to want to deny that: surely I am the exception! Surely I don't do this! That's okay. Acknowledge that reaction and let it go.

Return to the process of calling back your Energy from the cords you have created. As the cord-Energy flows back to you, use it. If you want to strengthen your connection with Source, just pitch the Energy out your crown. To strengthen your grounding, throw it out your feet. To propel you forward on your life path, jet it out of your sacrum in your lower back.

Remembering the power of repetition, go through this one more time. Call in another wave of Energy. To step it up a notch, have the intent to call in all the cords you have ever created, and all the cords you will ever create. If there's someone in particular that you doubt you would *ever* make a cord to, you know it *must* be him who would create this inappropriate link between the two of you, test that assumption. Call those cords in by name: "I'm calling back my Energy from the cords I created with so-and-so." How's that for an eye-opener?

To complete the process, use the Energy that you just called back. Throw it out your crown, your feet, or your lower back at the sacrum.

Did this help you release any judgment or criticism about "those bad people who make cords"? Were you able to gain some compassion for those people? That's what this part of the exercise is for: not to judge ourselves along with "those bad people," but learning to release judgment

of ourselves and of them. No judgment, just acceptance of what is, and the willingness to change it.

Cord Removal – Other Cords

Now let's move to the next stage. Form the intent to call back your Energy from the cords that other people have created with you. Hold the attitude of "I'm no longer willing to have that cord with you." If you're afraid this is going to harm your son or daughter or other Loved one who you feel is feeding from you, then ask that they be connected to Source instead of to you.

Remember to use the Energy that is coming back to you. If you feel overwhelmed, you have an excess of Energy in your field that is there to be used. Try the exercise of spinning your Energy field. Visualize the hologram of yourself between your palms, and compress yourself from end to end as if you were the child's top. Simply intending to spin your field while taking this action makes it so. Feel how it stirs your Energy really nicely so that gaps are filled in and clumps are released. Ground yourself and focus on the planet. Open your crown chakra.

If even after spinning your field you're still feeling buzzy and overwhelmed with Energy, consider this. You might be thinking of yourself as smaller than you really are, and as a result you're holding your Energy body too tightly. Have the intent to allow your Energy to expand to fill your entire field. Send that Energy out to the periphery of your field and notice how Peace and calmness replaces overwhelm. Notice how wonderful you feel.

Now that you have done what you can for yourself, ask the Cordmasters to use their fine art to relieve you of

cords and use the Energy for your optimal benefit. Simply call them with your intention. Ask the Cordmasters right now to come in and clear all of the cord Energies that you missed. Remember the power of repetition: continue to ask for help until it feels that what is going to happen has already been done. That's exactly it. Very good!

SPEAR REMOVAL – OUR SPEARS

Bring your focus back into the intersection of your heart chakra with your vertical channels. Take a breath or three. When you feel centered and ready, let's move on to spears. We'll begin once again with an exercise in humility and understanding, to help release our judgments about "people who make spears."

Form the intention right now to call back your Energy from the spears that you have hurled at others with your own anger. Try it with an open mind, and experience this for yourself just as I have. Call back the Energy from the spears you have created. We all do this. It is a natural human tendency to want to deny that: surely I am the exception! Surely I don't do this! That's okay. Acknowledge that reaction and let it go.

As the Energy of your own spears comes back, the reaction can be, "I don't want that spear headed back at me! I have enough troubles as it is!" Just remember, Energy is simply Energy. Just ball the spears up like play-dough and use the Energy. Use it to strengthen connections to Source, to the planet, and to move forward on your life path: toss it out your crown, your feet, or your sacrum.

Repeatedly call back all the spears that you have ever sent. Include the spears you have sent to yourself with hurtful thoughts: call those back as well. Know that this is

a layered process. What comes back today is the first layer. You can probably do this every day for two months and still have more to go. Please understand that is a statement about this phenomenon, not about you. When we really start working with the spears we've hurled over all our lifetimes, it can take quite a while to clean up the mess.

Did this help you to release judgment or criticism about "those bad people who make spears"? Were you able to gain some compassion for those people? To repeat, that's what this part of the exercise is for: not to judge ourselves along with "those bad people," but rather to release any judgment of ourselves and of them. No judgment of anyone, only acceptance of what is, and the willingness to change it.

Spear Removal – Other Spears

Now you are ready to deal with the spears that came to you from others. With your fresh compassion, it's easier to do this without criticism or judgment. The most helpful attitude toward these spears is to think of them as gifts of Energy. "Thank you, thank you for the gift."

With that attitude in place, draw all spears inside of you. Ball the Energy up like play-dough and pitch it out your crown, out your grounding connections, or out your lower back. Remember the power of repetition and repeat this many times, because things happen in layers. "Thank you for the Energy." Pull the spears in. Ball the Energy up. Throw it out your feet, crown or sacrum. Do it again. Repeat this until it feels the benefit has been received.

Once again, if you are experiencing Energy overwhelm, spin your field. If the overwhelm is still present, have the

intention to fill your entire Energy body, all the way to the periphery. Peace and calm will once again be present.

Now, ask the Spearmasters to remove all the spears that you missed. Ask them to use the Energy in the best way for your optimal well-being. Remember the power of repetition; ask for help multiple times until it feels the benefit has been received.

Having done what you could with the screens and with cord and spear removals, begin the Closing Process of creating a sacred seal on page 105. As you end the closing, put your attention on your feet; massage them. Bend and flex your ankles. Flex your toes. Bring yourself fully back into your body. Move your body. Stand up and walk around quietly and calmly, with the intention to ground fully. Have a drink of water, and give thanks.

My friend, this is a wonderful time to acknowledge the steps you have taken to learn and grow. Notice how different you feel now than you did before you picked up this book. Taking a longer view, recognize all the changes in yourself since you first began your personal journey of spiritual discovery, however long that has been. Be present with kindness, gentleness, and optimism. Notice what is. Know that you are on the path, that you are an eternal being, and that continued progress is inevitable. Feel the Peace that comes with that awareness. Simply BE.

CHAPTER SEVEN

BREAD AND BUTTER

As You Like It

All the world's a stage,
And all the men and women merely players;
They have their exits and their entrances,
And one man in his time plays many parts.
William Shakespeare

Almost everyone is hurting inside. Through this lovingly compassionate process of trauma release and soul fragment retrieval, we can help others let go of their hurts. As we do that, we ourselves are healed. By helping our subjects release the vibrations of trauma, matching patterns in our own system also release.

Trauma release and soul fragment retrieval are separate processes, but they are naturally linked. When we consider them as two parts of a whole, our understanding is more complete. Trauma releases are naturally followed by soul fragment retrievals because the fragments are willing to return when the trauma is gone.

For many subjects, this combined trauma release and soul fragment retrieval dance is at the heart of the Lightworkers Healing Method. This is especially true for subjects as they begin to experience LHM: their old baggage is still waiting to be cleared. As a subject receives repeated LHM healing sessions and his Energy body clears and strengthens, other elements of the LHM jewel will become more important. However, in the earlier sessions letting go of the past often takes center stage.

Underlying Phenomenon

Traumatic events are those that cause lingering hurt to the soul at some level. Physical events like a sports injury or a car accident can create energetic traumas. Emotional events do the same. Fear can be intensely scarring. Anger, either ours or someone else's, can create Energy injuries. Sensitive souls don't have to be beaten or molested to experience noticeable Energy loss. Hurtful comments can cause damage. Traumatic events can even be internal; it doesn't have to be something on the outside hurting us. We can be crueler to ourselves than anyone else ever would. We can also scare ourselves silly with wildly negative imagining.

Many children experience a lot of trauma through mental cruelty. For example, credible adults lying to a child traumatize him/her in a variety of ways. Often the child knows the adult is lying and therefore feels unsafe: "If my Mom is lying to me now, how can I count on her to protect me when I'm really in trouble?" Another common outcome is that the child's natural means of discerning truth from falsehood is disrupted. This dissonance is also traumatizing, leaving mental scars such as self-doubt and confusion that can last a lifetime.

When a traumatic event is happening, there can be parts of our soul that do not want to hang around for whatever is going on. This is a free will Universe; if parts of our soul want to go, they are free to go. In those cases, those aspects of the soul leave and go elsewhere, somewhere in the Universe. They will come back when they feel it's safe to return; in other words, when the trauma's roots are gone. Many traumas and their related soul fragments heal naturally through dreams and other means, but some are stubborn enough to linger for a lifetime and longer. These are the cases in which we can help our subjects transform their lives.

For some, the phrase "lost soul Energy" creates anxiety. My friend, it is normal for us to be missing part of our Energy. This is no big deal. Everyone you have ever met or will ever meet has soul fragments missing. It's only a question of degree. Think of it in the same vein as you would a vitamin deficiency. We don't have to be operating at 100% peak vitamin levels in order to be happy in life. However, life becomes difficult when the vitamin deficiency is extreme or when too much soul Energy is missing. The more Energy we have present, the stronger we are and the better we are able to fulfill our life purpose. Therefore, the more soul Energy that we can call back for our healing subject, the better his whole system works.

The most effective way to engage with life is not to deny that imperfect circumstances exist, but rather to mindfully engage with what is. Be empowered by knowing what to do about this situation, rather than afraid to admit it exists. You don't have to take my word for it; by the end of this chapter you will know enough to test this statement for yourself. At that point, go to www.lightworkersmethod.com and click on the *Experiential of Trauma Release and Soul Fragment Retrieval.* Nothing takes the place of personal experience. Right now, go to the website and receive the transmission entitled *Trauma Release and Soul Fragment Healing* to prepare yourself for the next section.

Healing Process Overview

The starting point to this entire healing dance is to realize that you are in the hunt for trauma. The process of finding the trauma follows closely. The next step is giving the trauma what it needs, in order to let go. Right after this comes the Joy of releasing the trauma. After that, the soul retrieval process begins with calling the soul fragments. Focusing on the fragments themselves, we help them let go of their pain; become transformed into clean, fresh soul Energy. Integration into the rest of the soul follows; the dance ends with a secondary release of any remaining pain.

Because there are more tricks, twists, and turns with the trauma release cycle of this dance, it can be both more challenging and more rewarding to the LHM practitioner than the second stage of soul fragment retrieval. Once the trauma release is complete, the soul retrieval phase is effortless and simple, and heals a life permanently.

A frequently asked question in the classes is, "If the soul retrieval is the easy and transformative part, why don't we just go straight to that?" We can, of course, facilitate a general soul retrieval. The soul fragments that are ready to heal will come in on a general call. This practice of calling in any or all soul Energy available is common in many ancient and venerated shamanic traditions. This is definitely helpful, but once a soul fragment is accessible enough to be healed by a general call, it will often heal spontaneously. Dreams and the between-life state are powerful vehicles for spontaneous soul healing. Therefore, the fragments that remain outstanding over lifetimes have a deep resistance to returning before the pain is removed. The vast majority of a subject's lost soul Energy at any point in time is in soul fragments that are still affected by their traumas. These fragments are not willing to come home until the pain that hurt so much is gone. This is why the trauma release doorway is the most effective way to get to that profoundly healing step of soul retrieval.

TRAUMA RELEASE

Persistent life pains, be they physical or otherwise, are clues that trauma is present. Pain isn't limited to our physical bodies. Have you ever had financial troubles? It's certainly a life pain. Chronic patterns of sadness, despair, anxiety, anger, confusion, fear, loneliness, and feeling disconnected from Spirit are also life pains, and all can be signals of buried trauma. "Dig here."

In our science-based society there is huge emphasis on the material causes of events. "Her finances are bad because the economy is in a shambles. His shoulder hurts because he has a torn rotator cuff. Her mind is confused because she inherited bipolar disorder." Right? To these explanations, we say, "Of course!" However, that is an incomplete interpretation. There is always another reason behind these simplistic analyses. Nothing is "just physical." The energetics of the situation precede the physical manifestation of the situation. Always. No exceptions.

Whatever is present in our lives is there for an energetic reason that gave rise to the physical dimension cause. For example, let's say I slip while walking down some stairs and I sprain my ankle. Obviously I have a pain in my ankle because I sprained it, right? Our society would like for us to declare the analysis complete. Just say "no" to this limitation of your exploration and continue on. *Why* did I sprain my ankle? There is always a more profound reason than "because I slipped." It's possible the reason is that a deeper trauma is present that is now ready to heal. That deeper trauma may have called for another event to bring my focus to the area so I can clear the entire injury on all levels. I don't want to over-simplify this; there could be other energetic reasons as well. Buried trauma is not the only reason for a painful event in our lives; it is simply a very common underlying cause of pain.

All brands of pain can respond to trauma release, if buried trauma is the underlying cause. When you are learning this healing art, however, it's nice to work with physical pain because it gives the facilitator immediate feedback. With some other life pains it's harder to tell in the moment that progress has been made, unless a bag of money falls through the ceiling and hits the subject on the head. Over time, of course, the progress becomes apparent, but when you are learning, immediate and clear feedback is very helpful. My recommendation is that you begin with something easy to measure like a physical pain.

That having been said, sometimes you don't have the luxury of working with physical pain. If there is none to be had in your subject's experience (congratulations to him), work with emotional pain. As the Energy shifts, the emotions will release. Often your subject will tear up. Tears are a beautiful indication of emotional healing. In general, a greater sense of Peace, Joy, and well-being are signals of healing for all non-physical pains, including financial stresses.

Locate and Understand the Trauma

After you create sacred space and with your subject's life-pain topic on the table, ask his Guides: what is helpful? As you gain proficiency with LHM, this part of the dance also becomes effortless because the Guides will start to lead you in some way. As the insights begin, your part is to simply play the game, to follow the Guides' lead, to follow the bouncing ball projected onto your inner screen by your subject's Guides.

Often the trauma needs to tell its story in order to be willing to release. Your mission is to follow the trail, to allow the understanding of what caused the pain to unfold. Trust your first impressions and go with it. Narrate the story out loud as it falls into your mind. Don't be afraid. Doubt stops you in your tracks. Take a chance and get in motion. If you "got it wrong," the story will grind to a halt. Think of it this way: you are trying to find your way through the tiny crooked streets of a medieval town. You feel you are headed in the right direction, but suddenly you find yourself in a blind alley. When that happens, no worries. Simply back up to the last thing you feel good about, reset your Energy, refresh your field, and try again. Go through the story of what happened until your subject's Guides say you have enough understanding to remove the trauma.

For example, let's say you are focusing on a subject's physical pain and you have asked his Guides what to do. Awareness is beginning to flow. It might unfold something like this in your awareness: "This pain feels like it has something to do with when you were a kid." "This pain feels sad and afraid." "This pain has something to do with running away from something big and bad." "This pain feels so old, this doesn't even feel like it's from your current life." Regardless of specifics, the point is that you'll start to have a sense that something is going on underneath the life pain the person is asking for help with. That's what you're looking for: what's really causing the pain?

My friend, please be clear about this: I do not mean for you to ask the subject, "Why does your side hurt?" He will tell you his "story" about it. If his story were the problem, that pain wouldn't hurt anymore. By definition he doesn't know the roots of the pain, or it would have already resolved. The true cause of the pain is rarely what the subject thinks, unless he is unusually insightful. In those cases, he might already know: "It has something to do with this situation in my life." Even so, since the pain is still present it's clear he isn't getting a full understanding, or it would have resolved.

Gently move past the conscious mind's story about the pain, and instead listen to the subject's Guides as well as to the body itself. Why do we listen to the body itself? We want the body to feel safe. Often the body has been traumatized, so it's not going to appreciate being ignored. If we ignore the body it might not trust us to help it; it might clench tightly around the pain. This is why we must relate to the hurting body like a loving parent relates to a hurting child, holding the pain with Love and comforting the body. If the body tells you what it believes it needs in order to release the pain, follow its instructions too, always checking back with the subject's Guides for verification. To ignore the body would be disrespectful. This is only a small step in the process, but it is a compassionate step.

We only need to listen to the body and follow its instructions so the body feels safe enough to allow you to proceed to deeper levels of truth. The body will know the truth better than the conscious mind. If you work with Body Talk or other methods of kinesiology you know this: you're accessing a deeper level of wisdom then by working with the conscious mind. That having been said, often the body itself is confused about why the pain is still there. Especially in cases of past life trauma in which the current body is not the one that experienced the original injury, it often doesn't know what to do to heal itself.

In the Lightworkers Healing Method we do not work with the wisdom of the body, because there are still deeper levels of truth available to us. The higher soul of the subject has more insight than the body does. Through various methods including certain hypnosis techniques, this higher soul can be accessed and healing can occur that isn't possible through working with only the body. Even that is not our goal, however. In LHM we look to the Guides for the answers, because they have still more objectivity, insight and wisdom than the subject's higher soul does. In LHM we do not even ask our own Guides about others. We listen to the subject's individual Guides to get the highest level of truth available to us about that particular person. Once you have a working inter-dimensional phone line from your subject's Guides, you have access to the deepest truths available for that person. Flash your learners' permit, trust what comes, and take a chance.

As you ask about what truly gave rise to the pain, the subject's Guides will start to tell you the root causes, in some way or another. If the insights flow freely, simply follow the bouncing ball. However, in the learning stages you may have inter-dimensional reception problems. This is normal, don't worry—you can break through this. Students who feel stuck at this point are often getting impressions, but having a hard time trusting those messages. Consider: is that what is going on for you? If so, your best option is to take a leap of faith and trust that your perceptions are real. Don't be afraid to sound like a crazy person. Fear blocks the flow of Divine Help and Guidance. Remember: that which simultaneously inspires and terrifies is exactly what you are supposed to do. Jump off the cliff and maybe you will fly. Besides, this part is really fun!

As the message begins to flow through you, start babbling it out: "Well, maybe it's something like this." If what you're saying is in the arena of accuracy, you'll get the next tidbit of information about the trauma. The Guides will feed the story to you, step by step. If you are on track, the messages will keep coming. The Guides are leading you down the path of discovery, telling you one little bit at a time until you get the full story.

If you misinterpret something, the misstep will become really obvious. It's like a brick wall across the trail; the flow of information shuts down. If that happens, don't panic. Just back up to the last bit of information that felt good and start again from that point. Know you took a wrong turn off the road of truth, get back to the road of truth and try again.

Be very aware: this is *not* the same as making up a story about the roots of the pain. Using your imagination is not the goal. Your goal is to be quietly receptive to the answers the Guides are beaming to you. This is also different than intuiting directly from the body itself: that's pointing your intuitive channels horizontally rather than vertically. Point your intuitive channels straight up with intention to connect to the subject's Guides. Follow the Guides and get a sense of the roots of the trauma.

As you do this, something fascinating will happen: the painful body will respond. This is why in a session it's very nice to be working with physical pain because the pain will start to shift. It might move around or it might diminish. If you are on the right track, the pain will do something. The pain's shifting will indicate, "Yes, you're on the right track."

How do you know this? From time to time, check in with your subject for feedback of what the body is doing. "Is the pain shifting? Is it better?" He might respond, "it's shifting, but it still hurts." That's fine. Don't expect the pain to be gone at this stage of the game. The shifting lets you know you are on the right path; keep going. Don't let the continued existence of the pain blow you out of the water. You are simply looking for signs that you are on the right road as you go. The road is however long it is; keep going until you reach the end. Each time the story stops, verify with your yes/no discernment to determine if there is more to come, or if the information-gathering stage is complete.

Don't be thrown by whether or not the subject's conscious mind has immediate memory of the incident. Hundreds of times in session I have been told by a client "that didn't happen," only to get the email or phone call later on with her amazed "Now I remember!" Don't be thrown if the person is another gender in the incident, or living in an impossible time or location. You might be viewing something that happened in another lifetime. Don't be thrown by any details. If it's true, the body will give you feedback that it is true. The results prove the theory: when the pain goes, it proves the truth of the message.

Eventually the Guides' explanation will come to an end. No further details are forthcoming. At that point, use your yes/no discernment from Chapter Three to determine if the trauma has received what it needs to let go. Sometimes the answer will be "Yes" and sometimes the answer will be "No." If the answer is "No," you will have to gather more information about that traumatic process (or perhaps about a second or third trauma) before you are ready to remove the Energy of the trauma.

Remember, this trauma can be a completely internal event. This used to throw me. The Guides would show me the subject at the age in which the injury occurred, just sitting alone in her room. Nothing would be happening externally. This is why simple clairvoyance is not what it's cracked up to be: just seeing events isn't enough. "I don't get it. There she is sitting in the room. Nothing's happening." Well, a lot is happening inside. She's messing herself up in her thoughts; that's what is happening. Trauma is defined by the recipient, by the one who experiences the trauma.

Keep a very open mind about what the contents of the trauma-stories are, because they vary widely. It could be, "when she was in eighth grade and they were playing field hockey she fell and landed on a rock right there," or it could be, "when he was five his uncle molested him," or it could be "she was so shy and fearful that when the stranger looked at her in the parking lot, she panicked." Who knows? Remember, the recipient defines the trauma.

Your subject also has a part in this healing journey. He is usually required to do something. Often that is simply to be willing to acknowledge the pain that occurred, to look it in the eye with awareness and acceptance. If he has spent a lifetime avoiding feeling this pain, he might need to feel it now in order to release it. That takes courage. With an open, compassionate heart, allow the subject's Guides to lead you through this stage. Ask, "Is anything more required from the subject before this pain can release?" Follow his Guides' instructions.

What if Clarity Isn't Coming?

My friend, don't be stopped by a perception that you can't do this. As you are learning this art, work with the subtle Energy skills that you have and know the others will develop as you continue down the path. If your clairvoyance and clairaudience are not yet developed, no worries. If "nothing is happening," take action rather than staying stuck. Assume that trauma is present if the subject has persistent life pains of any kind. If that assumption is incorrect this won't work. If the assumption is correct, it will. Let the results prove the theory.

To take action to remove traumas you don't yet have clarity about, use the powerful combination of your intention and hands. Set the intention to be shown where traumas are buried, and draw some screens of light through the subject's Energy body. Notice where the screens seem to snag or get stuck. That identifies a spot that is harboring trauma. If you do your best to reach for insight and none comes, simply flash your learner's permit, ask for the Angels and Lightbeings to help you, and proceed to the next step of removing the trauma. One caveat: while this is a good way to begin, it is important to not fall into the trap of relying on formulaic approaches any longer than is necessary. As we continually reach for more knowledge, our skills expand and we ourselves benefit exponentially.

Remove the Trauma

When you get to the point that the yes/no response tells you, "Yes, now I'm ready to remove the trauma," grasp all these traumas as if they were threads or ribbons. Wrap them around each other, like you're making a rope out of them. You want to get all of them out, and get them out whole. You don't want to leave little buried trauma-roots, so wrap them together into a rope to avoid leaving loose ends.

As you feel the trauma-rope coming together with solidity, then start to gently, gently pull on the rope. As you pull the rope, you can feel it pulling out of the subject's Energy body. Keep in mind that this is like pulling weeds. If you yank it roughly, you won't get the roots out and it will grow back. This is the same. Very gently pull the rope out with the intent to get it all out, roots and all. Sometimes the Guides say, "Pull this like it is wet tissue paper." A gentle hand is best.

Figure Seven: Trauma Release

As the trauma-rope comes out, give it up to the higher dimensions. Hand it to the Guides, to the Lightbeings, or send it to the Divine Recycling Bin. Send it to that aspect of the Divine that wants to take it. Then get feedback from your subject about that pain. It should have shifted dramatically. It might not be fully gone because it might still want the soul fragments back, but there should be noticeable change in the pain by now. If not, screen thoroughly to get all the roots of the trauma out. After you have done your best, ask the Lightbeings to remove the rest perfectly and completely.

Important points bear repeating. When you are in the learning process there will be times when you can't tell what the trauma is about or even feel where it might be lodged. If you have done your best but clarity still eludes, ask for grace and try this: assume there is some amount of buried trauma related to the pain or dis-harmony. With your powerful Energy hands and intention, grasp that trauma's Energy and pull it out, hand-over-hand, by feel. Ask the Lightbeings to grab the end of the trauma-rope and help you to pull it out fully. If you are working with physical pain, try drawing the assumed trauma out of the painful location. If you are working with another kind of pain (emotional, mental, spiritual, financial, interpersonal) and there is no obvious physical focus, you can use the crown as a default location through which to release the trauma. If your assumption is correct and there is a trauma to be released, you and your subject will feel the shifts happening. Results prove the theory.

As always in this method the key is finding the balance. What is for us to do? What is for the Angels and Lightbeings to do? What is for the subject to do? Finding this balance of allowing and doing allows us to maximize the healing benefits. If we try to do it all ourselves, we don't get best results. If we ask the Lightbeings to do it all, we don't get best results. If we don't engage the subject in doing his part, we don't get best results. We all have a part in the process.

There is one final thought about trauma release before we move on to soul fragment retrievals. Since trauma can build up in layers, it sometimes requires that it be released in layers. Whenever we get to the end we are done, but that might not be in one session. The releasing process might spread itself over multiple sessions before all the lingering bits are cleared away. This happens in cases where more Energy shifts are needed than the subject's body can process in one session. Schedule as many follow-up sessions as are needed to complete the process.

That having been said, be sure you aren't giving up too soon; check and double-check to be sure nothing more can be done in the current session. However, if the Guides insist, "This has to wait for another day," you have no choice but to accept their assessment. They are always right.

SOUL FRAGMENT RETRIEVALS

This is a naturally occurring step that follows trauma release. These are two sides of the same coin. You have just taken a clot of unhelpful Energy out of your subject's field. Now you need to fill that space with something. With what? The answer is, "with the subject himself." The parts of him that are missing are his soul fragments.

You'll sense there are fragments present in some way. Whatever signals your Guides give you are perfect; one way isn't better than another. Some LHM practitioners feel a hand signal from their Guides. Some practitioners are shown a particular color whenever there are soul fragments around. Other practitioners recognize a certain scent that is always present when soul fragments appear. Many facilitators see little faces. Those little people are soul fragments.

The point is, your Guides will develop a signal with you to indicate, "soul fragments." Be patient and let that communication system develop. In the meantime, assume that soul fragment retrievals are likely if you have completed a trauma release. Be on the lookout for them, and in that way you will learn to recognize the signals much faster.

This next part is easy. You've done the hard work. Even if you're really on the early end of that "how can I work with Energy" spectrum, you can do this. Even if your Energy sensing is still rough, you can do this. You have made it to the top of the mountain; now you get to ski downhill.

In summary, the basic steps are as follows: make a smaller bubble of Light and call the soul fragments into the bubble. Turn your attention away from the subject; focus only on the fragments for now, and help the fragments heal from their own pains inside the little bubble. Next, identify the doorway they will use to enter the body, thin the aura over the doorway, place a gold mesh funnel over the door as a precaution, pour the soul fragments through the doorway, toss the mesh funnel way up above the astral planes to Recycling, and re-thicken the aura. Now that the fragments are inside the body, help them find their right place, send a unifying frequency through to align the entire field, and ask for a secondary release.

This may sound complicated, but you'll find it to be easy and smooth. Let's break it down into its component parts.

Just as you created the big bubble of sacred space that you're always inside of in the Lightworkers Healing Method using intent and with Divine Energy, you now make a smaller bubble in your hands. This is normally about two feet tall and one foot wide. Next call all the parts of the soul who are ready to heal, to come into your new smaller bubble of Light. Invite them in. You can actually feel the bubble getting heavier as the soul fragments enter it.

One thing we absolutely know about this fragmented Energy is that it's wounded. Whatever was going on was bad enough that the soul fragments were willing to leave the body to get away from it. It makes sense that you wouldn't want to drop this traumatized Energy back into your subject's field as is. Although receiving one's soul Energy in poor condition is better than not having the soul Energy back at all, it can be quite disruptive in the short term if the Energy is still wounded. This disruption isn't necessary; we can quite simply bring grace and ease to the subject's integration process.

Stir the Energy inside the little bubble until it is circulating nicely, because movement supports change. Ask the soul fragments to converge on the pinpoint of Light at the center of the little bubble, because although they're all wounded, they're not all wounded in the same way and they're not all wounded in the same place. As they converge together they start to heal each other. It's like taking paper dolls with holes poked in them and laying them on top of one another. After a while you can't see the holes because no one hole goes all the way through the entire stack.

You have helped the fragments heal each other with your own actions first, doing what is yours to do. You have asked the fragments themselves to participate. To complete the balance of allowing and doing, next ask for the Angels and Lightbeings to improve upon your efforts, to bring the fragments into perfect optimal alignment. You will develop a sense of when that is done. The Guides will give you a sign to indicate the soul fragments are clean. These signs vary. The Guides may put a bow on a package, ring a bell, or give you a gentle nudge. There will be some way that you have of knowing, "It's ready." Double-check using your yes/no discernment, "Are the fragments ready to integrate?" When this step is complete the smaller bubble is full of clean fresh Energy of your subject's soul.

Always keep your subject posted on what you are doing as you work. Don't work in silence. Speaking out loud adds precision and power to your work and enlists the subject in the healing dance. Right now, be sure your subject understands what is going on. You're getting ready to pour his Energy back into him. His conscious mind has to be with you on this, or he might feel violated. Think about it: your shoving his soul fragments back inside of him without his conscious agreement is a violation, and often the trauma had to do with violation in the first place. At this point, it is important to have the subject's conscious mind understand and agree that he wants his fragments back. If he doesn't agree, you can't proceed. However, if you explain the process fully the subject will always want his Energy back.

There will be a spot in the subject's Energy field that wants to be the doorway for you to pour this Energy through. Typical locations are the heart chakra, the crown, or where the pain was. Unless you get another sense, choose one of those options as the doorway. Thin the aura over that doorway, so that there's no pushing and shoving required. Next call for a funnel-shaped mesh of golden Light, and put the mesh over the doorway. This is a safety precaution in case you missed something when clearing the soul fragments. If by chance you did miss something, it will get caught in the mesh of gold and not be poured into the subject's Energy body. Feel for the mesh funnel with your powerful Energy hands; it will be there. Pour this bubble of Light Energy through the mesh and into the subject. As that completes, send the mesh to Divine Recycling and re-thicken the Energy field over the doorway. Now the soul Energy is in.

When soul fragments leave, they leave from a precise spot in the Energy body. It is as if we are crystals, and the fragments are chips off the crystals. Each chip comes out of a precise spot, leaving a void. When the fragments come back, they move through the doorway, and then disperse to their exact right spots in the Energy field. Each fragment finds the spot it left from and settles back in. It's like a person making her way through a gigantic auditorium to find the exact seat her ticket is for.

There is still more we can do to improve upon the process. True, the soul fragments are inside the rest of the Energy body and back in their own right seats, but they are still very tenuous. They can pop back out with very little provocation. A minor scare in traffic might do it. We want to help the fragments fully integrate into the field, to weave them back into the fabric of the Energy body so they are stable.

One way of weaving them in is by drawing strands of the newly integrated fragment Energy though the rest of the body. Think of long threads that can reach from wherever the fragments have settled to the tips of the subject's body. Holding your hands a few inches away from the subject's body, draw your hands (and therefore the Energy) from the entry point along his torso, arms, and legs, all the way to the fingertips, toes, and head. In this way the fragments will be woven into the fabric of his Energy field.

Another way of weaving the soul fragments into place is to draw a wave of the subject's Energy back and forth over his body until it feels that all the fragments have absorbed into place. It can be similar to swishing water back and forth over grains of sand; the water is absorbed into the sand, filling the gaps between the grains. Whatever way you choose to weave the soul fragments into position, continue it until it feels complete. As always you will experience this in your own way. Your way is the right way for you. Whatever your way is, you'll come to recognize when the integration is complete.

So far in the soul retrieval process, you've identified the soul fragments, called them to your freshly made smaller bubble, helped them to heal themselves, located the doorway, thinned the aura over the door, placed a gold mesh over the door, poured the soul Energy in, sent the mesh to Recycling, re-thickened the aura over the doorway, and helped the fragments reintegrate by calling their Energy to the extremities. It would be tempting to call this complete, yes? But doing so misses a Glorious healing opportunity. Just a little bit more and we will have done the very best work we can do.

Remember the analogy of someone finding her seat in the giant auditorium? The fragments are now in their own right seats. They are calmer, less likely to hop up and run away. However, they aren't necessarily facing the front of the room yet. The next step is to send a unifying frequency through the subject's Energy field, to get all the Energy facing the same way so it is smoothly packed with no more problematic vacancies. There are many different ways you can do this. You can send a blast of Divine Energy through his body with your intention or your powerful Energy hands, or use your voice by toning or "Om-ing." You can invite a bell to sound or use tuning forks that emit a particular pitch. Send a unifying frequency of your choice through the subject's Energy field to align all those fragments with the rest of the field. It gets them facing the same way as the rest of the Energy body.

As your subtle awareness develops, you'll notice a puff of Energy like smoke coming off the body during that alignment process. This Glorious clearing is a secondary release. The unifying frequency often triggers the secondary release automatically, but asking for a secondary release to occur adds power to the process.

What is the secondary release? As those soul fragments assume their old positions in the Energy body, they push out the things that accumulated in their space while they were gone. Nature abhors a vacuum; nothing stays empty. When we have gaps in our Energy fields, something fills it. When you bring your subject's lost soul Energy back into its right place and help it to fully align, it pushes out the Energy that had occupied its place. The soul fragments themselves complete the healing process. Isn't that beautiful?

As always in this work, we want to find the balance of what is ours to do and what is for the Angels and Lightbeings to do. At this point it is a great idea to ask the Lightbeings to correct any mistakes you may have made, to include anything that was left out that should be included, and to bring the subject's Energy body to its perfect, optimal alignment.

By now, that pain is usually gone. Ask your subject, "How's the pain?" If the pain is gone, that's a good sign that you are complete with this topic for the day. As always, you would confirm this with his Guides, to be sure. If he has shifted a lot of Energy, you might be complete with the entire healing session for the day; this is a lot to have accomplished. Ask his Guides. They know.

Clearing long-standing life pains can often occur in layers. When it does, your subject will experience the pattern of incremental release. The life-pain might lighten, but may still be present. Alternately, it might go away for a period of time but then show itself again. Both of these patterns are a sign that there is another layer that needs healing. If the life-pain is better but not gone, ask the Guides, "Can we do more with this, today?" Sometimes the next layers are accessible to you that day, but not always. The Guides may tell you this is all that you are supposed to do with this topic today, that now it has to bake for a little bit, and then there'll be something else that can be done another day. This does not mean you did a bad job. It means the subject's Energy needs time to process this work before it can accept more.

My friend, please take the time to go to www.lightworkersmethod.com for the experiential exercise entitled *Trauma Release and Soul Fragment Retrieval.* It begins with a general call for all available soul Energy. This is followed by the dance of trauma identification and release, and another soul fragment retrieval process. Notice how much additional soul Energy comes back after the trauma release; notice the value of including that step in the dance.

There is a reason for your having to take this extra step to get to this particular experiential, which is a very significant exercise. It is placed online rather than included here precisely because it is so important to your mastery of the entire LHM process. This isn't to waste your valuable time, but rather to make the overall learning experience easier for you.

It's a thousand times easier to learn anything new if you have someone to help you through it, yes? The Lightworkers Healing Method website is the doorway to the mentors who will support you through the process of learning this healing art. My friend, our entire mentoring team is here and ready to help you learn the art. Take the time; it's worth it. Go online and work with the experiential

exercise for *Trauma Release and Soul Fragment Retrieval.* Then click on Request a Mentor. It is infinitely easier to have an experienced friend helping you with the twists and turns as you continue your journey.

NOT JUST THE CURRENT LIFE

In our western culture the topic of reincarnation can create some angst. If you would like to read about the topic of reincarnation, explore the writings of Ian Stevenson; he has set the gold standard in past life research. He traveled extensively over a period of 40 years to investigate more than 3,000 childhood cases that suggested to him the possibility of past lives. Stevenson was the author of several books, including *Twenty Cases Suggestive of Reincarnation* (1974), *Children Who Remember Previous Lives* (1987), *Where Reincarnation and Biology Intersect* (1997), *Reincarnation and Biology* (1997), and *European Cases of the Reincarnation Type* (2003). Reincarnation is a "theory" just as it was once a "theory" that the Earth revolves around the Sun. It has been proven and documented by Dr. Stevenson just as Copernicus proved the Sun is at the center of the solar system.

Some people "believe" in reincarnation; others don't. I don't propose you create a "belief" in reincarnation. Rather, I propose you explore the topic with an open mind, and experience past life memories for yourself. There's nothing like personal experience to open the mind to truth.

It's possible you already feel comfortable with your ability to connect into other lifetimes. It's possible the process has begun for you; you have glimmers of conscious awareness about other lives. It's also possible that you are at the starting line and feel, "I need some help with this." Any of these stages is fine. Opening up to past life memories is a natural process. Regardless of where you currently are on the spectrum of connection, it is possible for you to access other lives quite clearly. This is actually inevitable; the only question is whether you will achieve this now or later, in this life or some future life.

All of us already have past life memories. In North America, we typically don't identify them as such, because we don't have the frame of reference for it. Generally speaking, whenever our emotional response to a situation is out of proportion to current life events, it is because there is a past life component. There is truly no such thing as an out-of-proportion response; there are only situations in which we don't consciously remember all the background. As soon as the full truth becomes known, everything makes sense. Signals of past life memories include phobias; repetitive or unusually vivid dreams or daydreams; strong reactions to people, foods, movies, books, or places we travel to.

When you run into someone you knew in childhood, it brings back childhood memories, doesn't it? When visiting high school friends, you might remember events you haven't thought about for many years. Past-life memories are often triggered in the same way. When meeting an old friend from another lifetime, you quickly feel comfortable. Alternately, crossing paths with someone who hurt you in another lifetime can cause an immediate negative reaction. Running into people you knew in other lives triggers past-life memories, even if you aren't consciously processing it in that way.

This is good news when it comes to consciously remembering past lives: you are already linking to the memories. All that is still needed is to acknowledge the link and investigate it further.

Another common trigger of past life memories involves travel. Seeing the place in which you once lived happily can cause those reactions of "I could live here." Conversely, the idea of travel to a place in which you once suffered can be distasteful. This is not a reflection on the current reality of that location. Even lovely places such as Paris, Tahiti, or Machu Picchu can repel a person who had a traumatic past life experience there.

Have you ever read a book or seen a play you deeply connected with? Is there a movie you simply Love, and have watched repeatedly?

Consider: perhaps these indicate hidden past life memories. Examine what that book, play, or movie is about. Consider there might be a reason that particular story is hooking you. It could be that you lived in the culture it's representing. It could be it has a character that you really connect with; perhaps that character's life experience mimics yours in another lifetime.

Alternately, a movie, play or book with a similarity to a major past life challenge can be seriously upsetting. "Nightmares" can result. Often these are memories of traumatic or even fatal past life incidents. Dreams are a frequent doorway into past lives, especially if they are repetitive or unusually vivid. Both "good" and "bad" dreams can in fact be past life memories. Reflect on significant dream experiences with this awareness and be open to what happens next.

HOW DO I KNOW YOU IN A PAST LIFE?

Given that the people in our lives often trigger past life memories, it can be very useful to work with a friend when you are ready to open to other lives and times. It would be ideal to work with a friend who already has access to past life memories. Another ideal sharing partner is someone who is also engaged in learning the Lightworkers Healing Method, since the terminology, understanding, and energetic access will be similar. Once you have a partner to practice with, go to www.lightworkersmethod.com and absorb the transmission entitled *Past Lives* as many times as you wish. Ground yourself afterward, and you will be ready to proceed.

In this exercise it is important to trust your very first impressions, even if they don't make sense right away. They are coming to you from your Guides, your soul, and your subconscious mind. You will be stuck if you analyze. If you trust an impression, another will follow it. Follow the train of your hypothesis; any misinterpretations will clear up as you continue to let the awareness unfold. Stay in motion; don't stall out. A moving car is easier to steer than a stalled vehicle. Begin with the level of clarity you have to work with, and trust that your awareness will expand as you continue.

Once you are together with your friend, get centered and calm; use the Opening Process to open the connections between the two of you, and to create sacred space. Inside the bubble, both of you can turn your intuitive channels up and begin to ask your Guides to "show me a clear event from a lifetime the two of us have shared." Then ask yourself orienting questions: "Am I inside or outside? Is it day or night? Am I alone, with another person, or with more than one other person? Am I standing, sitting, or lying down? What type of surface am I on?" Be peaceful and receptive. Allow the thoughts to come. Speak out your impressions; your friend may be able to add her own insights.

Next, move into questions that help you establish culture, location, and time. "Are my feet bare or is there something on them? (What is on them?) Are my legs bare or is there something on them? (What is on them?) Is my upper body bare or is there something on it? (What is on it?) Am I adult or child, male or female? What about my friend: adult or child, male or female?"

Once you have a sense of how you both look, begin to assess the geography. "Is it hot or cool? Wet or dry? Flat, mountainous, or other? Is this countryside, village, or city? Is this North America or somewhere else? Asia or somewhere else?" In this manner, you will narrow down the location. As that settles into place, ask about the time: "What century? Approximately what year?"

Ask about the nature of your relationship with each other: "Are we siblings? Friends? Parent/child? Married to each other?" As these details fall into place, typically the connection to that past life is open enough that you can begin to ask: "What is important for us to know

about this life?" Follow the trail. Explore the life. Find the gifts it brought to you.

If both of you are opening up to past life awareness, this game is doubly fun. Be aware of one potential: that you have shared multiple lives. In this case one of you might be remembering one life you've shared while the other person might be remembering another life you've shared. In other words, if there's a discrepancy in the presenting scenes, don't make that be wrong. Choose one life for the first part of the conversation, and then when you feel like you've explored that to capacity, you can move on to the other life. When you feel complete, end your experience with the Closing Process (Appendix Two).

As you become aware of your previous connections to your sharing partner, it can be important to clarify the nature of your soul contract in the current life. This is especially true if your sharing partner is a friend of your gender preference, and you recall another time in which the two of you were married or romantically involved. If this occurs it is important to ask your Guides: "What is our connection about in *this* life, the current life?" Just because you and your friend were lovers once before does not mean that is your soul's plan in the current life. Investigate thoroughly. Be mindful. Don't jump to conclusions.

Playing this game with different friends on different days encourages the doors into past lives to swing open fully. As you explore your shared past with more and more people, a beautiful awareness will come: wherever we go, we're surrounded by people who we Love and who Love us. How wonderful!

What's the Point?

We aren't connecting to past lives for entertainment or curiosity. This is an important part of the healing process for the subject's current life.

Entrenched unhealthy patterns almost never began in the current life. There are almost always current life triggers, but that is not the same as the true cause. Almost invariably, really stuck patterns began in a previous life and have been carried forward into the current life so the learning can continue.

In working with trauma release, be alert to the potential for past life roots of current life troubles. Follow the path back to the previous life's trauma, and heal those traumas. Once that is done, look for links to current life patterns; making that connection is important in healing both the past and the current life. The techniques of trauma release when working with past lives are identical to those used for current lives. The difference in result is remarkable. The soul retrievals that follow a healing of multiple lives are much larger and more complete than when only current life traumas are released. Be thorough; don't limit yourself or your subject. All time is now. There are truly no limits.

Practice, Practice, Practice

Voila! Both trauma release and soul fragment retrievals are done! Practice, practice, practice these techniques. This is the heart of the healing process of letting go of the past. This can release decades-old entrenched patterns of all types of pain. This can heal "incurable" diseases. As we let go of our baggage, we are free to live in the present moment. We are free to be present for life.

Walk in Light, live in Light, be Light.

LEVEL THREE

USING THE POWERFUL FUTURE

CHAPTER EIGHT

CUT TO THE CHASE: THE SOUL PLAN

That Lives in Us

If you put your hands on this oar with me,
they will never harm another,
and you will come to find they hold everything you want.
If you put your hands on this oar with me, they will no longer lift
anything to your mouth that might wound your precious land - that
sacred earth that is your body.
If you put your soul against this oar with me,
the power that made the Universe will enter your sinew
from a source not outside your limbs,
but from a holy realm that lives in us.
Exuberant is existence, time is a husk.
When the moment cracks open, ecstasy leaps out and devours space;
Love goes mad with the blessings, like my words give.
Why lay yourself on the torturer's rack of the past and the future?
The mind that tries to shape tomorrow
<u>beyond its capacities</u> will find no rest.[1]

1 The feeling of helplessness creates the torture.

Be kind to yourself, dear—to our innocent follies.
Forget any sounds or touch you knew that did not help you dance.
You will come to see that all evolves us.
Jelaludin Rumi
From Love Poems From God, shared with thanks to Daniel Ladinsky

How do you think about your future? Most of us want our lives to go well. We want to be healthy, happy, reasonably comfortable and secure. We also know things don't always go according to that script. Accepting what life hands us is essential: when we resist what is, we create suffering for ourselves. However, in finding the balance, there are also steps we can take to improve the outcome of our life plans. Instead of just dealing with what comes our way here in the physical dimension, we can be energetically proactive.

In **Level Three**, we will explore how to work to improve the present by working with the future. The future chakra is almost always overlooked in chakra system descriptions, yet it is critically important in accessing the future. **Chapter Eight – Cut to the Chase: the Soul Plan** begins with a discussion of Energy anatomy, followed by an exercise to clear and improve your own future chakra. With that foundation in place, you will then learn to access and improve the life path, which is the energetic structure of the soul's life mission, or plan. Soul contracts (the verbal expression of that same plan) are also addressed to open another doorway of healing. A dynamic experiential exercise ends the chapter.

In **Chapter Nine – Using the Powerful Future** you will learn to access future selves for yourself and for others in order to bring healing to the present moment. The chain-link technique to connect to the ultimate future life is the most effective accelerator of life-healing and soul growth I have ever experienced. Exercises to open doors into future lives end the chapter.

Little things can make a big difference in the effectiveness of a healing system; **Chapter Ten – The Grand Balancing Act and Other Tricks of the Trade** covers some of these. The section on trouble-shooting tips is invaluable. The last technique of the book, working with the fabric of space-time to optimize and solidify outcomes, is absolutely cutting-edge material.

As with all aspects of the Lightworkers Healing Method, these techniques can be applied to others as well as to ourselves. What's the bottom line? We can improve our life experience and the lives of others with these very real hands-on tools.

How exactly do we go about improving the future for others and ourselves? Let's start with the future chakra, and with some background about chakras in general. Please resist the temptation to skip this section. Consider there might be something else to learn about this basic foundation.

THE PILLAR OF LIGHT AND THE CHAKRA SYSTEM

In the Lightworkers Healing Method, our primary focus is the Pillar of Light that runs through and around our physical body from Source to the center of the planet. A strong, balanced, clear, straight Pillar of Light makes it possible for us to hold space for the Divine Will to express itself here in the physical dimension. When our Pillars of Light are clear, strong, and well grounded, we are able to live in such a way that we do not express our will or any other person's will either—just Divine Will. Frequently repeating the Opening Process is a natural way of clearing and strengthening your Pillar of Light, and thus of creating a life centered in Spirit. Since both ends of the Pillar are grounded in Divine Energy (Divine Earth Energy beneath us, Divine Source Energy above us), the Energy that flows through the Pillar is pure Love and Light.

The Pillar of Light contains vertical pranic channels; these allow the upward-rising Earth Energy to move through and around us to Source.

They include both the intuitive channels and the closely-related kundalini channels. We are all engaged in an eternal process of straightening these channels until they point to Source. In this way our intuition is clear and our kundalini supports us in living a life based on our soul's plan rather than a life filled with the distractions of a search for sex and money. Please don't misinterpret this: sex and money are part of a healthy physical dimension experience. It is the obsession with sex and money that can destroy lives. When the vertical channels are flowing cleanly, our kundalini doesn't clog and these obsessions don't build up.

The Pillar of Light is peppered with chakras all up and down its length. Generally speaking, chakras are areas where an Energy exchange occurs between the living being and the rest of the Universe. You might think of them as openings in the Energy body, or as energetic input/output devices. The Energy body inhales and exhales prana chi/life force through both the vertical channels and the chakras. When the Energy body is functioning well, the living being is functioning well. Difficulties arise when either the vertical channels or the chakras are blocked or twisted. These challenges can be physical, mental, emotional, spiritual, financial, or interpersonal.

We have thousands of chakras that lie both inside and outside of our physical bodies. Different wisdom traditions will emphasize different chakras depending on the goals of that tradition. In the Vedic system of ancient India, the chakra system is often simplified to seven major chakras. Other wisdom traditions describe three, four, five, or six major chakras. Some teach eight or nine chakras. Most traditions depict chakras as reaching through the physical body, but there is variability in this as well. At least one lineage believes chakras don't go through the center of the body, and name the front and back halves separately. Knowing about this variation in how the chakra system is viewed, it is clear: the chakra system is malleable and multi-faceted.

Different traditions will explain chakra structures differently, depending on the goal of the system. While the Lightworkers Healing Method team discusses the chakra system from the perspective of this chapter, we acknowledge the ways it is taught in other systems. Although we discuss the chakra system differently than it is presented elsewhere, that doesn't make those other ways untrue. All ways can be true. It isn't either-or; it's both.

Let's discuss chakra structures first; chakra locations will follow. In the Lightworkers Healing Method way of relating to chakras, it's helpful to recall that all Energy, including chakras, conforms to our beliefs. How you expect chakras to be shaped is how they will shape themselves. Since this is true, it makes sense to choose a belief system about chakras that allows them to be easily cleared and healed. When my Guide Zoron was teaching me about chakras, he explained chakra structures as I am about to. When I began observing chakras in myself and in others, I found his explanations to be true. Since the LHM teaching works so well, it was easy for me to let go of my previous expectations about chakras. I encourage you to experiment and see if this can be true for you too.

In LHM, we observe that the chakras can open in all directions and there can be free flow through all parts of the chakras. There is never anything stuck at the back of the chakra because there is no back of the chakra. In other words, we can view the chakra from another angle and the back becomes the front. The Energy of the chakra can be cleared from any angle: back to front, side to side, diagonally, and so on. When a chakra is clogged, it can quickly and easily be cleared. Simply expand it, pull it open wider, and sweep the clog out with a River of Divine Flow. If there is a stubborn blockage, sweep it with Divine Love from another direction to wash it clear. Chakra clearing and balancing is quick and easy, not a big deal.

Chakras are not static. They twist, bend and move around. They're conscious living beings just as we are, and just as the cells of our bodies are. Therefore we have to acknowledge that chakras will not always open straight ahead; as a matter of fact, sometimes they will be looking entirely in the opposite direction. Fear is usually what causes the chakra to shield itself, and that's often the case when it's facing backward. It is afraid hurt is coming, so it tries to deflect the pain. When we observe this configuration, we simply draw enough Love into the chakra that it can release its fear and open back up to life. It is easy to work with chakras to bring them into their optimal condition. Love heals all wounds.

In my observations using this belief system, I notice that chakras are often significantly larger than they are commonly represented. Many drawings of chakra systems show the major chakras as roughly grapefruit-sized. While it is possible you will find people with chakras that small, that is not the norm for the people I work with. The chakra diameters are commonly at least hula-hoop sized, and frequently much larger than that. Therefore, most if not all of the commonly referred-to chakras are actually large enough to encompass the entire torso of the individual. Hold a hula-hoop in front of you for a nice visual representation of this. Focusing on the full hula-hoop sized chakra during clearing yields a much better result than simply flushing the core of the chakra clear.

Let's now consider chakra locations. Energy-healing traditions emphasize the chakras that influence the goal of that system. The simplest chakra system I have awareness of is that found in Traditional Chinese Medicine (TCM). TCM presents three dantien (chakras). There is a lower dantian low in the torso, a heart dantian at chest level, and a higher dantian in the head. No bells and whistles; just the foundations of health at all levels.

Many Energy systems discuss seven basic chakras: the root chakra at the floor of the torso pointed downward, the second (also called sacral or sex) chakra from the lower abdomen through the lower back, the mysteriously moving third chakra, the heart chakra running through the chest, the throat chakra at neck level, the third eye in the forehead and out the back of the head, and the crown at the top of the head pointed upward.

Have you noticed that the third chakra's location seems to shift? One book will describe it as being at the solar plexus. Another will position it at the navel. Still others will drop it down a few inches below the navel into the hara. Actually, major chakras exist at all three of those locations—the hara, the navel, and the solar plexus. Most authors, however, chose only one "third chakra" location in an effort to fit into the "seven chakras" model.

If we step back and take a larger view, it's clear that we have literally thousands of chakras in our core and in our extremities, as well as above and below our bodies. The larger chakras are centered roughly every two inches up and down the midline of the head and torso, and continue at regular intervals down the legs as well as above and below the body.

All Energy schools emphasize the chakras that are significant to that particular healing art. None of these systems are wrong, my friend. Each system simply works with the most relevant chakras for its modality.

FUTURE CHAKRA

The overall goal of the Lightworkers Healing Method is to bring our Energy into alignment with our life mission. An important factor is to work with the part of life that has not yet occurred. In other words, with the future. There is a chakra that's important to emphasize that is typically not discussed in other systems. It is centered halfway between the heart chakra and the solar plexus chakra, on the sternum at the level of the nipple line. This future chakra deals most directly with our future in this life, as well as with future incarnations.

Improving the Future Chakra

When you are working to heal your subject's future, the starting point is to check her future chakra, centered at the sternum. See that it is open, balanced, and flowing freely. If it is squeezed shut or twisted around, healing the future will be harder than it needs to be. When you optimize the chakra first, you are working smart rather than hard.

Straighten the future chakra, help it open, help it clear, and balance the flow of Energy through it from side to side. How? With your intention to do so, and by drawing Divine Love through the chakra. In the Opening Process of creating sacred space (Appendix One), you learned how to clear and balance a heart chakra by opening to the River of Love that wishes to flow through it. Simply apply that identical process to any chakra, and you can clear and balance it, too.

Like all chakras, the future chakra extends all the way through the body. Just as with all chakras, at first we relate to it as a tube from front to back. Of course, as with all chakras, it can open in all directions. It is common to relate to the future as being in front of us, and the past as being behind us. When you think of the back of the future chakra, some mind-chatter might occur. You might wonder, "What does the back of my future, my past future, have to do with now?" When you were a child, you had a future that has now partially become your past. How you related to your future then is still carried in your Energy body, in the back of your future chakra. It's important to clear those old views as well as the current views, to truly clear the future.

Friend, an experience is worth a thousand words. I'll talk you through an exercise to clear your own future chakra so you will know for yourself how this works and then be able to apply it to help others. To prepare yourself, go to www.lightworkersmethod.com and absorb the transmission entitled *Life Paths and Soul Contracts* as many times as you wish.

Begin with the Opening Process (Appendix One) to create sacred space. Then bring your focus to the future chakra, halfway between your solar plexus and the center of your chest. This should be on your sternum, roughly at the nipple line. It can help to actually place your finger there, touching the center of your future chakra. Remember the hula-hoop guideline for size, and expand your focus beyond the chakra's center to include all of it.

Now start to breathe in and out through that entire chakra. Give it your loving attention. Let it know you notice it, and that you Love it. Draw Divine Love through it exactly as you did with your heart chakra in the Opening

Process. Flush the chakra with Love back to front and front to back.

It is normal for the chakras to be a bit twisted or bent at the start of a meditation or healing. It is unusual to find a chakra completely straight, open and aligned to begin with. Knowing that twists and bends are normal, you won't be afraid to search for them. Using your powerful Energy hands and your intention, straighten your future chakra. Chakras respond to gentle loving touches of pushing, pulling, shaping, smoothing. Don't be harsh with it; be loving and kind. If the chakra is twisted to one side or the other, it can be helpful to not only bring it straight, but actually overcompensate, drawing it a little bit past the midline. In this way when you release the chakra, it comes back to straight alignment. As it straightens, flush it with more Divine Love.

Include the back of the future chakra in your focus; straighten and align it as well. If this is difficult for you, imagine a hologram of yourself floating in front of you, so that you are able to see your own back. In this way you are the outside observer to your own Energy body. From this perspective, reach out and straighten the back of your hologram's future chakra. This is a surprisingly helpful maneuver. Alternately, you can imagine the hologram "you" behind yourself. From this perspective, the hologram of you is lovingly straightening the chakra on your behalf. In this way you are still inside your Energy body, but have awareness of the outside observer who is also you. Either way is fine.

As you bring the entire chakra-tube of your future chakra into straight alignment, flush it clear with the River of Divine Love. Draw Light and Love from Source into the

front and out the back of your future chakra, letting the River of Love flow. Now switch the focus; draw Love from whatever element of the Divine you are most comfortable with into the back and out the front of the future chakra. Let that River of Love flow through the chakra. Finally, invite those streams of Love to flow simultaneously in both directions, doubling the amount of Love present in the future chakra.

If you feel like coughing or exhaling or yawning, that is a sign of Energy releasing. Just let that happen. Don't fight the cough, the sneeze, or the yawn. Stifling these body reactions to an Energy shift stifles the Energy shift itself. Let it out and feel your Energy body improving.

Friend, are you feeling this in your future chakra? Are you able to connect to it? If not, reset your Energy body and give yourself a second go with this exercise. If after your second try, you are still struggling to experience and connect with your future chakra, don't worry. This can happen, and there are a few reasons for that. First, perhaps you've been ignoring this chakra for a long time and it isn't as fluffy and full as your other chakras. Second, there could be an element of fear about your future, or fear about some element of your future, that is complicating this for you. Again—that's common. No worries.

If you feel you might have some fear about the future, just acknowledge that fear right now. Don't make it wrong and don't try to push it away. Instead, Love the fear like a perfect mother Loves her crying baby. Acknowledge, "I feel fear here." Open the door into the fear, not to push it out, but to ventilate it so the fear can feel Divine Love flowing through and around it. Trying to push the fear

out doesn't work. It works to allow the fear itself to receive Love. That's all it needs. It just needs Love.

When you have done your best work, ask the Lightbeings to improve upon your efforts: to clear the future chakra, straighten it, and optimize it. As always, we intend to find that point of balance between what is ours to do and what is for the Lightbeings to do. Put a sacred seal on your work with the Closing Process, Appendix Two.

Whether working with yourself or with a healing subject, the process of clearing the future chakra is identical. Having done this for yourself, you now know what it feels like and what a wonderful gift you will be able to share with others: opening to the Divine Future.

LIFE PATH

Your work with the future chakra has laid the foundation. Now you can begin working directly with your subject's future to align her with her life mission. First things first: we *never* decide on our own to work with the life path of a healing subject, or for that matter with any of the techniques in this system. We are not the "deciders" in this system. After we are past the initial learning stages, our only decisions are to clarify the healing intentions, to begin the healing session by creating sacred space, and to end it with a sacred seal. Everything that comes between the opening and the closing is up to the subject's Guides; we simply follow their instructions. In this way, we are most open to Divine Guidance.

Nonetheless, when we know the types of things the Guides can tell us to do, it's easier to understand the instructions that come. Working with the life path of the subject is something that can come up. The more you know about this in advance, the easier those healing sessions can go. With that caveat, let's begin.

Perceiving the Life Path

By now, you have at least one method of subtle Energy sensing that works for you. You might even be comfortable with more than one method of subtle Energy awareness. Again, it doesn't matter what system of sensing you rely on. What matters is that you have a system that you can start to work with, and that you're open to the other systems developing as well.

Now that you know life paths exist, you can bring your subject's path into your awareness using your powerful intention. As you start to focus on it, you can perceive the path like a ribbon or a road that the subject is on. It goes behind them (the road they've already traveled), and it extends in front of them (the road still to come).

There's nothing like personal experience to make new concepts clear, so try this with yourself as your subject, as you read along. Get calm and centered, right now. Use the Opening Process (Appendix One) to create sacred space. Then form the intention to work with your life path as a learning exercise.

The obvious starting point is to perceive, to locate, the life path. Set your intention to find the life path; ask the Guides to give you awareness of it. Use your powerful energy hands to feel for the path; it is tangible. As your hand brushes against it there is a subtle resistance.

Different subjects' paths are shown to us differently. The locations will shift depending on how the Guide wishes to show it, how the subject relates to her path, and how we relate to the paths. There isn't a right place or a wrong place for this path. The most common perception of a life path's location is at the feet. The second most common perception is that the path comes out from the future chakra. Those are the two most common places, at the feet or at the future chakra—but roughly a third of the time, people sense them in a variety of other places. Don't stress about this. You don't need to shift its location to a "better place." Simply notice it where it is. Wherever you perceive the path is perfect.

Right now, experiment with different ways of perceiving your path qualitatively. If you are visual, simply look at the path: what does it look like? If you aren't visual, feel it with your powerful Energy hands like you're feeling a shape, getting to know the shape with your hands. Next, try listening to the path: what does it sound like? Then see if you can smell the path: with the intention to connect to the path, take a whiff. See if you can taste it, too. You'll be surprised what paths can taste like.

Perhaps you will feel it emotionally. Open your heart to the life path; have the intention to feel the emotions of the path, whatever they are. Sometimes, people feel anxious when they first connect to their life path. As they work with it, the obstacles start to clear and the way smoothes and eases, a sense of optimism and Peace arises.

If you are having difficulty connecting with your life path, simply ask right now for your Guides to clear whatever it is that's hindering your awareness. Ask your Guides to let you sense very clearly whatever it is there is to notice, and to help you trust what you're perceiving. Almost always the discernment is present but it is clouded by doubt about one's ability to sense. Ask your Guides and Angels to clear away the doubt.

If you are still struggling to connect with your path, it is possible you have a fear that "this might not be something I am supposed to do." Consider this, my friend. If this were not for you to do, why would you have this book in your hands? Would your Guides and Angels have led you to it if this weren't right for you? I doubt it. Try this: ask your Guides to reveal your path to you only if it is in your highest and best good, and then try again with an open mind and a light heart.

After locating the path the next step is to perceive its quality. Is it straight? Is it clear? Is it wide? Is it bright? Does it seem like something that you can easily dance along, or does it seem like something that could use some improvement? The first time someone's life path is observed, often it's not pretty.

If your perception is either visual or tactile, there might be boulders in the road, giant craters, sharp twists and turns, a cliff, and ogres in the road. These are metaphors for life challenges. If you're sensing the path emotionally, it might feel not-so-great: anxious, unhappy, fearful, angry, or irritable. It might smell rancid or foul. It might sound like scary noises, crying, or alarm bells. On the other hand it might not. It might smell like pine trees, have happy Caribbean music playing, taste like chocolate, and be clear Light. Don't get hung up in any preconceived idea of how it will be. It is how it is.

Improving the Life Path

When we are instructed to work with a life path by the Guides, our goal is to bring it into better alignment. Clear the obstacles, fill the potholes, smooth it, widen it, and straighten it. Make it shiny and bright, a joyous, sweet path of Light. Bring it into harmony in as many ways as possible. You can do this with your intention and with your mental focus. Keep your second senses sharp and notice the changes happening. Keep at it until the shifts feel reasonably complete.

As always, keep in mind that there's a balance between the do-it-yourself method and asking the Lightbeings to do the work. After you do your best to improve the path, ask the Lightbeings to optimize it. It's always an eye-opener to see what they can do to improve upon our very best efforts. It keeps us humble. Don't be surprised if you see huge shifts at this stage, even though your work was very thorough. This doesn't mean your work was sub-standard; quite the opposite: it is an indicator that you have, in fact, done your best. That is when the Lightbeings can do the most for us: when we have already done our very best. This is the true meaning of the phrase, "God helps those who help themselves."

Let's walk through this life path improvement process so you get the feel of it. You may engage with this either for yourself or with a healing subject. First, get centered. Repeat the Opening Process (Appendix One). Ask your Guides to work with you, to support you in this process of learning how to work with your life path and how to

work with the life paths of others. Knowing that intention counts for so much, form the intention to locate your life path. Begin by checking around your feet and around your future chakra with your powerful Energy hands, or with another sense if you prefer. Notice how much easier it is to find the path, this second time around. Wherever you find it is perfect. There is no wrong location.

Start to get a sense of your life path once more. How does it seem? If you feel it with your hands, how does it feel to the touch? If you open your heart to it, how does it feel in your emotions? If you listen to it, how does it sound? If you smell it, what is its scent? If you want to taste it, you can taste it. If you're visual, you can look for it. What does it look like? Get a perception of it. Simply notice its quality.

Form the intention to sense whatever blockages there are in the life path in whatever way is helpful for you to notice them. Also ask your Guides and Angels to help you perceive these barriers, so that you have both the personal intention and the higher-dimension help. You can feel blockages with your hands, you can feel them with your emotions; you can smell them, you can hear them, you can taste them, you can see them, however you sense them is perfect.

Notice the changes that occur as you begin the following clearing process. Start with your powerful hands and the do-it-yourself method. If a blindfolded person wanted to clear a countertop of grains of sand or pebbles, he would just move his hand back and forth. Eyes aren't necessary; he can simply clear the countertop. If your other subtle senses are sharp, use them too—but you can make a big difference with your powerful hands alone.

Reach your hand forward, trust it will find the path, and clear the path in front of you. Use your hands to swish it clear from side to side. Next sweep its length clear in front of you with a motion like a breaststroke when you're swimming. Keep going for a while until it seems you have done enough for now.

When you feel ready, take a moment and reassess. Is there some perception of difference? Does the path feel lighter? Does it feel more clear? Is there less blocking the way? Does your breathing come easier when you're sensing your life path? Almost always the answer will be "yes," and you will have had your first successful run-though of the do-it-yourself method of clearing the life path.

If you are ready to step up the level of precision, ask the Guides, "What is needed in order for the remaining blockages and obstacles to clear?" As you perceive an answer, follow the instructions. When you complete that process, once again assess. Did even more improvement occur?

Having done what you could to make a difference, move to the second stage. Ask the Lightbeings to clear the life path of whatever obstacles remain. Ask that the obstacles be cleared, be released, be lightened, be brightened, that the load be lifted. Ask for whatever is necessary, and notice your felt sense of the path. It should feel noticeably lighter and brighter. If something is releasing at the emotional level right now, that's perfect, too. Just let it go and breathe it out. Don't hold it in. Open your crown, exhale, and let it go. Have the intention to release and know it will happen.

If significant blockages still remain, this can mean one of many different things. This can mean that whatever blockage is there needs to tell its story. In other words,

you might need to have the cognitive awareness of what the issue is. You might need to learn the lesson. It could also mean that it is not time to clear whatever is there now, although that line of thought can often cheat you of a healing opportunity.

It can also mean that you're simply not noticing the shift that has occurred. That can happen. Reset your Energy body, and try this technique. First ask to be shown how the life path was before. Then have the intention to perceive how it is now, and compare that to the first perception. It's like comparing two cartoons: what's different in these two pictures? Using all your subtle senses, compare the "before" and "after" versions. Notice the differences. Notice how much it has improved, with all your efforts and intentions and the assistance from the higher dimensions. Then, my friend, create a sacred seal for your work with the Closing Process (Appendix Two).

By now you realize this is a process that you have begun, but not completed. Knowing there is power in repetition, you can repeat this process many times. Have fun experimenting. Try different approaches. Take your time. Remember that we are all eternal beings engaged in an eternal process of growth. Don't get frustrated if there are still obstacles when you have done your very best. Rome wasn't built in a day. This is a process; try it again tomorrow. Notice how your life changes over time, as you repeatedly clear the Energy pathways.

ALIGNING WITH THE PATH

My friend, for purposes of this section I will assume you are working with yourself as the willing subject. I do this because you may find this technique to be especially useful as you self-treat. Because it focuses exclusively on the structure of the Energy, it is easier to use than other methods that more readily engage your thinking mind. It is also a powerful technique to use in working with others, and I recommend you practice that way as well. That way, in an actual healing session when a subject's Guides suggest you work with his life path, you will feel ready to do so. If you are blessed to work with someone else, adjust the language accordingly.

After having smoothed and improved the life path, the next step is to check your position with regard to the life path. We are almost always rotated to some extent; very rarely are we facing it straight on and ready to go. Why? As with the future chakra's twists and turns, this is almost always about protecting ourselves from a perception of future pain. Since our life plans are designed to encourage growth, they are a series of changes, sequences of letting go of the old to allow the next stage of life to emerge. Sometimes we wish to resist change, to view it as "bad," and therefore to resist our life plans and view them as "bad." Nonetheless, the Divine Plan for our lives is The Plan because it is the best plan. If there were a better plan, it would be The Plan. Therefore, to the best of your ability, you will want to face your path fully. It is by far the path of ease and grace. By far.

Many people want to do only things that are comfortable. They misinterpret fear as "No" guidance, but that is not usually the case. Those things that both inspire and terrify show us our life path. Therefore, to march down the center of the life path we should do the scariest, most inspiring thing on our to-do list first, then move on to the second scariest and so on. That keeps us from weaving side to side down the path as many people do in their futile attempts to avoid fear.

As you know by now, I believe in the value of experience, so let's go through this together. Center yourself; repeat the Opening Process (Appendix One). Ask your Guides to support you in your work today, and begin.

Have the intention to perceive your life path that you just worked with one more time. Having connected with it

before, it is infinitely easier to connect with now. Feel for it with your powerful Energy hands if you wish, look for it with your subtle eyes, listen for it, smell for it, taste for it.

When you find your life path again, notice yourself standing on it. Become aware of your feet with regard to the path. Are they standing evenly on the path? Does one foot feel lighter than the other? If so, put more emphasis, more weight, more focus in the other foot. Does one set of toes feel farther ahead then the other? If so, bring the lagging foot forward. For many people, it's the left foot that's lagging behind, but not always. Using your intention, bring your feet even on the path. Make the adjustments that feel necessary until your perception is that your feet are evenly aligned and facing your life path fully.

Having done your part, you may ask for Lightbeings to improve the alignment of your feet with regard to the life path. Do you perceive a difference in the orientation of your feet using either the do-it-yourself method or with Lightbeing assistance? If so, great. If not, once again: the issue is almost always in your belief that you can't perceive the changes. Know it is possible, know you can do it, reset your Energy field, and try again to perceive the shifts.

After aligning your feet, bring your focus to your hips and hipbones. Have the intention to straighten yourself so your hipbones are evenly facing the life path. There is often a powerful shift as the hips align. This is your root chakra, which holds your foundation for your life belief pattern. As you have the intention to bring your hips even, let any unhelpful or limiting beliefs release. Let the Vortex carry them away to be recycled into clean, fresh Energy. When you have done your best, ask your Guides, Angels

and the Lightbeings to bring your hips into perfectly even alignment with the path.

Once again reset your field. Pulse the Vortex; pulse the Living Waters. When you feel reset, bring your focused attention to your shoulders. Have the intention to bring your shoulders square with the life path. Just as the hips have to do with bringing your root chakra into alignment, your shoulders often have to do with bringing your heart into alignment with the path. Keep in mind many of us have the habit of shielding our hearts, and so this shoulder rotation with regard to our path is very common. Be gentle with yourself. Don't be forceful, don't be cruel, but bring your shoulders gently into even alignment with the path. When you feel like you've done as much as you can, you can ask your Guides, Angels, and the Lightbeings to bring your shoulders into balanced alignment with the path. Let everything that is releasing go out your crown or root or heart or anywhere else, for that matter. Don't hold it in.

Ask the Vortex to pulse and clear away everything that is being released. Ask the Living Waters to pulse and flood your space with Divine Love. Reset your Energy body and get ready for the last step of aligning with your life path.

Bring your attention up to your ears. Have the intention to balance your ears to the life path. We use the ears as the point of reference because of where they're geographically located on our heads. This step brings your head into alignment with the path. Therefore, this step is about clearly perceiving your life path. Your head contains many of your perceptive senses—your subtle vision, your subtle hearing, your subtle smell, and your subtle taste. As

a result, as you bring your ears even with your life path, you bring in more precise awareness of your path. Now you can perceive clearly what your path is. This has to do with self-honesty. No more fooling yourself.

As you gently but firmly bring your ears even with your life path, let everything out your crown that wishes to come out. When you have done your part, ask for the Guides, Angels and Lightbeings to help you align your head with your life path, and notice the changes.

Now let's ask that you be brought into perfect overall optimal alignment with your life path. Ask that you be brought into optimal alignment with your life path on all levels—physical, mental, emotional, spiritual, financial, and interpersonal. Knowing there is power in repetition, ask again that your feet, which often have to do with action, be brought even on the life path. Ask that your hips, which often have to do with your foundations for life and belief patterns, be brought even with the life path. Ask that your shoulders, which often have to do with emotions and your heart, be brought even with the life path. Ask that your ears be brought even with the life path, so your subtle perceptions are clear and you aren't deceiving yourself. Now create the sacred seal with the Closing Process (Appendix Two) and declare your practice session complete. Very good!

Notice you have un-torqued your field, clearing the twists that were present before. We started at the feet, and we straightened up through the crown. You may notice that as you go through this un-torqueing there's a release coming out your Energy body, like wringing a sponge dry. Often the release is out the crown. Probably for months to come, every time you go through this process you will notice that same releasing effect.

It's like wringing a sponge dry out through the top of your head. Intend to have that Energy strengthen your connection to Source as it passes up and out.

My friend, it is common to notice there is a lot of room for improvement the first time you work with a life path and with the alignment to the path. Applying a new technique like this will give you a huge opportunity to create significant positive changes in your life and the lives of your subjects. You are becoming aware of a process and you're starting to notice how much more you can do with this to help yourself and others. Becoming aware of the state of your life path and your alignment with the life path starts the journey; it doesn't complete the journey. Be open to your life transforming more quickly than you think is possible.

SOUL CONTRACTS

Working with the life path is a structural way of relating to life. We observe the path without actively conceptualizing what's going on. We simply move the Energy structurally to improve the path, and to improve our subject's alignment with the path. It's a Glorious means of treating ourselves and our Loved ones without our minds getting in the way.

In this section to do with soul contracts, we work with the same project from a different perspective. Now we're looking at the life plan conceptually, with words attached. It is, in fact, the same thing. There are two ways of perceiving the life. One is structural, the other conceptual. In both ways we are working to improve the life; we're simply working with it differently.

Because our minds are not the friends we think they are, it is almost impossible to effectively treat our own soul contract. There is way too much attachment to the result. It's almost always easier to work with the life as a structural path rather than a contract, because there is less emotive content. You can perceive its structure and you can tell how to shift and adjust it to improve the situation. You don't necessarily know what you're shifting and adjusting. The tendency to meddle and get involved is far less when it's just structural shifting. As soon as the concepts are involved, things get trickier. Therefore, this section is written assuming you will be working with a practice subject, someone who is preferably not your spouse or child. That way you can get a feel for the process without getting too snagged by your emotions.

Background

Choosing to incarnate is an important decision for a soul. The soul is never doing this lightly. The soul always has clear intentions of what it wants to accomplish by coming into a body. Working with our Guides, we (as our higher souls) come up with a plan for the life that we're preparing to live. The soul contract is the plan that we as our higher soul have formed for our life, with the help of our Guides.

Soul contracts can present themselves in a number of different ways. If you have a background in business, these contracts might appear similar to a business contract here in the physical dimension. They might look like lesson plans to a teacher. Sometimes they look like scrolls. You may perceive it simply as mental concepts without any visual element. However you experience these contracts is fine.

As you start to become aware of a soul contract, you will notice there is a short list of goals for your practice subject's life; bullet points of topics that soul wishes to work on. The short list is not for us to mess with; leave that to the Guides. It is not our work. Typically there are between four and nine of these topics. Six is an average number of topics in the soul contract. The short list includes topics such as humility, generosity, patience, endurance, compassion, honesty, courage, surrender, stepping out on faith, peacefulness, loving-kindness, and connection with others.

The rule is that the short list should not be modified. There can be temptation to want to work with the short list, but that is never for us to do.

Never.

After the short list there can be reams of detail that follow, pages and pages of all the details of how the bullet points are going to be accomplished in the life. The bullet points are lifelong goals and do not change; the details can and do shift as the free will dance unfolds in the physical dimension.

The contract details include the promises we as souls have made to each other. For example: "In this life to come I'm planning to have a certain soul as a friend. I'm going to help her open her heart, and she will help me be honest with myself." That's a typical promise, a typical soul contract agreement. Another example: "I'm going to be married to a certain someone, and we're going to help each other with compassion and patience." The details will usually get quite specific, showing events that we have planned to help us with these goals. As free will intersects with the contracts, the details shift. Life extends us a series of opportunities that we can take or pass by. All of us pass by opportunities all the time and that's fine; the details of the plan shift as we go.

Caution

This section comes with a warning label. There can be a tremendous temptation to monkey with soul contracts. My dear friend, it is important to keep in mind that Source knows better than we do what is needed in every single situation. As you are learning LHM you have the support that comes with your learners' permit, but once you have it mastered this technique should not be used unless the Guides suggest it to you. When the idea comes from us, it often comes with the intention of making the subject's life easier. This can result in slowing or stalling growth rather than assisting it. In the long run this doesn't help. Therefore, please use extreme caution before trying to change a contract. Confirm and reconfirm the idea with the Guides before proceeding. Consider: whose great idea is this? Is it coming from you, or from the Guides? Be sure of your motives. Double-check your sources. Be sure the direction is from above. Then proceed with caution.

Working With the Soul Contract

Rule #1: follow your subject's Guides to the very best of your abilities. If the Guides bring up the soul contract, they will lead you through what needs to be done. Be alert to the importance of being a clear channel when working in this arena. Point your intuitive channels straight up. Set a very strong intention that in this process you are going to be as clear a channel as you can be, giving your very best efforts, following the instructions to the height of your abilities. Do exactly what the Guides say, no more, no less.

Often how this topic comes up is that your subject will ask about his mission, life plan, or purpose. He has stated his intention; the Guides know the intention; intention is powerful. Your subject's objective of clarity on his soul contract is a powerful call for help. Often the Guides will address it. In those cases it can be possible that adjustments may be suggested that will improve the subject's experience of life.

Adjustments to soul contracts typically occur for one of three reasons. The first reason is that there is an area of the soul contract the person is avoiding, delaying, or simply not giving the appropriate amount of effort and focus to. The second reason is that there is a part of the contract that is complete, but the person is still beating that dead horse. It's time to move on to the next step. The third reason is that there is a part of the contract that has to be let go of. It was part of the original plan, but the overall plans have shifted to the point that we simply have to let go of that detail and move on.

SOUL CONTRACT WALK-THROUGH

If you wish to participate in this learning exercise, please find a suitable subject: someone who has a wish to know his/her life purpose, who is not you, your spouse, or your child. Then proceed, my friend. You have your learners' permit; the Guides and Angels are with you. You will be aligned with Source. All will be well as long as you don't try to steer the boat. Trust the Plan is the Plan because it is the best Plan. Detach; let go, let God.

Begin with your Opening Process (Appendix One). Ask your subject's Guides if some preliminary screening (Chapter Six—Screens of Light) might be helpful in order to achieve the level of clarity you will need for this work. Follow their instructions in that regard. As that draws to completion, ask for permission to view your subject's soul contract. Ask for it to be placed in front of you very clearly, perhaps in your hands. You will feel the tangible weight as the contract appears. Once you have a perception of the contract, ask your subject's Guide what it is he needs to know about it.

If you have the contract but "nothing's happening," ask the Guides, "Is there something that he needs to focus on, an area that he has overlooked? Is there an area in which he has begun to work, but that needs more focus?" That question can get you in motion again. If the answer is "Yes," follow the bouncing ball of guidance. Be alert to the trap of the conscious mind wanting to help. Keep your Energy body in its optimal alignment and do your best. If you are ready, the awareness will come. Work with getting clarity on the area the subject needs to focus on until you have the level of understanding that satisfies your subject's Guides.

When that understanding is in place, give the subject the opportunity to give this area new focus if he wishes. Ask him right then and there. If your subject agrees he does wish to work on this, ask the Guides, Angels, and Lightbeings to help him right now to support that process. Repeat that request several times, noticing the Energy

changing, until the benefit stabilizes. Get feedback from your subject and ask for more Lightbeing help as needed until the Guides and your subject both feel complete with this step.

Refresh your sacred space; pulse the Vortex, flush your combined Energy cross. Ask the Guides if you are complete with the contract. If the answer is "No" but nothing is happening, ask your subject's Guides, "Is there anything in this contract that is finished, and that he has not realized is complete? Is there something he has been pushing himself to accomplish that has already been accomplished? Something he can let go of?" If this is the case, you will once again be in motion.

If you perceive there is something to declare complete, offer your subject the opportunity to do so. Almost always, he will have to make some kind of energetic mark or signature to indicate completion: cross it out, check it off, sign the form, cancel the debt. Get feedback from your subject and check with his Guides to see if this stage is complete. When it is, move on.

Once again refresh your sacred space. Use your Energy sprays or other tools, and repeat the Opening Process as thoroughly as feels necessary to be fully present and clear. Ask again if the topic of the soul contract is complete. If the answer is "No," ask the Guides, "Is there any expectation my subject needs to let go of? Is there any situation he needs to release? Is there anyone he needs to release from his/her promises? Is there anything at all that he is holding onto that it's time for him to let go of?"

My friend, if the answer to this is "Yes," now is a time for extra compassion. Sometimes the soul contract contains items that someone else was supposed to help

the subject with or to do for him, something that other person has not done. We all have things that we as souls are supposed to do that we can't quite get ourselves to do. You do, I do, and the people in our lives do, too. We're not perfect. They aren't perfect. There are things that people have promised to do for us that they are not able to deliver. If we are holding them to their promise at the soul level, it's hurting us. We're waiting for them to deliver something that they aren't able to deliver. We can instead choose to let them go, to say, "I release you from your promise." Try that now: "I release you from your promise." Ask your subject to join you in saying, "I release you from your promise."

Perhaps your subject was abandoned, hurt or betrayed by another. He might still be in a lot of pain over that, but holding onto the betrayal, not the betrayal itself, causes the pain to linger. The betrayal is over. Holding onto it keeps the pain present. He has the opportunity to let that go right now. "I release you." As we let go, the pain disappears. This can be quite difficult for your subject to do; not everyone is ready to let the people who hurt them off the hook. Whether or not he does so is not your choice to make. It is your subject's call. However, if he wishes to let go there is a lot of help available to support him in that process.

If your subject wants to let go, ask the Lightbeings to support him in the process of letting go. Suggest he say these words out loud: "I release you. We are complete. Thank you for the lessons." Feel the changes happen as he repeats the statements several times. As that settles down, ask again, "Is there anyone or anything else he is ready to forgive, let go of, or release? If so, please help him do that

right now." Continue to ask for Lightbeing support. Use the power of repetition until the work is done for the day.

My dear friend, soul contract work can be very intense. As you complete it, sit in the Divine Flow for a bit. Allow the Vortex and Living Waters to cleanse and clear you and your subject for a while. Don't be in a rush to end the session. Ground deeply and fully. Be extra-thorough with your Closing Process (Appendix Two). And give thanks. It is a miracle.

BOOKS OF KNOWLEDGE

Everyone, whether physically incarnating or living in the non-physical, is bound by soul agreements. Our Guides are also bound by the soul agreements they have made with us. These agreements define how they're supposed to help us. In some areas they have agreed to help us automatically, whether we consciously ask for help or not. Conversely, there are some things the Guides are not allowed to help us with, even if we ask. This can occur in areas in which we are stubbornly refusing to do our personal work. In those cases, we will have to put forth some effort before they will be able to do more. Finally, many topics are in a midway zone where the Guides can help us if and only if we ask for help. If we don't ask, they can't help. If we ask, help is available. "Ask and it is given." The books of knowledge are in that middle zone. If we ask for these, the Guides can give them to us. If we don't ask, they can't offer them.

Books of knowledge contain that which we need to know, that we don't yet know. The book's knowledge can be absorbed into the subject's Energy body to enhance his innate wisdom. This helps him know what it is he needs to do in upcoming life situations. It is as if a new operating system has been properly installed in a computer. Your subject doesn't necessarily need to know how to run the program; it runs itself automatically.

If we ask the Guides for a book of knowledge for the subject, frequently they will give us a little book. Often these books are very beautiful, with gold or jewels on the covers. We aren't shown what's in the book; these aren't for us to read to the subject. As facilitators and often as subjects, we're not privy to the details of the gift with our conscious minds. It's completely between the Guides and the Energy body. It is a gift of grace.

As the book appears, ask the subject if he would like it. His conscious mind must be with you on this; even a gift of grace forced upon someone does not feel like a gift. If his answer is "yes," place the book in the heart, the crown, the abdomen, or wherever the Guides and the subject agree it belongs. Allow it to absorb fully. Don't rush. Call for a secondary release as the wisdom absorbs in. That may or may not occur, but it is a wonderful opportunity for additional healing.

If you would like to experience this for yourself right now, get centered. Repeat the Opening Process (Appendix One) to create sacred space. There's no need to beat around the bush: simply ask if there are any books of knowledge your Guides will give to you. Open your crown and heart chakra (or other preferred location) to receive. Feel the shift as the book settles and absorbs. Ask for a secondary release, and create the sacred seal with the Closing Process (Appendix Two).

My friend, I know that this chapter may be pushing your limits. Don't accept anything I tell you "on faith." Do keep an open mind and try it for yourself.

Life is full of miracles. Own this one. Make it yours. Claim it. Change your life, change the lives of others, and change the world. You can do it.

CHAPTER NINE

USING THE POWERFUL FUTURE

The distinction between the past, present and future is only a stubbornly persistent illusion.
Albert Einstein

LET THE FUTURE HEAL THE PRESENT

My friend, this series of techniques has the potential to transform lives more fully and rapidly than anything else I've yet discovered. As you read this section, first know that it is possible to do this, that many other people have learned to use these techniques, and that you can do the same. People who tell you it can't be done simply don't know how to do it, that's all. That having been said, our beliefs create our lives. If you believe "this can't be true," you will not achieve results. If you believe it is possible, you will be amazed.

When you began working with past lives in Chapter Seven, you had the experience of breaking through the veils and seeing that our existence is simply a long continuum through time. You discovered it's possible for you to get awareness of what happened in other bodies and other times. You discovered that it's possible for you to heal those oldest wounds and patterns.

We also know that all time is really now. Einstein proved this, the genius that he was. Our concept of time is simply a way of keeping track of events in our heads so the totality of our experience doesn't overwhelm us at any moment. We think of the past as already having happened, and we think of the future as not having happened yet, but it's really all happening right now. All time really is now.

Therefore, there's no difference between accessing the past and accessing the future. We just go the other direction in the hallway of time; it's no big deal. Having already accessed the past, you'll easily move through the "future" door, too. It's the identical concept; you've already done this. This is true for accessing future events of the current life as well as for accessing the future in other bodies.

I suggest you try this out for yourself right now. Find a willing friend to practice with, someone who also has a wish to open the doors to the future. Either together or separately, go to the website at www.lightworkersmethod.com and absorb the transmission entitled *Future Lives and Space-Time Fabric.* Repeat it as many times as you wish until you feel ready to proceed. Then go back to Chapter Seven's exercise of How Do I Know You in a Past Life (page 188). Change the wording from "Past" to "Future" and begin. Apply a different intention—to reach the future rather than the past—and the identical process will get you to the future rather than to the past. All time truly is now. Truly, we can all do this. Don't take my word for it. Open your mind to consider it might be possible, move into believing it can be done and that you can do it, and then try it.

Focus on Healing Rather Than Information

Often when students start to work with the future, the first thing they want to do is find out how their current challenges will turn out. Sometimes the Guides will play this game, but not always. If it isn't in our best interests to know what's coming up, we will not be shown the future, even if we ask. The Guides know what they are doing in this arena; you can trust that they will show only what is helpful. When I was learning this lesson, there was a challenge in my life that I really wanted to know the outcome of. I begged my Guides, "Just tell me how this is going to turn out, and I promise I'll do what I need to do, regardless. Just tell me."

Jade-Su cautioned, "It doesn't work that way."

"Yes, yes." I insisted. "I promise I will put in the same effort either way."

"You'll see," Jade-Su shrugged.

Then, to give me the chance to learn this lesson, Jade-Su told me the outcome of that particular challenge: it wasn't going to work out. Remember my promise? "I'll do what I need to do, regardless." Well, my friend. Bad news. I am a very disciplined person, well beyond the norm, and I did not have the self-control to do what I was supposed to do once I knew that it wasn't going to work out. I thought, "I'm not going to make myself sick over this; it's all a waste of Energy anyway." I couldn't give my full effort. As a result I made extra work for my Guides and extra pain for myself. They had to recreate another situation identical in vibrational quality, although different in detail, for me to get the lesson the first situation was designed to provide. I had to go through two painful life experiences rather than one. Lesson learned: when our Guides say, "Best not to know," we can give up the attitude of "I have to know how this is going to turn out before I can proceed," and trust it is true.

This having been said, many parts of our future are accessible to us. Many of us stall out in our lives because of fear. If this is your pattern, it can help you to see that your life *is* going to work out, that your challenges are solvable. That knowledge can keep you on track, keep you moving forward. Your Guides may Love the opportunity to soothe your soul, to show you it *will* be fine, that you *can* relax. Bottom line: sometimes it's helpful to know the future; sometimes it isn't. Since we don't know the big picture we can't be the ones to decide when it's helpful to know the future or not. Our Guides know when it's helpful. Once we know how to access that information they will show us what we need to know, and no more.

Why the Future?

The real question is, "What good is it to access the future?" My friend, while looking into your healing subject's future can provide helpful assurance that everything truly will be fine, that provides 5% of the benefit. As in all aspects of the Lightworkers Healing Method, 95% of the benefit comes through actually changing the Energy.

For example, in working with past lives we go back in time to help that past life resolve and heal issues. That resolution and healing comes through time to heal our subject in her current life. As your subject releases her old baggage, she is free to move forward in life. The Energy has shifted. If you continue to work with this same subject over many different healing sessions, something remarkable occurs: the focus turns away from letting go of the past and toward accelerating into the future.

In our current lives, all of us are working on certain issues this very moment. We all have our list of growth topics, whatever they are. Since we are eternal beings on an eternal growth path, by definition at some point we will have mastered the challenges we're working on right now. We may not master them by next Tuesday, next year, or before we are fifty—but over our eternal growth process mastery will eventually occur.

In this chapter's technique, we present our client's current self to a future self of hers who has mastered what she is struggling with right now. We ask that more evolved future self to help the current self, to share his/her mastery with the current self. The wiser, more powerful future self is delighted to do that because as the future self helps the current self, it's also helping the future self. This is the flip side of the process in which we reach back into the past lives to help them heal, which therefore heals the current life. Consider that the current life is a past life to all future incarnations. It's a win/win situation, a cycle of healing that benefits the current life as well as the future life.

If your head is spinning, remember Einstein's words: "*The distinction between the past, present and future is only a stubbornly persistent illusion.*" He was a genius; he was speaking the truth. All time truly *is* now. This is grounded in hard science. Einstein proved the fabric of space-time is flexible and can bend back on itself. If you are still shaking your head in disbelief, Google "fabric of space-time is flexible" and read to your heart's content. You don't have to believe me; you can believe Einstein and believe NASA. But, my friend, since belief creates your experience, now is the time to work with your beliefs on this topic. Please do whatever you need to do with regard to believing that all time is now before you read on.

(Pause; insert Jeopardy sound track. Exits on either side of the auditorium; watch your step. Until we meet again, walk in Light, live in Light, be Light.)

Take-Off Time

Wonderful. Glad to have you with us on this exciting adventure. Put your seatbelt on, my friend. The acceleration is beginning.

First and foremost, when you are actually using the Lightworkers Healing Method for yourself or for others, let the Guides lead you through this. You never have to decide how to go about this, because they will tell you step by step how to proceed. Nonetheless, when you know what's possible, you will "get it" faster. That's the benefit of this book: to know that these techniques are possible, to recognize the Guides' instructions, and to know how to apply their in-the-moment instructions.

Let's start gradually, by working with the future of the current life. If your subject is struggling with a particular issue now but will have mastered it before she re-emerges into the non-physical, her Guides might take you to the end of her life. If she will have mastered the lesson in her older age, the vibration of mastery will exist in her Energy body in that future life stage.

There are two ways of bringing that vibration into the present moment from the future. In the do-it-yourself method of shifting the Energy, use your intention and your powerful Energy hands to connect with the vibration of mastery that she already has in the future, and pull that Energy into the present moment. Feel the changes occurring.

When the changes stabilize, shift techniques. Ask that future self to help the current self of your subject with her intentions; observe the changes occurring. Be the witness. This is the flip side of facilitating childhood healing in which you go back to childhood to heal traumas. The difference is that you are now promoting adult healing by using the power and wisdom of old age.

My friend, there are many different levels of lessons. Some of our life lessons are quick little segment-lessons. In these cases we might be struggling with a lesson right now at age 53, but by age 77 we'll have it handled. Other lessons take lifetimes worth of learning. In these cases, going to the end of this life is helpful, but it isn't enough to create a real breakthrough.

In those cases of long learning cycles, you will have to reach beyond the end of your subject's current life. Reach ahead to find a lifetime in which the point is mastered. Once the link to that life is open, the techniques are the same as reaching to the end of the current life and finding proficiency. Begin with connecting to the Energy of mastery and drawing it into the present moment with your powerful Energy hands. As that benefit stabilizes, ask the future life to help the current life with the intentions. Be the witness to the changes that result.

There will be cases where you can't find the mastery point at first: searching as far into your subject's future as you can reach, the issue is still in process. You might note improvement but not mastery, even four or more lifetimes into the future. This does not mean it is impossible to bring the vibration of mastery into the present moment; it simply adds another step to the process.

Here's how to proceed. First make contact with your subject's most distant future lifetime you can find; I'll call him/her FL4 (Future Life #4). If FL4 has made progress but is still working with the issue, then—with permission—simply merge with FL4 just as you did with your healing subject. Now reach forward again from inside this newly merged Energy, as far as you can perceive from the vantage point of FL4. This gives you access to another four or more lives even farther into the future. If this person who is now perhaps eight lives ahead of your subject (Future Life #8) still doesn't have the issue mastered, just repeat the linking process. Merge into FL8, and move forward in time again to the point of mastery.

Link life to life to life, as many times as is necessary, to find the point in which the vibration of mastery exists. We are all eternal beings, so there is always a point in time in which the lesson is mastered. When you connect to that point, first use your powerful Energy hands to draw the vibration of mastery from the future into the present moment. This does not steal the vibration from the future, but rather overlays the vibration of the future into the present time much as a copy machine works. As that vibration stabilizes, ask that future life to help his/her past life who is your subject's current life. Invariably the future life turns around, comes back to the current lifetime, and helps her master her issues.

Once you have done all of this, as always it is appropriate to ask for the Angels and Lightbeings to make it not only right but actually perfect.

If you feel spacey and ungrounded right now, congratulations! Your Energy body has just expanded rapidly. Now stabilize the expansion so it benefits you immediately. Ground down fully and completely through the outer edges of your Pillar of Light, as if you were staking down a tent. As you ground the newly expanded edges of your Pillar of Light into place, your head should clear once more.

My friend, you may need to re-read this section many times over for it to sink in fully. That is normal. At this stage in the Level Three class, we have an extended question and answer period to allow everyone to wrap their heads around this process. Connect with something solid in your thinking. Remember Einstein; remember NASA. This is based in solid science, not freaky-fringe psychobabble. Take a break if you need to. Use the "Day's End" processes from Chapter Four to re-establish your grounding and balance your Pillar of Light.

Read on when ready for my personal favorite growth technique. Because I Love this as a self-treatment process, it is worded that way—but don't let that confuse you. This technique can be applied to your healing subjects for equal benefit. Share the gift when the Guides direct you to. No need to be stingy. There is unlimited Divine Flow; we can all have this powerful experience.

ULTIMATE FUTURE LIFE

As you know, we are all eternal beings. Our Energy continues on forever. But there is eventually a point, which could be 50,000 lifetimes from now, where we are truly complete with the growth process and we merge again into Universal Oneness. Therefore by definition there is going to be a last life. In or out of body, physical or non-physical dimension—there is an ultimate future life. I have never seen an ultimate future life who is still incarnating into the physical dimension; in my experience these ultimate future lives are all in the non-physical. It is possible there are exceptions to that rule. I don't claim to have all the answers by a long shot. I know a tiny fraction of the knowledge that exists. However, if you are connected to a life that is still in the physical dimension I would suggest you look farther into the future. Keep going.

In this extraordinarily powerful growth accelerator, you chain-link through the future lives as you learned to do above, and contact that ultimate life. With that connection made you can then stand in front of your ultimate future self, which is a Glorious experience. You are a fully enlightened being by the time you are living that ultimate life. Begin by noticing what that person feels like using your subtle senses. Drink it in: that magnificent being is YOU! That amazing Light-filled powerful Avatar of Grace is YOU! That embodiment of Love and wisdom is YOU!

When ready, begin to ask your ultimate future self for the help and gifts s/he has for you right now, today. By all definitions this is a fully enlightened being, and s/he has every reason to help you. S/he *is* you, so his/her willingness to help you is 100 percent. How Glorious!

At this point in the classes, invariably someone asks: "Why would we bother with any other techniques if we have this one? Why not simply connect to the ultimate future life where all our issues have been resolved and all our growth is complete, and draw that into the present moment?" This is a great question.

One hundred percent of what I'm presenting in this entire book only works if the Guides approve of the process. We are not the "deciders" in any of this work.

When my Teachers and Guides first showed me this technique, I thought this was the ultimate Energy-healing process. I went back to that well over and over again in my own self-healing treatments. Then one day, it didn't work. My Guides had decided, "Cut her off. She's had enough. Happy Hour is over." Now I pace myself. Periodically I ask my Guides, "May I?" In those moments once again I am blessed beyond belief to receive gifts from that amazing being who truly is me, who is my ultimate self.

Try it for yourself, my friend. Go to our website at www.Lightworkersmethod.com and absorb the transmissions for Level Three and particularly the one entitled *Future Lives and Space-Time Fabric* as many times as you wish. Play the game of "How Do I Know You in a Future Life" by modifying the Chapter Seven past life exercise. Follow along with the experiential exercise of working with future lives on the website. And then share the gift with others.

Remember the words of Rumi: "... *time is a husk. When the moment cracks open, ecstasy leaps out and devours space; Love goes mad with the blessings...Be kind to yourself, dear—to our innocent follies. Forget any sounds or touch you knew that did not help you dance. You will come to see that all evolves us."*

My dear friend, if you are trying but have not yet mastered these techniques, have faith. I am simply describing a natural process. Work with your belief systems using the positively worded questions you learned about in Chapter Five. As your belief patterns shift, try again. Disbelief and giving up are the only things that will block your success.

Go online to receive the related transmissions as many times as needed. Find an LHM class series near you and participate. The day will come when all these doors and more will open for you. As you continue to explore working with your future through all of these techniques, you will hasten your evolution and bring dance back into your step. Your life path can be bright and smooth. The challenges that remain will be those that your soul has planned for your evolution. You can rise to meet the challenges. You can win at the Game of Life, and you can help everyone around you win, too.

CHAPTER TEN

THE GREAT BALANCING ACT AND OTHER TRICKS OF THE TRADE

With that Moon Language

Admit something:
Everyone you see, you say to them, "Love me."
Of course you do not do this out loud, otherwise
someone would call the cops.
Still, though, think about this, this great pull in us to connect.
Why not become the one who lives with a
full moon in each eye that is always saying,
with that sweet moon language,
what every other eye in this world
is dying to hear?
Hafiz of Shiraz
From Love Poems From God, shared with thanks to Daniel Ladinsky

My friend, as you begin to practice the Lightworkers Healing Method, moments will occur in which you know there's more that can be done to help your subject, but you can't tell what that "more" is. This chapter contains some possibilities; give them a try. Each situation is different; what works one day might not work the next. You will know when you find the answer *du jour* by what occurs in the session as well as how you feel both during and after the session.

Have a light heart about this as your Guides present you with different practice situations. Don't "make it wrong" when you realize there is more to be done but you don't know what that "more" is. It is a *good* sign, not a bad one, that you are being offered this lesson. It is confirmation that you are ready for more, not proof that you are "no good at this." Each healing session is a practice opportunity for you so that you can improve.

Key to the Kingdom #2: Rather than asking for the sessions to go perfectly, ask for the right number of things to go wrong: not so many errors that you are overwhelmed, but enough so you can progress as quickly as Source wishes you to. This is also a good way of relating to life, my friend.

THE POWER OF THE QUESTION

What we ask for and how we ask it makes a huge difference in the outcome. There are two basic facets of the Power of the Question: the Power of Repetition, and the Power of Precision.

The Power of Repetition

The Power of Repetition applies at all levels of the LHM process. If you are working at the basic level, this is an extremely helpful tip—but even at the more involved levels, repetition can have a big impact. Let's take the example of working with a subject who has an intention to receive Divine Help with their finances. The first time you ask the Guides and Lightbeings for help, the Energy of the situation will be what it was when your subject walked in your door. Asking the Lightbeings to "help him with his finances" (either in the foundational way of Level One, or with the techniques of Levels Two and Three added) will generate some energetic improvements. The vibration of the financial situation will change, and you will know this with your subtle sensing. Often, simply repeating the identical request ("help him with his finances") will improve the situation even more. You can perceive the additional changes with your methods of subtle Energy awareness.

Why does this work? It may seem as though you're making the same request, but because the starting point is different, the call for help is different. The new intention is to "help it from *here*." There is power in repeating requests until you sense you've wrung enough benefit out of that request and it's time to move on. Your yes-or-no discernment comes into play. Ask, "Is it time to move to the next step of this financial healing process?" When the answer is, "Yes," it does not mean you have done all you can do to help with his finances. It means that you can now move to the next step so you can continue to help with his finances.

The Power of Precision

In many teachings it is said, "Ask and it is given." In other teachings, it is said, "Be careful what you ask for because you might get it." Both of these aphorisms point to one basic truth: how we phrase the intentions and requests really makes a difference.

In the healing sessions, you might present one request and achieve a small amount of success, while having that nagging feeling of, "I know there is more available here." The feeling can be one of sensing a flood of blessings backed up behind an unseen dam. Asking your subject's Guides if the request needs to be worded differently can be a great way to get the session moving again. Often, the answer is, "Yes." If so, try improving the precision of the request. For example, perhaps you are asking, "Tell him what to do to help his finances," when what is really helpful is, "Help him with his finances. If it's in the Divine Plan for the finances to improve, please make it happen right now." When you feel the dam release and the blessings start to flow, it's clear: that was an effective way to put it. Until that moment occurs, work to find the optimal perception, and therefore the optimal wording.

When considering this topic of how to word the question, it can be helpful to think of your subject's healing intention as a multifaceted crystal, like a giant diamond with many facets to it. What you're really trying to do is get into the very heart of the diamond, to explore that whole diamond. Each healing request opens a facet and gets you into a part of the diamond, a part of the wholeness of the healing opportunity. Some facets only allow superficial healing, but there is always a way to get to the heart of the crystal. As you continue to improve your precision by tinkering with the phrasing, you can achieve a result that's impossible to reach by repeating the identical request over and over again.

If you feel stalled out, consider: perhaps improved precision is needed. If the Energy shifts are meager, assume there is a better way into the heart of the diamond, and find another doorway. This is a fun game of tinkering with phrasing and following the Energy of the situation to discover how you can be more accurate or effective in your requests. It's like finding your way through a labyrinth.

Don't feel that you have to master this art of phrasing right away. You are in the learning mode and therefore there's a huge amount of grace available for you. At first, as long as you are truly doing your best and the phrasing is remotely close to what's needed, almost any request works. A lot of adjustment will be made on your subject's behalf.

However, over time as you become more capable, more accuracy will be demanded of you. This is a good sign; a sign that you are no longer operating with a "LHM Beginner's Permit" but now have an "LHM Intermediate Learner's Permit." As you leave the "LHM Beginner" stage and move into the "LHM Intermediate Learner" phase, confusion might arise. Your conscious mind may think, "I was better at this at the very start. Now I stink. What happened?" Your training wheels are coming off, my friend. Don't let that throw you; it is supposed to happen. It's not that you're getting worse, it's that you're getting *better*. We must always do our best to open the floodgates of Divine Assistance, and your "best" is now better.

My friend, don't get stuck in "I *can't* do better" thinking. You *can*, or your Guides would not ask you to. They see the beautiful, powerful co-creator that you truly are. Trust them, and step it up. You absolutely can do it. Understanding the Power of Precision is enormously helpful in living life successfully. As you learn the art of modifying the requests, it helps you achieve precision in your own goals, and therefore have the life that fits you best. As you step into co-creating breakthrough for your healing subjects, through the miracle of simultaneous healing you will co-create breakthrough in your own life.

As you pursue this healing art, at various stages in the journey you will have breakthroughs. The thoughts of, "Oh my goodness, now I'm really getting it" alert you to the breakthroughs as they occur. Guess what happens next, my friend? Something new, something more, is going to be expected of you. It will usually take some time to figure out what that is. Be both patient and persistent. Be willing to make mistakes. Ask for the right number of things to go wrong, so you can learn and grow. This is true in learning LHM, and it is true in the Game of Life.

ENLISTING THE SUBCONSCIOUS

Engaging the subject in his own healing is a critical part of this healing art. Often, the subject's mind is not his helpful friend. In these cases, changing his subconscious mind's thought-patterns can be a pivotal point in his healing, because our subconscious minds are really driving the buses of our lives. The conscious mind, the part of us we normally identify with, is just along for the ride.

Remember how the subconscious mind operates: it responds to questions much better than to statements. The subconscious immediately categorizes statements into "Truth" and "Lie," *not based on reality but instead based upon how close the statements are to the underlying belief patterns.* "Truths" are accepted; "Lies" are rejected. However, when we ask ourselves a question, the subconscious mind perks up. "A question? I'm on it!" This is a *new* area, a *new* venture. New territory can open up. Off the subconscious goes, driving the bus of life in the direction of the question.

Continuing with the example of the subject wishing healing for finances, if his foundational belief is, "I am a successful person; I'm simply in a slump right now," the affirmation, "I am successful and abundant" might work. His subconscious mind might accept that statement as being reasonably true, and turn the bus in the direction of abundance. However, if his underlying belief is that he doesn't have a clue of how to succeed financially, his subconscious will respond to the affirmation, "Successful and abundant" with, "That's a big fat lie."

Consider the types of questions we typically ask ourselves. To continue the example of financial healing, the usual questions our subject might have been asking himself would be along the lines of, "Why don't I have any money? Why is my business failing? What is wrong with my business? What is wrong with me?" *Ay yi yi.* Off the subconscious mind goes, driving the bus in the direction of finding the answers. "Well, you idiot, you don't have any money because when you were five and you lost the grocery money, your mom told you you'd never have any money." "Your business is failing because no one can make it in this economy, just like CNN said." "What's wrong with you? You're dumb just like your high school Math teacher told you."

Changing the questions we ask ourselves is extraordinarily powerful, because it gets the buses of our lives moving in the directions we desire. You can help your subject understand this. He can begin to take responsibility for his own healing by asking himself positively worded "why" questions in between his LHM sessions with you. Continuing our example: "Why am I so successful? Why do I have so much money? Why is my business so successful?" "Well," responds the subconscious, "You always were a clever boy, just like your grandma told you." "Remember when you found the quarter under the chair in the movies? Money comes to you easily." "You care so much about your customers that your business can't help but be successful!"

The point is *not* to hear the answer to the question. The point is to get the subconscious to perk up and steer the bus in that direction. This begins to pull the life into alignment with the desired vibration of health, happiness, abundance, and harmony. This is one slice of the subject's part of the dance. This is one thing he can do to help himself. This is part of his homework to practice until your next healing session together. This supports the energetic shifts that occur in the healing sessions so they continue through his life. It helps to keep his vibrations positive and healing.

Working Within the Confines of the Subject's Belief System

While it is the subject's responsibility to heal his beliefs between sessions, inside the sessions themselves you have the responsibility of working within the confines of his beliefs as they stand in that moment. If you offer healing that he does not believe to be possible, his subconscious mind will reject the healing. Therefore, how you frame issues is important.

The first time you work with a new subject, clarify up front if he is open to the topic of reincarnation. If not, no worries; you will need to work within the confines of his belief system but you can still get the job done. His past life wounds can still be healed, but you must frame them in terms of metaphor rather than fact. Similarly, if your subject doesn't believe it's possible to connect into the future, he will block the benefit. Again, phrasing the healing as a metaphor can get around this mental block.

A common confusion about the LHM sessions is that the greatest benefit comes from the guidance aspects that arise in sessions. "Tell me what to do" requests abound. When your subject presents a list of "tell me what to do" requests to you as his intentions, this can be a neon sign: he doesn't believe the Universe can actually help him resolve the situations. He believes it's all on him to Make His Life Work. Regardless of the truth that messages provide 5% and the actual Energy shifts provide 95% of the benefit of an LHM session, your subject can make the reverse true for himself with his limiting belief. He can ignore the giant Energy gifts on the table and leave, clutching the tiny scraps of clear messages in his fists like gold.

My friend, I understand this way of being. I was a very Hard Worker. I did not believe Divine Help was available to me. I was *sure* I could Make It Work if only my Guides would tell me what to do. It's a painfully hard way to go through life, but it is an available option. If your subject presents you with a "tell me what to do" list—privately, silently, ask his Guides how to handle the situation. Listen intently, and follow directions. Almost always the directions are to gently help the subject reframe his requests and beliefs into those that will allow him to receive Divine Help. Almost always his Guides will assign him homework on working with his subconscious mind.

Another very common limiting belief has to do with the topic of whether or not simultaneous healing "steals" from the subject. No judgment! I was hung up on this for a long time myself. If the subject believes simultaneous healing steals from him, even though it doesn't and actually increases the depth of his healing, he will block his ability to receive benefit to the extent that he is aware you are also benefitting. He will create the situation of decreased benefit for himself. Therefore, be alert to your phrasing. Let your subject know you are "with him" in his healing, that you are also experiencing his process, feeling what he feels, with and for him. "Let's do this now, together" is the tone, rather than "I am also benefitting from this process." This gently acknowledges the fact of his belief barriers, and allows him to receive full healing. It is a way of wording the truth of simultaneous healing in a way most people can accept.

Expanded Beliefs Yield Expanded Results

Your beliefs impact the success of the healing session even more than your subject's. If you believe you won't be able to help him, you can create that situation. If, however, you know that all you have to do is open up and let the higher dimension beings use you as a vessel, the full power of the Universe will move through you. As you come to deeply and fully know that there are truly no limits, that reality will manifest in your work. You will have a front-row seat to the best show on Earth: the spectacle of multi-dimensional Divine Energy healing manifesting for you and for the people in your life.

Consider the questions you wish to ask yourself, for your healing practice and for your own life. "Why do miracles happen in my presence? Why do people heal so easily? Why are there truly no limits? Why am I so vibrantly healthy? Why is my life so full of Love? Why am I so fulfilled? Why am I so joyful? Why is my life so wonderful? Why do I deserve all good things?"

Although the point of asking the questions is not to find the answer but rather to train the subconscious, breathe this in.

> **The answer to all these questions is the same, my dear friend: "Because the Universe LOVES you and CARES for you and wants you to be JOYFUL!"**

My friend, this is True. Your subconscious might categorize this as a "Big Fat Lie," but it is True. Ask yourself, "Why does the Universe Love me, care for me, and want me to be joyful?" Apply the Power of Repetition to that question, and watch your life transform precisely into your wildest, most inspiring dreams.

FINDING THE BALANCE

This healing art is a dance between the subject, the higher-dimension Guides, Angels, and Lightbeings, and the LHM practitioner. Finding the balance in LHM is like balancing a plate on a pole: there is a perfect point of balance in which you're doing what's yours to do, the higher-dimension beings are doing what's theirs to do, and the subject is doing what is hers to do. That balance point is the zone in which true healing can and does occur. When you are in balance and in the zone, the work is effortless. Insights come fluidly; Energy shifts quickly; the subject's symptoms release and her life heals.

If something is out of balance, you could be doing too much or too little, or the subject could be doing too much or too little. The Lightbeings are always doing what's theirs to do as long as you have asked them to do so. They already understand how to play this game. We LHM practitioners are the ones that have to learn the game of finding the balance. It is up to us to properly enlist both the Lightbeings and the subject so everyone can join in the dance.

How we are in this work is how we are in life, my friend. We all have our patterns: we can tend to do too much, or we can tend to do too little. By working to find the balance in these healing sessions, you will start to notice what your own pattern is, and learn to compensate for it. Learning how you are in this work can be a wonderful eye-opener for how you're living your own life, and a powerful catalyst for balancing your life more effectively.

Let's break this balance point down into its component parts. It can help to visualize this three-dimensionally. Between the Lightbeings and you there's a vertical connection and balance point. You are here in the physical dimension; the Lightbeings are higher-dimension beings. Between the subject and you, the connection and balance point are horizontal since both of you are here in the physical realms.

Vertical Balance

In the vertical connection between the Lightbeings and you, the trick is to find the balance between allowing and doing. You will be doing either too much, too little, or the right amount. When you're doing the right amount and allowing the right amount, you're in the flow, the Energy is shifting, things are happening. It's clear; you're at the balance point. Conversely, if the session feels stuck, if you have the feeling that "Nothing's happening," it can be very helpful to check the balance.

The easiest way to check the balance is simply to change your tactic in the moment. If you've been repeatedly asking the Lightbeings to create a change for the subject and nothing's happening, try applying a do-it-yourself method to create the change. On the other hand, if you've been using the do-it-yourself methods and nothing's happening, ask the Lightbeings to handle it. Simply try the other way of interacting in the vertical connection. Very often that is all that is needed for the flow of the session to pick up again.

Those of us who are inclined to do too much may have an overreliance on the do-it-yourself methods. We are really thorough with the screens and the cord-sorting and the trauma-releasing, but forget to ask the Lightbeings to create miracles, to correct our mistakes and bring in what we've forgotten and to optimize. We're busily working away and not asking for help. The cure is to ask the Lightbeings for help, and to trust them, the Divine, and the Divine Plan. Often we are Hard Workers; sometimes we are righteous and indignant about how hard we work and how easy everyone else has it. No worries! All of us are doing our very best, in every moment. Especially in the moments it seems we aren't doing our best: in those moments that is the best we're able to muster up. In this pattern of Hard Work, we don't usually trust the Plan or life or the Divine in our own lives. We feel we have to create it all with our own efforts, and that if we slack off for even one day our entire life will fall into shambles.

Conversely, for those of us who are inclined to do too little with regard to the vertical connection between us and the Lightbeings, we ask them to do everything. We stay stuck in Level One mode, in which we ask the Lightbeings to handle it all. We aren't stepping up to the plate with what is ours to do, in sessions and in life. We can confuse ourselves by thinking we are Trusting The Divine, but in reality we are being too passive, perhaps even lazy, and not doing what is ours to do. Again, no worries! We are all doing our best, and this is especially true in moments like these in which we feel unable to generate good results and therefore don't try. Have compassion, be understanding – and we still have to put forth our best efforts and intentions, both in healing sessions and in life. This is not the intention for a specific outcome, but rather the intention to do what is ours to do, so the Divine Plan comes to pass. Once we have done our best, *then* we may ask the Lightbeings to do what is theirs to do, and trust that the outcome will be perfect.

Another way of not doing enough in the vertical balance is playing it safe by not speaking the requests out loud, not narrating to the subject what you are doing. If this is the case, you are playing the game silently in your head. If you recognize yourself here, have some compassion, my friend. Almost always, this is because you're afraid. "What if I got it wrong; what if the subject thinks I'm crazy." You aren't really committing to the process because you are afraid you can't make it work. This can be a self-fulfilling prophecy because at this level of engagement the work often is ineffective. To truly be powerful in this work, you must claim it, step into it, and speak it out. Commit with words and actions. Don't beat yourself up about this—would you beat a scared child?—but do work to change your subconscious belief patterns and be willing to risk failure in order to succeed.

When you step over this line you'll find that something interesting happens. Thoughts tend to be much more vague and amorphous than spoken language. Speaking will force you to step up your level of precision, not be general in your intentions, but rather to be very focused. You don't have to be perfect; it's okay to make a mistake. You can always correct yourself and adjust course. What matters most is that you do your best to commit and to be precise, and that you maintain the balance of doing what is yours to do. When you are doing your best, the Lightbeings will correct your mistakes.

There's a lovely quote from W.H. Murray, in which he also loosely quotes Goethe: *"Until one is committed, there is hesitancy, the chance to draw back, always ineffectiveness. Concerning all acts of initiative and creation there is one elementary truth, the ignorance of which kills countless ideas and splendid plans: that moment one definitely commits oneself, then Providence moves too. All sorts of things occur to help one that would never otherwise have occurred.... Whatever you can do or dream you can, begin it. Boldness has genius, power and magic in it."*

Be bold. Speak out loud what you are doing in the healing sessions.

Horizontal Balance

The horizontal balance is between your subject and you. You are to match the subject's investment in the LHM process as precisely as you can. Whatever effort she is putting into her healing is how much Energy you put into it. You can suggest she do her part, but she must step up and do it. In the session her Guides will indicate what is hers to do; your awareness of how fully she complies will naturally develop. Between sessions her part typically consists of training her subconscious mind, and of completing the other homework instructions her Guides have passed on. If she isn't willing to do what is hers to do, you can't force her to be willing. You can't force an Energy change upon a subject who is not ready to change, no matter how obviously helpful and important that change might be. That is doing too much. This is exactly how our Guides treat us: they match our investment in ourselves to the quark. In the healing sessions you are to adopt that behavior since you are the conduit for the subject's Guides to work through.

Ways of doing too much in the horizontal balance include enabling and forcing changes upon others. Sometimes your subject wants a change in her life, but she isn't willing to put her own Energy into it. This type of subject wants to come to you and have you wave magic wands and make her problems go away for her. That's enabling and it doesn't work, no matter how much you might want to help her. You can't effectively help someone who does not want to help herself, because there is nothing in her own Energy body to anchor the changes in place. You would be trying to fix her problem for her rather than matching her investment. Therefore the Energy changes don't last.

The tendency to do too much for the subject is especially strong when working with Loved ones. If you are working with a stranger and she doesn't want to fix her life, it's a lot easier to let that go than if you're working with your child and he doesn't want to do what is needed to fix his life. When someone you Love is hurting himself, there's a huge temptation to do too much and force an Energy change.

Unfortunately, this feels abusive to the recipient. It is doubly upsetting to him because it is abusive at a very subtle Energy level. Not only does he feel angry and violated, he is also confused about why he feels that way. Not only does forcing a change on someone create problems in your relationship; it doesn't last. The change that you have just forced on your subject, albeit with loving intent, isn't anchored into the physical dimension because he has rejected it. The change evaporates. All you've done is create a problem in your relationship with him, and no good has come of it.

As you become experienced in this work, you'll continually be trying to stay in the balance point. When you're in the balance point, things are flowing as if by magic. The work is almost effortless. When the session feels bogged down, try changing your tactic. If your habit is to do too much for your subject, ask her to engage with you. Paying attention to how her mind and body are feeling in the moment can help to identify healing opportunities. Forceful exhaling can help in Energy releasing. She can work with her subconscious mind. She can turn to meet the life path. There is always something she can do. Ask her Guides what she can do; suggest it; engage her. Find the balance point.

One way of doing too little with the subject is by giving a reading rather than doing a healing. Giving her a message and telling her what to do is helpful information, but that's not what we are supposed to do in LHM. In this healing art we put our own effort into allowing the Divine Plan to come to pass at whatever level we can, at whatever level is ours to do. Rather than simply telling the subject, "You should do this in your life," help her take the step by shifting the Energy. Take the responsibility. That which simultaneously inspires and terrifies is yours to do.

Another way of doing too little with the subject could be telling her what to do to shift her Energy, rather than shifting the Energy with or even for her. She should participate to the extent she is capable; you provide the rest. If she is an energetically weak person, her full effort will not produce much. Therefore, her part of the load will be smaller than it is if she is energetically strong. If you are stronger than she is, you might be carrying the bulk of the Energy-shifting load, but that is not what determines balance. It's a balance of effort, not of result. Your role is to encourage her to do what is hers to do, and to match her efforts, not her results. If her efforts are all-out, yours should be too.

At the balance point, you are doing your part, you have engaged the Lightbeings so they are doing their part, and engaged the subject so she is doing her part. This is the zone in which miracles occur. You do not create the miracles; that is up to the Universe. You do, however, create the perfect point of balance that will allow the Universe to act.

After the Session

During the session you have merged with your subject; that's a powerful way of connecting. After the session you must separate from her equally powerfully, and that is a process. This begins with the formal Closing Process at the end of the healing session. However, typically after a healing session there is conversation: scheduling the next appointment, at a minimum. Presto-change-o, the connection between the two of you is open again. Therefore after she goes out the door, it's time to separate again. You might need to do it repeatedly until the merger is truly ended. How can you tell the connection is still open?

You keep thinking about the session or about the subject herself, while simultaneously feeling drained. If this occurs, it's your responsibility to complete the separation.

Ways of doing too little after the session include thinking, "She is a bad client, she drains my Energy," rather than taking your own responsibility to keep your Energy body clear. If you have "bad-client syndrome," you aren't taking enough responsibility for your own well-being. When you find a cord from a client in your Energy body, you can choose to be grateful to her for showing you where your Energy field is weak, rather than being upset that she corded you. "Thank you for the lesson; you're not getting in next time." Then maintain your Energy body: fill the spot where the cord was with your own soul fragments, ground more, engage in that eternal process of straightening your vertical channels that occurs in the Opening Process, and draw in more healing Source frequencies. Strengthen your Pillar of Light. This is your garden to tend, your corner of the Universe to maintain.

Ways of doing too much after the session include letting the subject continue to enlist you in her healing process. Don't re-open the Energy of the session to "help" the subject. If you closed properly, all your errors and omissions have already been corrected. The Energy has already been optimized and grounded in place in the Divine Plan. How can you top that? Leave it be. As a general rule, don't go back into the session.

Sidebar: sometimes your Guides will suggest you go back to the topic for your own growth and learning. Perhaps you missed something that is also relevant to you; perhaps you left the gift of simultaneous healing on the table. In those cases your Guides may lead you back into the session, but that is not the same as the subject herself pulling you in. She must learn to get her Energy from Source and from Earth. She doesn't need it from you. Discourage her from using you as her detour to Source. Your subject is also connected to Source. We are all children of God, after all.

FEEDBACK IS FABULOUS

This is a joyful three-way dance of co-creating healing between you, the higher-dimension beings, and your subject. As you turn your focus to the subtle realms it is important to ground the healing benefits into the physical dimension, i.e. into the healing subject and his life. If the healing subject's interpretation of the words you choose is different than yours, this process can be slowed or stopped. If a subject believes *any* aspect of the healing is impossible, he will create that reality for himself. Therefore, it's important to repeatedly check back in with your subject.

Each time you feel you have made progress, touch base to see if this is manifesting in the physical dimension. If his healing request involves physical pain, ask for status reports as the session unfolds. "How's that pain?" When you are headed in the right direction, the pain will be changing. It may still be present, but it might shift locations or change from sharp to dull, or vice versa. When the session is complete the pain is almost always either gone or significantly improved, but as you are working with it, there should be shifting.

If the pain is unchanged after you feel a shift has occurred, something has blocked your subject's ability to receive it. It could be that the way you are expressing the situation uses different words than he would use. Let's say you have awareness that an issue involves your subject's mother. Your subject does not feel anything shifting, even though you can sense a change has occurred. Ask something along the lines of, "How does what I have said feel to you in terms of truth and relevance?" Through gentle, compassionate investigation you discover he can't identify the incident or pattern you are referring to, and he is getting hung up on that. His conscious thought of "That's not true" is blocking his ability to be healed. Intuitive channels up; check your message with his Guides. "Did I get that right?" Usually the answer is, "Yes"—but begin by verifying. Nothing else has integrity. Assuming it is a valid message, ask his Guides how to proceed. As the communication is cleared up and your subject feels the description is in fact true, his Energy body opens to receive the changes and you are back on track again.

Another common cause of a blocked healing is that you have bumped up against a limiting belief system. Remember, we must work within the confines of our subject's belief system in order to be able to help him. Let's say your subject is not open to the concept of reincarnation. Blissfully unaware of that state of affairs, you are waxing eloquent about a past life trauma and skillfully removing it. Nonetheless the subject feels nothing. Flashing light: ask him what is going on. Through kind, mindful discussion the limiting belief is revealed. Intuitive channels up; ask his Guides what to do. It might not be right for you to "talk him into believing in past lives." Changing his belief system might not be for you to do. You might be instructed to frame it as a metaphor to work within the confines of the belief system so healing can occur. What is for you to do is to frequently touch base to ensure the Divine Gifts are reaching all the way down into the physical dimension.

If your subject's healing intention does not involve physical pain, you can still get feedback to gauge your progress. Let's say his presenting issue is work-related stress. As your session unfolds, ask him to think about work and gauge how he feels. There should be progress throughout your time together. By the end of the session, he should be able to think about work and feel peaceful, optimistic, and even invigorated.

The point is, asking your subject for feedback is the necessary first step to revealing whatever it is that is preventing the Energy healing from manifesting physically. The more frequently you ask for feedback, the smoother your sessions will go because you and your subject will remain in sync. As you master the rhythm of eliciting feedback at each natural pause in the healing session, your sessions truly become a beautiful, flowing dance of grace and blessings, a Beguine.

OPTIMIZING AND STABILIZING A SESSION USING SPACE-TIME FABRIC

My friend, by now you have experienced for yourself that Energy is tangible. You have experienced the Rivers of Divine Love flowing through you. You have felt the Energy bodies of your practice subjects. You have felt soul fragments land in your hands to be healed. You have felt the lumps and bumps of life paths. You know this to be true: Energy has substance. You have also experienced the changes that occur in the present when we heal the past and invoke the powerful future. By this point in our journey together, it is clear that space-time can be worked with in many ways. Putting these two concepts together, you will experience that space-time itself is tangible, and that you can work with its Energy just as you can with screens and with soul fragments.

Toward the end of a session, after the Energy has shifted and the pain is gone but right before the formal Closing Process, sometimes the Guides suggest we solidify the healing. Solidifying or stabilizing the healing is like wearing a retainer after the braces come off; it helps the healing benefit stick around. This is the most powerful stabilizing technique I have learned so far. This final technique of the core curriculum involves working with the actual fabric of space-time to improve and solidify the healing benefits you have allowed to flow through you to your subjects. Knowing that Energy is tangible, this is just one more little step. You can do this. We can all do this. Truly, we are naturally co-creators with Source, and this is a tangible way to experience that fact. I will explain this step-by-step so you can follow along. You will feel the changes occur and that will help your conscious mind believe this is really happening.

Having done what you could inside the rest of the session, use your powerful hands to connect to the

Energy exactly the way it is in that moment without analysis. Simply reach out in front of you and connect to the tangible Energy. Drawing your hands from front to back, have the intention to pull that Energy vibration from today into yesterday, last week, last month, last year, two years ago, four years ago, six years ago, ten years ago, 20 years ago, and beyond. Draw the healing farther and farther back in time until you have drawn it into the first breath of life. In so doing you create the experience of having been free of this issue for the entire life. You can feel the Energy tangibly; there is a strong pulling sensation.

Now bring your hands and your focus in front of you again. Once again reach out in front of you and gather up the tangible Energy exactly the way it is in this new moment. Notice that it feels different than it did just a few minutes ago: more solid, more secure, stronger in the new vibration. Apply the Power of Repetition and again draw this more stable vibration into yesterday, last week, last month, last year, five years ago, ten years ago, first breath of life.

Repeat this process of solidifying the healing through space-time into the past until the Energy feels very solid and strong. Then take another step into stabilizing: reach beyond the current life. Continue to draw the Energy back: 100 years, 200 years, 500 years, 1,000 years into the past. Now your subject's healing benefit has been with them for 1,000 years; it is stable as stable can be.

This is already enormously powerful, but we can do more. Reach an equal distance of 1,000 years into the future; find the optimized vibration of your subject 1,000

years from now. Since we are eternal beings on an eternal growth path, that Energy will be better than his present state of affairs, no matter how good that is in this moment. Draw that future optimized Energy into the present moment; feel the vibrational pitch amp up as the future benefit flows into the present. Don't stop there; continue to draw the future optimized Energy through the present and anchor it into the past and equal distance of 1,000 years ago.

Repeatedly reach forward 1,000 years into the future, gathering up the optimized future vibrations, draw them through the present, and anchor them 1,000 years into the past. Let the coughs and yawns occur as the Energy bodies absorb these powerful shifts.

Gradually reach out farther and farther to the left and right, including more and more beings in this blessing, until you are reaching as far out to the left and right as possible and all beings everywhere are blessed. May all beings everywhere benefit.

Yes, this is wonderfully stable—but we can do more. All of this has occurred in a horizontal dimension; you have been working only with time. If you can visualize a graph, all our Energy stabilizing has occurred on the "x" axis. Now draw Source Energy vertically through this stable horizontal plane from the center of the Universe to the center of the planet, and vice-versa. Repeat this vertical stabilizing process; now you are stabilizing the Energy along the "y" axis of the graph.

The moment will arrive in which the Energy will feel perfectly balanced and stable. That is what you have been working for. At that point, begin the standard Closing Process (Appendix Two) to create the sacred seal.

My friend, this is the last technique in the core curriculum of the Lightworkers Healing Method, and the end of Level Three. We have done all we can do to prepare ourselves to be vessels for Divine, higher-dimension beings to work through. We are done with doing. What remains has nothing to do with doing or techniques, and everything to do with simply being.

Walk in Light, live in Light, be Light.

LEVEL FOUR

LIGHTBEING CONNECTIONS

CHAPTER ELEVEN

GUIDES, ANGELS, LIGHTBEINGS, AVATARS, AND HELPFUL DEAD PEOPLE

Every blade of grass has its angel that bends over it and whispers, "Grow, grow."
The Talmud

Congratulations, my friend; you have made it through Level Three. That is the most challenging part of the Lightworkers Healing Method core curriculum because it presents ideas for which most of us do not have a pre-existing frame of reference. Since you are reading these words, you must still be with us on this journey of healing, growth, and discovery. If you have engaged in the exercises presented in the previous chapters, you have done your very best to prepare yourself for Level Four, the culmination of the core curriculum. For the moment, you are finished with techniques and effort; now you have the opportunity to open to become vessels for Source in the form of higher-dimension Angels and Lightbeings.

My dear friend, being a vehicle for Source to work through is a blessing beyond belief. You will *feel* the indescribable Love, wisdom, and power of these higher-dimension beings as they move through you to help others. As this happens with more and more healing subjects, *you will come to know beyond a shadow of a doubt that Divine Help is always here for all of us.* This is the true miracle of simultaneous healing: as you become a vessel to help more and more people, the moment will come in which you realize that there is absolutely no doubt that you are continually held in the loving arms of the Divine. You are completely safe, completely secure, completely Loved and cherished in every single moment. As are we all. Fear evaporates. Life feels safe, joyous, and blessed. Each event is simply an event. Nothing is "bad" or "wrong." All truly is as it should be.

To properly prepare yourself to be a vehicle for higher-dimension beings to work through, you must show them you are trustworthy. There are three major areas the Divine will require of you to use you as a vessel: to keep yourself out of the way, to keep others out of the way, and to live with integrity.

First, will you keep your own ideas out of the way? Will you avoid second-guessing these enlightened beings, and substituting your judgment for theirs? Will you be able, in effect, to say, "Not my will but Thine?" In sessions, it's never for us to decide what the subject needs, or what he needs to hear. That is for his Guides to handle; we are simply instruments. We are not the "deciders" of anything. We don't generate anything. Our purpose is to be a clear channel for Divine Will, not to impose our own ideas on the situation.

My friend, this does not mean you have to be perfect. We all make mistakes. There is nothing wrong with making a mistake. How else can we learn? When you find yourself "giving great advice," simply notice that you are imposing your will. No worries as long as you stop when you catch yourself doing it. Just clear your field, reset your Energy, and try again to be a vessel. All is made right when the intention is pure.

The second area of trustworthiness these higher beings look for is your ability to stand your ground against the opinions of others. Will you be a strong steward for the Divine, not allowing others to exert their will as you release your own? Will you be able to say, "Not my will, but not anyone else's either; just Divine Will"? In LHM sessions and in life, there will be moments in which you are clear, you know what Divine Will is and you are not substituting your judgment for Source's. Then your healing subject (or spouse, or business partner, or parent) will exert *his/her* will on the situation. This is the moment of truth: are you strong enough in your grounded Pillar of Light to be a steward for the Divine? Will you be able to stand up and declare, "That does not feel true to me; I do not agree"? Of course, after that you must still take all actions to resolve the conflict, but it is crucial to hold space for the Divine, to defend the sacred intentions.

Again, mistakes are fine. We all wobble from time to time, especially in the presence of powerful personalities. However, we must have a pattern of holding space for the Divine in order for higher-dimension beings to feel it is wise to send their Energy through us. In LHM sessions if your subject disagrees with your interpretation of what the Guides are presenting, first back up to the last clear message and try again. But if you do that and still come to the same conclusion, take a deep breath. Perhaps now is the time to practice standing firm in your truth. If your channels are pointed up, if you have verified the instructions with the Guides and they are firm, don't allow yourself to be derailed. Don't doubt the vertical communication between you and the Guides. Instead, gently, compassionately investigate what the flaw is in the horizontal communication between you and your subject. That is where the issue is. Clear that up, regain consensus, and move forward again. Hold the space for healing.

My friend, the more you practice LHM, the easier it is to trust Spirit. As you witness more and more lives change, trust develops naturally. The more you tend your Pillar of Light, the easier it is to be a strong steward for the Divine. Inside of a solid Pillar of Light, *only* Divine Will can come to pass. Therefore, as your Pillar grows and aligns, Light solidly grounds into the planet and you *are* a strong steward for the Divine.

The final area of becoming trustworthy involves integrity. In *Conversations with God,* Neale Donald Walsch laid down the challenge of complete integrity. I was a CPA when I read that book; I believed I already was a living example of integrity. And yet when I took his challenge, I found hundreds, if not thousands, of areas in my life in which my thinking was sloppy and therefore my life was out of integrity.

As we increase our precision in thought, word, and deed, our ability to live with 100% integrity increases and we become more trustworthy in the eyes of the Divine. Precision leads to clear thinking, clear thinking combined with clear intention leads to integrity, and integrity is what Source is looking for to know it can trust us. The more precise we are, the more trustworthy we become in the eyes of the Divine, the more access we will have to the Universal Source, and the more miracles can happen through us. When we trust Source and Source trusts us to be clear channels, our ability to access Divine Flow and therefore our results improve exponentially.

My friend, you *are* worthy. You *are* good enough. You do not have to be perfect. None of us is perfect. We all make mistakes, and that is wonderful! How else can we learn? Intention is what counts more than anything else. If you have the intention to be an appropriate vessel, flash the learner's permit and move on. Be alert to signals that a mistake is in progress and be willing to adjust course as those signals arise—but have heart. You can do this. Your Guides want you to do this, or you would not be reading these words. This is for you to do. You can do it. We can all do this. It is a natural, inevitable process for an eternal being on an eternal growth path. Why not in this life? Why not now?

Reset your Energy. Flush your heart chakra clear with Universal Light and Love. Draw up Earth Energy to strengthen you, open your crown to allow healing Source frequencies to flow through and around you to the planet, and read on.

POCKET GUIDE TO NON-PHYSICAL BEINGS

The true Teachers of the Lightworkers Healing Method are higher-dimension beings, and they have very precisely laid out the entire LHM curriculum for us. Each section has a higher vibration than the steps preceding it. The curriculum draws you upward into the higher dimensions just as my brother Allen led me up the same pathway. If you have engaged in the exercises in Chapters Two through Ten you are now able to reach above the confusion of the astral planes into the clear dimensions and bring that Light solidly down to the world. "Not my will, not anyone else's either, just Divine Will."

The order in which you are introduced to the higher-dimension beings is precisely determined. You have already worked with the Screenmasters, Cordmasters, and Spearmasters; these are Lightbeings that will greet us at the doorway and train us to work with Energy. Now, if you wish to, you will move even farther into the higher dimensions and open to the Lightbeings that are waiting just beyond. However, before we take that next step it is important to establish some foundational definitions. Because the identical words can mean different things to different people, we will begin with a definition of terms.

Helpful Dead People

Often the first other dimension experiences we have are with out-of-body Loved ones: dead friends and relatives, close soul friends, teachers or gurus, and the like. They can help us, but are not Angels or Lightbeings. They are almost never our technical Guides. They are dear friends who Love us and are trying to help. Because they left their bodies behind and re-emerged into the non-physical, certain confusions have been cleared away and their perspective is clearer than it was when incarnated. Even so, they still have their personalities, perspectives, preferences, and limitations.

When we ask them for advice, we get their opinion. This is a wonderful source of comfort and Love, but is not our best source of assistance. These are our dear friends with all their flaws, still loving us and trying to help us. They still have their own agendas, and bring them to the communications. Nonetheless, because we know and trust them, they can often be doorways to all the other higher dimension beings.

Out-of-body spiritual masters, healers, gurus and the like can often help us, but are not usually our Guides in the technical sense. They are never Angels or Lightbeings. They are helpful dead people at varying stages of advancement. As with other non-physical friends, because we knew them in a body, because we Love them and know they Love us, it can be easier to relate to them and therefore to open up to them. This is why helpful dead people can often be doorways to the rest of the Universe.

We are most closely connected to one particular helpful dead person: our own higher self. There is a portion of our soul that does not come into the physical dimension, who stays "home" in the non-physical. This is our higher self. Like other helpful dead people, our higher self certainly has more clarity than our incarnate self does, but not as much clarity as our Guides do. Go for the Guides; they are the highest dimension help that is directly accessible to us, and therefore to whom we should reach.

Higher Dimension/Higher Vibration Beings

In the Lightworkers Healing Method, we access various types of beings in the higher dimensions to ask for help. They are all higher in vibration, clearer in intention, closer to Source, and can access pure Divine Energy better than we can. This becomes apparent in the "Tune Your Food" exercise (page 127) in which we first attune the Energy to Source, and then ask the Lightbeings to optimize it. Nothing has a higher vibration than Source—but Lightbeings have greater access to that vibration than we do, which is why that last step yields such powerful results.

In a healing session we are working under the instructions of the higher dimension beings, not the reverse. We all work to help the subject, but the higher dimension beings are in charge, not us. They are not "helpers" in the subservient sense of the word. They help the subject and help us too, but from the advanced perspective of generous, enlightened beings. Respect is appropriate. Not my will, but Thine.

Most people group all higher dimension beings together and call them all "Angels." When we first open up to these beings, from our perspective they are all the same: amazing beings of Light. "Angels!" As we progress, however, more precision is expected of us. Guides instruct; Angels, Lightbeings and Avatars heal.

I have been corrected when I have referred to Guides as "Angels." They declare, "I am not technically an Angel; I am a Guide." Although Guides are frequently labeled "Guardian Angels," there is a very distinct difference between the two that will be explained below.

Lightbeings have also made it clear that they are technically different than Angels, although almost everyone in the physical dimension includes them in that category. Many "Angelic Channels" are in fact channeling either Guides or Lightbeings. Don't get me wrong: that's a huge gift to the planet in and of itself; hats off. It is simply that precise definitions allow us to improve our results, so we are defining these terms precisely. Lightbeings, Guides, and Avatars are not technically Angels; neither are Nature Spirits, Devas, and so on. You will discover this for yourself, or perhaps already have. The more we increase our level of precision, the more accurate and effective our work becomes.

Guides

Guides, sometimes called Spirit Guides, are wise, loving beings that have been continuously associated with and helping the subject for many eons. They are the ultimate day-to-day authority on what the subject needs. They are the ideal go-to person on the higher dimensions, and in charge of LHM sessions. Guides come to the relationship with a much higher perspective than the subject's out-of-body Loved ones. They are always looking out for their subject's best interests, rather than their own best interests. They completely and unconditionally Love their subjects beyond our ability to comprehend. Their agenda is always their subject's soul growth and well-being.

All Guides have experience living in the way their subjects are living, which in our case means as humans. They know what it is like to be human. They have walked the walk. They understand. This is one difference between Guides and true Angels; Angels never incarnate into the physical dimensions in the normal sense. That having been said, Guides rarely incarnate by the time they are full Guides. Your subject's dead grandmother was almost certainly not her Guide, no matter how wise, wonderful, and loving she was.

In a healing session, both sets of Guides are present, yours and your subject's. In the early stages, you may not have awareness of the different voices of the Guides. You may feel them speaking to you as one voice. This is fine. As long as that lasts, go with it. One day you may notice there are multiple Guides present. At that point it is time to learn to distinguish the voices. If you can tell the difference, your subject's "Tell me what to do" questions should be directed to her own personal Guides since they are the experts on her, and don't have another agenda. If you can't understand your subject's Guides, no worries. Your Guides are present during healing sessions to support you in your well-being and your work, and can provide a translation of your subject's Guides' instructions.

In the early stages, it is normal to have confusion about which higher-dimension voices to be listening to. No worries, this will work itself out as you gain proficiency. These are wise, loving beings. They know you are doing your best. They will help you find your way in this art. If you ask your subject's Guides what to do for yourself, they will channel your Guides' instructions to you, just as you might channel your subject's Guides' instructions to them. Once you are past the early stages, your subject's Guides may gently tell you, "Ask your own Guides." Once you are past the early stages, Angels, Lightbeings, and Avatars will also direct you back to your Guides if you ask them what to do. They will do their job, which is to shift Energy and create change—and gently direct you back to your Guides for answers.

Angels

Many of us, especially in the Abrahamic traditions (Judaism, Islam, Christianity) have grown up with a belief in Angels. Guides, Lightbeings, and Avatars are all commonly referred to as Angels, but are technically different higher-dimension beings. Angels never incarnate in the traditional sense, and never have. They are from other dimensions; they aren't living lives here in the physical dimensions, they have always and will always live in the higher dimensions. This is one easily definable difference between a true Angel from a Guide.

If we call for Angels when we really need some other kind of higher-dimension help, support will still come—but it will not technically be Angels. Whoever is appropriate for the situation will show up: perhaps a Guide, perhaps a Lightbeing, or perhaps an Avatar. My friend, don't let this confuse you. All these higher-dimension beings are representatives of Source, of Spirit, of the All-That-Is. When you call for help, appropriate help will come. As you become more precise in your thinking, your ability to create change increases—but in a moment of crisis when you call for *HELP*, Source knows what to do. The right higher-dimension help will be there for you.

There are many varieties of Angels, but this is not the place for a complete discussion. We will crack open the door into the Angelic realm. If you are ready, more will naturally unfold for you. Remember: opening up to the higher dimensions is natural and even inevitable. You are an eternal being on an eternal growth path; this will happen at some time. Why not now?

Avatars

All healing arts are created by an Avatar, a higher-dimension being similar to Angels and Lightbeings but technically neither. From Western Medicine through Chiropractic, Traditional Chinese Medicine, Yoga, Reiki, and the Lightworkers Healing Method, every single healing art has its Avatar. These Avatars are available to support practitioners in those arts. Call for them; notice what happens. It's fascinating and awe-inspiring.

Lightbeings

Lightbeings are not technically Angels, although almost everyone labels them that way. They are from a different high vibration family tree. Like Angels, they never incarnate. Like Angels, their Joy is to reach down from the higher dimensions to help those of us who are in bodies. The only reason I distinguish between Lightbeings and Angels is because they ask me to do so. Sometimes it is not clear which type of Lightbeing is helpful in a particular situation; in that case simply ask for Lightbeings who know exactly what to do, to come. Then observe who shows up and learn.

The Lightbeings in this chapter are listed by the names I use for them. You might already call them something different, and that is absolutely fine. Your labels are equally valid. The Lightbeings are being presented in a precise order; the groups most willing to work through new channels come first. As you pursue this work, many more groups of Lightbeings will come to you. The Higher Level classes always include at least one transmission from another Lightbeing group. Also, as you continue to grow in this work more groups will spontaneously show up in your healing sessions.

Lightbeings You Have Already Worked With

Screenmasters use screens of Light to clear Energy fields of people and places. Cordmasters dissolve Energy cords, the unhelpful connections through which physical dimension people tend to take each other's Energy. Spearmasters transmute the Energy of anger, resentment, and irritation into clean, fresh Energy. All of these higher dimension beings work much faster than we do and of course do much better work than we can. That having been said, they are eager to teach us how to work with

Energy. They know what we are and are not ready to tackle. Sometimes they want us to watch and learn, sometimes they prefer for us to assist in the process, and sometimes they tell us to do it ourselves. They know what we are capable of doing and what each situation calls for; you can trust them. They are always right.

NEW HIGHER DIMENSION CONNECTIONS

This section will lead you through some of the higher-dimension beings who are willing to use us as vehicles to heal the world. After a thorough introduction to each family of higher beings, you will be directed to the LHM website so you can absorb the energetic transmissions that are available from these Loving, wise, powerful celestial beings. In this way, you offer yourself to these blessed beings and ask if they will use you as a vehicle to heal yourself, your Loved ones, and even the world around you if that should be your desire and calling.

Tiny Hands Lightbeings very gently and thoroughly optimize the Energy body, and help it open up to receive blessings. Small and non-threatening, very few people resist them. Miners ground us so we can hold our Energy strong and true in the physical dimension, shining Divine Light into the world around us. Medics support physical well-being—without that, life is hard. Magnetic Services support soul growth and Lightbody expansion. Protective Angels—ahem—protect.

With all these higher beings, we provide the initial connection, the introduction. The rest of the relationship is up to you. Be respectful and appropriate. Don't try to enlist these higher dimension beings to impose your will on a situation; that is a showstopper. Stay humble, stay grateful to be used as a vehicle for Divine Healing, don't think you know better than these higher beings do what is needed. Don't let others impose their will either; be a proper steward for the Divine. Do your best, correct your mistakes as you notice them, keep your integrity, and all will be well.

For each of the groups of Lightbeings that follow, there is a description to give your conscious mind a frame of reference. After you read the description, go to the website at www.lightworkersmethod.com and listen to the transmission for that Lightbeing group. After the transmission, gentle movement will help you get grounded. It is ideal to practice with a subject immediately afterward. In that practice, have the intention to be a channel for the Lightbeings you just connected to. Invite them to help your subject with whatever his presenting request is. You'll be amazed to discover how much help is available as these beings come into the healing session. Truly, it is a blessing.

Tiny Hands Lightbeings

The Tiny Hands Lightbeings are some of the first high dimension beings that approach us to help with healing. Perhaps because they are so small and therefore not intimidating in the least, very few people have resistance to them. They are gentle, tender, loving, and very clear channels for Source. The Tiny Hands are generalists and can help your subjects in almost all areas of life.

Often the first sign of the Tiny Hands Lightbeings is that we get an impression of tiny hands doing work in the subject's Energy body. These Lightbeings are approximately the size of Tinkerbelle, with appropriately tiny hands. Because of this, they can do extremely delicate and precise work in a person's Energy body. They help with meticulous repairs and make subtle improvements to an Energy body that full-sized fingers can't accomplish.

If you follow the Tiny Hands up the arms to the rest of them, you might notice that some of them have wings, like Angels do. Some don't. There are many types of Tiny Hands. They often come in large numbers. If they have wings they can flutter in a healing flock. Their sounds are often high-pitched or bell-like, and they can smell like fresh air.

My friend, go online and absorb the transmission for *Tiny Hands Lightbeings* as many times as you wish. Ground yourself, and then practice. Begin with the Opening Process and end with the Closing process. In between, call for the Tiny Hands Lightbeings to come help with your healing subject, and relax. This is a natural process; you have done your best. Detach from results. What will be will be. Enjoy!

Miners

The Miners are the most commonly available grounding Lightbeings to work with, although other groups also exist. Grounding can develop through many different layers, and its benefits can be expanded in many ways. Strong grounding forms the chalice to firmly hold the downward flow of Source Energies, to be a strong steward for the Divine on Earth. The more strongly we are grounded, the more Light our systems can hold in the physical dimension, the more we can be a Pillar that brings Light to the planet. The Miners are here to assist in that process.

Miners know their job isn't glamorous, but is absolutely necessary. Even more than other Lightbeings, they appreciate being properly thanked for their help. They reach their hands up, grab our feet or ankles to pull us down, and ground us properly. They are humble, unusually strong, patient, kind, loving, and extremely effective. Their combination of physical strength and emotional gentleness makes it clear that when they are with us, we are safe in the physical dimension. We can go ahead and be grounded. The Miners are here.

Miners typically appear to us as full-sized physically fit adult men; they have low-pitched, male voices. They live inside the Earth; they show themselves to us dressed as if they work in mines. They have helmets with built-in flashlights and wear dark clothing that doesn't show dirt.

Visit the website and absorb the transmission for *Miners Lightbeings* as many times as you wish. Ground yourself, and then practice. Begin with the Opening Process, call for the Miners to come help with your healing subject, and relax. This is a natural process; you have done your best. Remember to thank the Miners, end with the Closing Process, and detach from results. What will be will be. Enjoy!

Medics

The Medics work at the level of the physical body's Energy, healing the ills of the physical form. They help with Energies lodged in the physical body down to the cellular, molecular, and atomic levels. They can shift beliefs, traumas, and emotions lodged in the cells, molecules, and atoms to create healing. The Medics will sometimes take the subject to the "hospital in the sky" for deep work. During this time the subject can feel immobilized. If that creates anxiety for your subject, help him understand it's perfectly fine, he is safe, higher-dimension healers are working on him, and normal feeling and motion will return in a few minutes.

The Medics typically wear white scrubs and appear as full-sized human beings. They can signal their presence with the thought of an operating room, or with stretchers or ambulances. You may detect a very clean antiseptic scent. Medics don't want us to learn their techniques, but prefer to do the work themselves. They are in-charge, capable, competent, expert, thorough, confident, compassionate, and Loving. Stand back and let them do their job.

If subjects have had a bad experience with a hospital or another aspect of western medicine, they can feel resistance to the Medics. It is helpful to explain that the Medics are high dimension Lightbeings and therefore pure LOVE. There is nothing harsh, painful, disempowering, or demoralizing about their healing process. These experiences are miraculously blessed and Loving.

Although their style of work is similar, Medics differ from the beings that work through John of God, most of whom appear to be ascended human masters of healing (helpful dead people in our fancy lingo) as opposed to Lightbeings as we use the term. The Medics are Lightbeings in the technical sense of the word. This is significant because there is something very special about John of God that very few people have. Few of us could create the miracles he manifests while working as a channel for helpful dead people. I certainly don't have that ability. Thankfully, you and I don't have to be John of God for the Medics to use us. We can still be vessels for Spirit.

When you are ready, go to the website and absorb the transmission entitled *Medics Lightbeings* as many times as you wish. Ground yourself, and then practice. Begin with the Opening Process, call for the Medics to come help with your healing subject, and relax. This is a natural process; you have done your best. Detach from results. What will be will be. Remember to close properly, and enjoy!

Magnetic Services

Magnetic Services Lightbeings work with the electrical system of the Light body. They repair as well as upgrade individuals' electrical systems, which include the acupuncture meridians and nervous system, but extend far beyond the physical body in many different ways. These electrical systems include the merkaba, for example. Their work typically results in an expansion of the Energy body, and therefore a spurt of growth. Growth typically results in life changes, which the subject will either welcome or resist. Free will choices and working with the subconscious mind are the subject's contribution to the process.

When they appear, Magnetic Services reps may show up in orange jumpsuits such as electricians might wear. There might be an impression of electric circuitry or wiring, a feeling of static electricity in the air, the smell of lightning, or a current such as giant magnets might generate. They are extremely competent and efficient but have a great sense of humor and often crack a string of jokes as they work. Like the Medics, they don't want us to learn their techniques, but prefer to do the work themselves. It is dangerous work; they work with electricity. The tone is, "Kids, don't try this at home." What a blessing to have them simply do the work for us and for our healing subjects.

Go online and absorb the transmission from *Magnetic Services Lightbeings* as many times as you wish. Ground yourself, and then practice. Begin with the Opening Process and end with the Closing

Process. In between, call for Magnetic Services to come help with your healing subject, and relax. This is a natural process; you have done your best. Detach from results. What will be will be. Enjoy!

Protective Angels

Protective Angels are true Angels, and opening to them opens the door into the true Angelic realm. They have offered to extend their hand through to you, to provide that link. Protective Angels provide the highest levels of protection in many different ways. When we shout for help in times of perceived danger, this is often who comes.

Our goal is to be so strong in our Pillar of Light that we are invulnerable, but growing into that is a process. Until we are able to keep ourselves safe with a strong Pillar of Light, Protective Angels can fill the gap exponentially better than any shielding techniques. We have to be doing our best to build our Pillar—to do what is ours to do—but in the meantime we still have the right to live our lives in sacred space and the Angels will help if we ask. They can protect both spaces and people against unhelpful Energy intrusions. They can be with us for short or long periods of time.

Protective Angels can be the size of a full-grown human or larger. They are as big and as numerous as is needed for us to both be safe and feel safe. They always seem to have angel-wings, but they present a variety of different ways. Sometimes they look like big, burly, winged bodyguards, sometimes like winged secret service agents, sometimes like classic Angels with robes, but always winged, always strong. An unmistakable feeling of security is present wherever they are.

When you are ready, go to the website and absorb the transmission from the *Protective Angels* as many times as you wish. Ground yourself, and then practice. Begin with the Opening Process, call for the Protective Angels to come help with your healing subject, and relax. This is a natural process; you have done your best. Detach from results and remember to close properly. What will be will be. Enjoy!

Further Learning

While there are many other categories of higher dimension beings, it is not my place to draw your attention to them today. When the time is right, your Guides will open those doors. Curiosity, trust, respect, and gratitude are a powerful combination. When you are curious to learn more, that vibration will draw more learning to you. When you trust that what comes is in your highest and best good, you will resist it less and come to understand it more quickly. Being respectful keeps you from derailing the Lightbeings' process, and optimizes your working relationships with them. Gratitude acts to magnify the presence of that which we are grateful for.

Walk in Light, live in Light, be Light.

CHAPTER TWELVE

NEXT STOP, NIRVANA

Wring Out My Clothes

Such Love does the sky now pour,
that whenever I stand in a field
I have to wring out the Light
when I get home.
St. Francis of Assisi
From Love Poems From God, shared with thanks to Daniel Ladinsky

A few years into my process of learning how to teach the Lightworkers Healing Method to others, one of my very favorite long-time clients brought me a beautiful gift. In his session he asked his Guides to explain what was really going on in a challenging situation in his life. The way his Guides responded was to explain the Game of Life as clearly as I have ever heard it put. With his permission I can share these excerpts with you.

"You and everyone you know are on a train going somewhere. When you got on the train, all any of you wanted to do was to get to the destination. You all shook your heads at the posted schedule, chuckling at how silly it was: only one station was posted. 'Obviously the Station Master left things off.' None of you believed that the next station could possibly be the station that you wanted. You believed it to be a long journey so you settled in for a long haul.

Now you are on the train, and to pass the time you are playing poker with the people close to you. All that really matters is the train ride, but the poker game is compelling and fun with its combination of chance and free will. The game creates an exciting feeling of adventure, and gradually takes more of your focus than the train ride itself. You and your poker companions are getting excited about the game, standing up and shouting at each other, accusing each other of all kinds of things. You have completely forgotten this is just a game to pass the time while you are on the train. You now believe the game is important.

All around you, the train is full of people all playing their own poker games. Periodically a Conductor comes through, calling out something in a language that no one understands with his or her mind, which makes him easy to ignore. Most people are intent on the poker games. Very few people notice the Conductor as he passes through the train, calling, 'Surrender!' in the language of the heart. Only the ones that are not drawn into the poker games notice him. Of those, only the ones that can listen with their hearts can understand what he is saying. Of those, the very few who are willing and able to truly surrender can follow the call of the Conductor and actually get off the train. Everyone else is still playing poker, forgetting their original goal of reaching the next station.

For the ones that surrender and follow the call onto the station, they pass under a welcome sign in many languages, displaying words like Heaven, Pure Land, and Nirvana. At first you are entranced and astounded. This is a wonderfully fabulous place, so much better than any other place you have ever been in. You walk around with your arms, eyes, and mouths wide open.

Then something interesting happens. After a while, although it's still a wonderful place, you have gotten used to it. It starts to feel humdrum and normal, and you start to want something more and better. You know there's always another train pulling into the station. You get on the next train, thinking it will take you someplace different. It's an illusion, however. All the trains go into a big loop like toy trains circling a Christmas tree and there is only the one station.

Back on another train, not much has changed. People are playing their poker games and the Conductor is coming through and calling the word that means, 'Surrender' in the language of the heart. Almost no one notices him, but now you know the drill a little better. You think, 'Here we are, people playing poker and shouting—but wait a minute, I remember this. There is something I'm supposed to do here.' Now it happens faster. You stop paying attention to the poker game, wait for the Conductor, and then—as if in a dream—you get up and follow his call. Surrendering, you disembark at the next station, which is the only station.

Having arrived at Nirvana, at first you are entranced and astounded; it is the most wonderful place you have ever been. But then you get used to it, another train pulls in, and it starts over. Each time you get off and on the train, and even each time you sit down from the arguing, the air in and around you clears more and more. The vibration becomes finer, quieter, and develops more of an inner focus.

You have asked us today how to truly help all these people on the train with you. First, you yourself must let go of your own feelings of trappedness, anger, fear, etc. and sit down. Sit down, stop shouting, and begin to listen for the Conductor.

Next, establish the link between yourself and another, one of those trapped in the illusion. Notice: how are you exactly like him? There is always a link, always a shared pattern. Then align with his Energy and find how you yourself are exactly like that. Sometimes it's easy to find it and sometimes you really have to dig for it, but it is always there. Find the match inside of you: the fear, the anger, the need to strike back, and then sit down again. Let it go. Surrender. Say, 'Yes, this is the way life is, and I can still be happy.' Sometimes that is really hard and you will have to ask it as a question rather than make a statement. Ask your subconscious, 'Why am I like this too, and still happy?'

When one person sits down, the people around him have a better chance to change. As one person awakens, it creates more potential for the people around him to awaken. In this way you help yourself become free, you help the ones around you become free, and you help all beings become free."

This explanation of life from an enlightened Guide has moved me to tears many times. Its last three paragraphs encapsulate the Lightworkers Healing Method in which we align with Source, merge with our subject, and once again surrender and let go. We let go of all the old baggage, of insisting we know what is supposed to happen in the sessions and in our lives, of our fear, and of our resistance. We open up to receive Divine Assistance and Love. We learn to step over fear, move forward on our life paths, and live fully. In so doing, we help our subject let go as well—and in this way, in this small little way, we help all beings become free.

LHM is a way of learning to perceive, listen for, and understand the Conductor as he comes through the train of life. Each time we engage in LHM, by either giving or receiving an LHM session, we have the chance to get off at the station. Each time, our vibrations become finer and quieter. Each time, as we learn to listen for the Guides and to follow their directions rather than imposing our ideas on the sessions, it becomes easier to hear the Conductor in our daily lives and to realize, "Yes, this is the way life is, and I can still be happy."

My dear friend, the Lightworkers Healing Method is both a healing system and a spiritual growth vehicle. Through this method it is possible to learn to live in the Light so that Joy is always present regardless of life circumstances. It can lead you into the space inside of yourself where no matter what happens, you are not only fine but actually thriving, living with Peace and Joy as your default setting. Beauty and wonder will manifest throughout your entire life, filling you with bliss as you realize you are truly One with the Universe.

I tell you, my friend, it's been a long journey for me. 22 years and counting. It has been a journey full of fear and resistance and, as a result, full of challenges and pain. I came here through tragedy and grief, business reversals and disability, but I now know what it is to surrender. To see, feel, and experience life with all its Gloriously intense pain, and to still be happy. In the words of St. John of the Cross, "To hold beauty in my soul's arms." I know that it's there for all of us, for absolutely all of us.

Growth is a series of things falling apart and coming back together in a new configuration. Certain turning points in the growth process are pivotal; once past these pivotal points, we can't turn back to the way things were before. For me, I'm past the decision to teach this healing art to all who wish to learn. There isn't any going back, only moving forward. Since this is what I'm called to do, I'm giving full multi-dimensional effort to the assignment, and trusting that whatever occurs is what is supposed to happen.

Some of you reading this are called to master this art; others are not, and that is fine. If you feel the call, it is very possible that reading this book is *your* pivotal point, one from which there is no turning back. My friend, if you are called don't stop here. You have read the framework of the method, but there is so much more to be learned. You truly can bring LHM to life in and around you. This is not a gift but rather a skill, a naturally learnable art. If you are called, go online. Find the classes nearest you. Begin to participate. Ask for a mentor. Share the book with a friend so you have someone to practice with; give and receive the gifts of LHM sessions. Decide to master the art, and relax into the process. Let it unfold within and around you. Let it lift you up, strengthen you, and bring you Peace. You are not alone. As we each do our part, the world transforms.

My friend, this is the end of the core curriculum of the Lightworkers Healing Method. Congratulations for coming this far—but, my very dear friend, this can be the beginning, not the end, of this incredible journey. If the idea of being a channel for Divine healing simultaneously inspires and terrifies, it is what your soul wants you to do. You can learn this skill; we can all learn this. It is natural and inevitable. Why not now? Moment by moment, our attitudes determine how much is available to us. Decide you can learn the Lightworkers Healing Method as many others have. Incorporate it into your life and see it transform into your wildest dreams. Use it, learn it, claim it, own it, become it.

Be who your soul wants you to be. Live the life you came here to live. Walk in Light, live in Light, be Light. Next stop, Nirvana.

AFTERWORD

CORE MESSAGES OF THE LIGHTWORKERS HEALING METHOD

Love, peace, and joy are our natural states of mind. Everything else comes from temporary confusion and fear.

We are the creators of our experience. We create, attract, or allow everything in our lives.

Our mission at the Lightworkers Healing Method (LHM) is to help people live the life their souls intend to live, to be who they came here to be, and thereby to bring the overall Divine Plan to manifested reality on Earth.

We are all supported and guided by higher-dimension beings. Labels don't matter; whether we call them Guardian Angels or Spirit Guides is irrelevant. What matters is that we learn to trust them, to trust life, and to say "yes" to life.

It is natural to be connected with our Guides and with Source. Channeling Divine healing and guidance is a learnable skill, not a gift. There is an amazing amount of higher-dimension support when we commit to learning LHM. We can *all* learn to do this, not only to help ourselves but also to help others.

You are more capable than you know. You can tend your energy body to improve your life and to live your soul's purpose. Focus on your vertical

Pillar of Light to live a life guided and supported by Spirit while also being grounded into the reality of the physical dimension. Create a vortex to create sacred space for yourself and your life; to create a fertile ground for a Divinely led life to grow in.

To get clear guidance about anything including your life path, point your intuitive channels UP to your Guides rather than out into the world around you as is typical. It is natural to be able to distinguish "Yes" from "No" in the guidance, and you can live your life's purpose with guidance at the level of "Yes" and "No." Just point your channels UP to get the highest level of messages available, and practice. You can do it.

Life messages abound to supplement direct, subtle guidance. That which both inspires and terrifies you shows you your life path. Our life Plans include challenges but also the expectation that we will succeed. Our lives develop as we progress through the Plan while making our free will choices.

Life presents us with an endless series of beautifully designed growth and learning opportunities. In each moment we have the free will choice of accepting the opportunities or passing by them. Every situation has a gift; find it, appreciate it, and accept it.

Saying "yes" to life—accepting the opportunities life presents to us—allows an increased flow of Divine energy through us and through our lives, and creates a life that works. Saying "no" to life—resistance to the opportunities life presents to us—creates life challenges, illness, and pain.

Most people have a pattern of saying "yes I'll do it" to life in a moment of inspiration followed by saying "no I can't possibly do this" when fear arises. This creates painful dis-harmonies at some level of life, which can be physical, mental, emotional, spiritual, financial, or interpersonal.

The secret to living a fear-free life: do the scariest thing on your to-do list first, right now, and then nothing else is as scary. Then do the next-scariest thing on the list, and so on until all the frightening items are taken care of. Nothing left to fear!

Your beliefs create your reality. Choose empowering thoughts. Everything is possible; there are truly no limits. When we do what is ours to do, some element of the Divine supplies the rest to create miracles.

All time is now; everything can be healed. It's never too late to ask for Divine help to correct our mistakes, to make the impact of our actions not only right but actually perfect.

Everyone, without exception, is doing his/her best. You are too.

Unconditional love does not mean ignoring "flaws" in ourselves or in others. It means acknowledging the "flaws" and loving anyway. No blame or judgment, just acceptance of what is. If the topic is our own "flaws," add willingness to improve to this recipe for best results.

Helping others is the easiest way to heal ourselves. Through the paradox of simultaneous healing we can be helped with the issues we are blind to in ourselves.

The wonderful and blessed thing about LHM is that we never have to decide anything. We simply point our intuitive channels UP to the Guides and follow directions.

Doubt and trust are both equally accessible in any moment. Choose to trust your Guides, and to trust life. Choose to say "yes."

The instant we are truly ready for life to be different, it is.

You can do it, you can do it, you can do it.

Walk in light, live in light, be light.

THE SOUL PLAN CHALLENGE

Our mission at the Lightworkers Healing Method (LHM) is to help people live the life their souls intend to live, to be who they came here to be, and thereby to bring the overall Divine Plan to manifested reality on Earth. Will you join us in our mission by accepting the Soul Plan Challenge?

The Basic Challenge

Before you came into your body, your soul formed a plan for the life you are currently living. That plan, of course, includes challenges, but your soul intends to rise above the challenges and experience a life of joy. As you live your life plan, you feel peaceful because you know everything is unfolding as it should, and you feel joyful because you are doing what you came into a body to do. Remember: the Universe LOVES you and wants you to be JOYFUL!

Will you commit to discovering and
living your personal soul's plan?

If so, please go to www.lightworkersmethod.com, click on Soul Plan Challenge, and click to record your commitment.

The Bonus Challenge

Because the overall Divine Plan for Earth is the amalgam of all the individual soul plans, living our individual plans helps the greater good. When we are all living our soul plans, the Divine Plan will have manifested here in the physical dimension.

Most of us assume that only enlightened beings—maybe the Dalai Lama or people like Mother Teresa—are responsible for manifesting the overall Divine Plan. Therefore we don't even try to help all beings live a life of joy. However, we are all connected; there truly is only One of us here. By helping our brothers and sisters here in the physical dimension, we help ourselves in the deepest possible way. Like the Dalai Lama, we can all commit to helping everyone live a life of joy.

Feel the difference for yourself that personal responsibility makes. Say, out loud, "May all beings discover and live their soul plans." Then say, out loud, "Like the Dalai Lama, I will personally help all beings discover and live their soul plans." This is a much more powerful, and also a scarier, statement. There is no pressure to do this! However, if you feel ready, this is a bonus opportunity. You can help the world. You can be a part of the wave of people who are committed to all beings living their soul plans.

And the Universe can align with you and support you in an even more powerful way.

Will you commit to helping all beings discover
and live their individual soul plans?

If so, please go to www.lightworkersmethod.com, click on Soul Plan Challenge, and click to record your commitment.

Take the Extreme Challenge

(Not for the faint of heart)

Our world needs help now, not later. Because work expands to fill the time allowed, it is important to have a deadline in mind. Feel for yourself the difference in urgency a deadline makes. Say, out loud, "I will personally help all beings discover and live their soul plans." Then say, out loud, "I will personally help all beings discover and live their soul plans by January 17, 2017." While this is the date we on the LHM Team are working toward, if you prefer another date, choose it. As long as it is reasonably soon the urgency is still there.

Can you feel how powerfully compelling this statement is? There is absolutely no pressure to do this! However, if you feel ready, this will trigger an amazing experience of soul growth for you.

Will you commit to helping all beings discover and
live their individual soul plans by January 17, 2017
(or other reasonably soon date of your choice)?

If so, please go to www.lightworkersmethod.com, click on Soul Plan Challenge, and click to record your commitment.

Now What?

If you have accepted the Soul Plan Challenge, congratulations! No matter whether you are at the Basic level, the Bonus level, or the Extreme level, your next step is the same. Through www.lightworkersmethod.com, request a mentor. Then register for a class near you, or take a distance learning module. Relax into this process. Let it unfold within and around you. Let it lift you up, strengthen you, and bring you Peace. You are not alone.

Walk in light, live in light, be light. Next stop, Nirvana.

ABOUT THE AUTHOR

Lynn McGonagill is the physical-dimension Founder and Teaching Channel of the Lightworkers Healing Method. To date, she has gratefully invested twenty-two years in training with higher-dimension healing beings, twelve years in joyfully practicing LHM full-time with thousands of clients, and five years in lovingly teaching the method to others. Lynn is nearing the end of a three year, three month, three day at-home retreat in Sarasota, Florida, during which her sole focus has been teaching, writing about and practicing the Lightworkers Healing Method.

APPENDIX ONE

OPENING PROCESS

This is a living, growing process. It will continue to evolve. Don't freeze it into this format. Let it live.

1. Calm and center yourself with the breath
2. Notice your Energy body's condition; give Love to any tenseness or pain
3. Find the other person's Energy body in your awareness
4. Notice its condition and have the intent to merge with it at this level
5. Open what is now the joint heart chakra to the Universal heart of life and Love
6. Invite a River of Love and Light from this Universal heart straight into the front of the joint heart chakra, filling the chakra with so much Love that it expands before exhaling out the back in a River of Love
7. Reach out the back of the heart chakra and connect to another element of Divine Love: Christ Consciousness, Buddha Nature, or whatever suits you and your subject best; no need to identify it
8. Draw that River of Love into the back of the joint heart chakra, filling it with so much Love that the chakra expands before it exhales out the front

9. Notice the streams of Love flowing simultaneously in both directions, creating turbulence, clearing and cleansing
10. Reach through the joint feet into the center of the planet; draw up Father Earth and Mother Earth Energies
11. Draw these up through all the vertical Energy channels and through the entire Pillar of Light and out the crown; let this River of Love run Earth to Source
12. Reach through the joint crown and draw in from Source all the healing frequencies you currently have access to, have ever had access to, and will ever have access to
13. Draw these down through the vertical Energy channels and Pillar of Light and out the feet; let this River of Love run from Source to the center of Earth
14. Notice the streams of Love flowing simultaneously in both directions, creating turbulence, clearing and cleansing
15. Focus on the intersection of heart chakra and central channels; let a critical mass of Love build
16. When the bubble of Light pops from that focal point, notice it is electrified
17. Claim the interior as sacred, safe, private healing space
18. Invite the Guides, the Angels and Lightbeings to join you in the bubble
19. Ask your own Guides and Angels for permission to do this work today (for your own highest and best good)
20. Ask for guidance, support and protection during the process
21. Call in the Vortex. Notice it continually clearing the bubble as the Energy spirals up to Recycling
22. Call in the Living Waters down the middle of the Vortex. Notice them creating a foundation of Love for healing
23. Locate the subject's higher self; notice its majesty; feel gratitude

24. Ask the subject's higher self for permission to work in their Energy body and with their Guides, acknowledge you will honor any limitations they create
25. When the Energy opens, that is where you have permission to work
26. Ask the subject's Guides and Angels to join you in the bubble and open the channels of healing, support, and communication wide
27. Ask the subject's Guides to make any improvements in your Energy body they notice, and that you are willing to allow

APPENDIX TWO

CLOSING PROCESS

1. While your Energies are still merged with the subject's, ask for any errors or omissions to be corrected. Ask for poorly done work to be done well, and well-done work to be made perfect.
2. Ask that the subject's Energy body and yours both be brought into its optimal alignment
3. Have the intention that the Energies be stabilized and set; draw them through skin, soft tissues and organs into bones for both of you
4. Begin the grounding process and ground as fully as possible with your intention
5. Ask the Lightbeings to help both you and the subject ground optimally
6. Separate your Energies from the subject's; his/hers back to him/her, yours back to you
7. Continue to ground, stabilize, set and separate until it feels complete
8. Focus on the bubble of Light; expand it 1,000 times over so there's so much Light it's more than enough for all
9. Split that Light into individual bubbles, one each for you, the subject, and all others you touched
10. Ground those bubbles down into the Divine Plan until they click in place
11. Declare the session complete and give thanks

GLOSSARY

A-COAT—(Acronym) Five step process of working as a conduit for Divine Energy Healing: **Align** with Divine Energy; **Connect** or Merge with another person's energy; **Open** the channels to the Guides and Lightbeings; **Ask** for help on behalf of the subject; and **Trust** the outcome.

Beguine—Two traditional definitions. First, a graceful partnered music and dance form originating in the French West Indies. Second, a group of semi-monastic communities without formal vows active in Europe in the 13th and 14th centuries. Hence Beguine's combined meaning: a lovely, passionate dance with God. To *Begin the Beguine* is to begin to dance passionately with God. In the Lightworkers Healing Method, we begin the Beguine using the Opening Process of creating Sacred Space.

Chakras—areas or points of energy exchange that run perpendicular to the Pillar of Light. Earth chakras are below the physical body in a chain that reaches to center of the earth, and sky chakras are above the physical body in a chain progressively reaching toward Source. Life Force (chi/ prana) is inhaled and exhaled through the chakras as well as through the vertical channels of the energy body.

Conduit—within LHM, an individual who serves as a channel or vessel for Spirit to work through.

Energetic Transmissions—Powerful calls for Divine help that open the connections to Source and to higher-dimension beings including Guides, Angels, and Lightbeings. Energetic transmissions draw Divine help into the physical dimension. This combination of prayer and energetic access is especially effective in activating your innate healing gifts.

Felt Sense—An "inner knowing" of phenomena which could be past, present, or future.

God Code—A hidden message within the fabric of life itself, down to every atom, that links every living thing together, and to God's name.

Guide—Wise, Loving higher-dimension beings that have been continuously associated with and helping the subject for many eons. They are the ultimate day-to-day authority on what the subject needs. Also commonly referred to as Guardian Angels and Spirit Guides. See page 265.

Merkaba—Merkaba, also spelled Merkabah, is a divine light vehicle that can be used to connect with and reach the higher realms. It is part of the electrical system of the Lightbody and therefore intricately interwoven into the Pillar of Light. "Mer" means Light. "Ka" means Spirit. "Ba" means Body. Mer-Ka-Ba means the spirit/body surrounded by counter-rotating fields of light, (wheels within wheels), spirals of energy as in DNA, which transport spirit/body from one dimension to another. An activated Merkaba is one of many ways of reaching the higher dimensions.

Physicalize—To draw into the physical dimension, to give physical expression to.

Pillar of Light—the vertical component of the energy body that contains intuitive and kundalini channels, running vertically through the energy body, from Source to the center of the Earth. A good visual image or representation of the appearance of the Pillar of Light is of tightly packed vertically running fiber optic cables.

Sacred Space—in the Lightworkers Healing Method, sacred space occurs inside the protective "bubble" of light and love that surrounds the practitioner and subject in a healing session. The space is created by asking for and initiating the flow of the Rivers of Life and Love, first flowing in both directions through the heart chakra on the horizontal axis, and then from the center of the earth to the center of the Universe on the vertical axis. This "energy cross" of Divine Source Energy culminates in a bubble of Light and Love, within a more encompassing Pillar of Light. This bubble that is created is claimed as private, safe, sacred space in which Divine healing work can be accomplished.

CREDITS

Illustrations by Luci Belknap.

From the Penguin publication *Love Poems From God*, copyright 2002 Daniel Ladinsky, and used with his permission: *The Essence of Desire* (St. John of the Cross), *That Lives In Us* (Jelaludin Rumi), *With That Moon Language* (Hafiz of Shiraz), and *Wring Out My Clothes* (St. Francis of Assisi).

From Heron Dance, www.herondance.org, and used with Rod MacIver's permission: an excerpt from *This Ecstasy* (John Squadra), and an excerpt from *Interview with Balbir Mathur.* Balbir Mathur, Founder of Trees For Life, also granted permission.

Excerpted text from *The Tao of Equus* by Linda Kohanov, modified and used with her gracious permission.

Excerpted text from *The Scottish Himalayan Expedition* by W.H. Murray, published by J. M. Dent, currently part of Orion Publishing Group. All efforts at tracing the copyright holder were unsuccessful.

Ingram Content Group UK Ltd.
Milton Keynes UK
UKHW041629250523
422344UK00021B/266